DISCARD

UNEQUAL EQUITIES

UNEQUAL EQUITIES

Power and Risk
in
Japan's Stock Market

Robert Zielinski
and
Nigel Holloway

KODANSHA INTERNATIONAL
Tokyo and New York

Distributed in the United States by Kodansha International/
USA Ltd., through Farrar, Straus and Giroux, Inc., 19 Union
Square West, New York, NY 10003. Published by Kodansha In-
ternational Ltd., 1-17-14 Otowa, Bunkyo-ku, Tokyo 112, and
Kodansha International/USA Ltd., 114 Fifth Avenue, New
York, NY 10011.

First edition, 1991

Printed in Japan.

ISBN 0-87011-976-1 (USA)
ISBN 4-7700-1476-7 C 0033 (Japan)

Library of Congress Cataloging-in-Publication Data

Zielinski, Robert, 1958-
    Unequal equities : power and risk in Japan's stock market / Robert
Zielinski and Nigel Holloway.
        p.   cm.
    Includes index.
    ISBN 0-87011-976-1 (U.S.) : $21.95
    1. Tōkyō Shōken Torihikijo.   2. Financial institutions—Japan.
3. Stockbrokers—Japan.   I. Holloway, Nigel, 1954-   . II. Title.
HG4597.Z54 1990
332.64'252—dc20   90-40222
                                                         CIP

Grateful acknowledgment is made to following: the Toyo
Keizai Shinposha for permission to reproduce the sample of
company outlooks from the *Japan Company Handbook;* the
Nihon Keizai Shimbun, Shuppan Kyoku, for permission to
reproduce the face used for purposes of stock analysis from the
Kaisha Joho; the Jitsu Nichi Research Center for permission to
reproduce logarithm graphs from the *Tsukiashi nijunen;* Toshi
Radar Corporation for permission to reproduce charts from
the *First Section Chart Book;* Golden Chart Company for permission to reproduce charts from *Tsukiashi shu;* and JAMA
for permission to reproduce the map from the "Analysis of
Japanese Industries for Investors, 1990."

For our parents

CONTENTS

Chapter 1

RICH COUNTRY, STRONG STOCK MARKET

Unlike Sony or Toyota, the Industrial Bank of Japan is not a household name—even to the Japanese. The bank's wedge-shaped headquarters is unprepossessing, tucked behind the Tokyo branch of another bank. But let not appearances fool, for IBJ is, without doubt, the most powerful company in Japan.

IBJ wields its power discreetly. Its men are directors at 103 publicly owned companies. It is the biggest lender to listed Japanese companies and is a major shareholder in more than 600 of them, including such illustrious names as Nippon Steel, Hitachi, Nissan, and Fujitsu.

Since it was set up by the Japanese government in 1902, IBJ has acted as the venture capitalist for Japan Inc. It financed the new companies which colonized Manchuria and Korea. After the Pacific War, it bankrolled the heavy industry which generated Japan's modern-day growth.

With power has come responsibilities, and IBJ has fulfilled them well. Whenever an industry or its corporate clients have been in trouble, the bank has been ready to serve. It has never allowed a client to go bankrupt. When the bear market of the mid-1960s threatened the survival of the entire securities industry, IBJ took control of most of the big brokers and nursed them back to health. When Keisei Railway speculated too heavily in real estate in the early 1970s, IBJ helped arrange for Tokyo Disneyland to be built on Keisei's land. And when the big shipping company Japan Line was foundering badly in the late 1980s, IBJ brought about its merger with another big distressed shipping company, Yamashita Shinnihon Steamship, writing off ¥160 billion in loans in the process.

From power flows wealth, and vice versa. IBJ's equity base is four times the size of Citicorp, America's largest bank. Over the years, it has accumulated ¥4.1 trillion in unrealized capital gains from investing in the shares of companies it lends to. This has not only made IBJ rich, but it has also made the bank's own shares valuable. At the peak of the market in December 1989, IBJ had a market capitalization of almost ¥16 trillion—second largest in the world.

Virtually all of IBJ's shares are in turn held by the companies it lends to. These shares are a form of insurance, since its shareholders know IBJ will stand behind them in times of financial difficulty. Their loyalty has been richly rewarded. Although the bank neither earns large profits nor pays high dividends, its share price rose by 18 times between 1984 and 1989. This performance afforded IBJ the freedom to call upon its shareholders twice during that six-year stretch to raise ¥496 billion through two rights offerings, despite a back-breaking price-earnings ratio that averaged 80.

By the end of the 1980s, IBJ had become a symbol of Japan's growing financial might. It was also a symbol of something more basic—the way in which Japan's stock market works to enhance the power of corporations and thereby Japan. Because of its shareholdings, IBJ has the equity base to support its ¥43 trillion in assets, the financial resources to absorb loan losses, and the right to influence other firms. Because its shares are held by its corporate clients, IBJ need not worry when it chooses to help its borrowers at the expense of short-term profits. Even if this were not the case, the surge in share prices over the past decade, irrespective of profitability, greatly increased the value of their holdings, just as it did IBJ's own share portfolio, and made them willing to buy new shares.

With Japan's economy booming and its stock market soaring at the end of 1989, IBJ's power was growing daily. Nothing seemed to stand in the path of its ambition to become the premier investment bank in the world.

The loftier the aspiration, the harsher the disappointment. When Japan's stock market plummeted by 29 percent in the first three months of 1990, IBJ's share price fell by half, causing its shareholders to lose ¥8.5 trillion. The bank's own portfolio shrank in value by ¥1.5 trillion. Without the bulwark of a strong stock market, IBJ suddenly had the look of vulnerability. Aside from its share portfolio, the bank's leverage appeared excessive, with shareholders' equity equal to only 3 percent of assets. Its low level of profits could be expected to fall further, as it derived at least half from selling part of its shareholdings.

Such a dramatic change in fortune was being repeated across the length and breadth of corporate Japan in the early months of 1990. The country reeled from the shock of finding ¥150 trillion wiped off the value of the Tokyo Stock Exchange.

THE MAKING OF A MARKET

For 15 years, Japan's stock market had seemed irrepressible. It shrugged off the second oil crisis in 1979 and the profit slump caused by the rise in the yen in 1985. It bounced back from the October 1987 Wall Street crash faster than any other major stock market in the world, climbing 26 percent in 1988 and 24 percent in 1989.

By the end of 1989, the Nikkei Average of 225 leading Japanese stocks had reached ¥38,915—some 590 percent higher than at the start of the decade and 17 times higher than in 1970. There seemed to be only one direction shares could go: even higher. The market-weighted price index of all stocks quoted on the First Section of the Tokyo Stock Exchange (TSE) increased 200 times in the 40 years following the reopening of the exchange in 1949. In contrast, Standard & Poor's Index of 500 representative stocks listed in New York appreciated only 20 times over the same period.

At the pinnacle, 716 of the 1,136 companies listed on the First Section of the Tokyo Stock Exchange had a price-earnings ratio (PER) greater than 50. Fujitsu's PER was double that of IBM, Kawasaki Steel's was seven times that of Bethlehem Steel, and Nippon Telegraph and Telephone was worth three times as much as AT&T despite earning 40 percent less. Japan's top 16 commercial banks had a market capitalization six times greater than the 50 largest commercial banks in the United States.

TOPIX versus Standard & Poor's 500

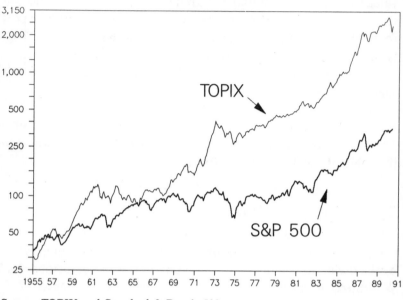

Source: TOPIX and Standard & Poor's 500

Japan's stock market symbolized the country's new status as a financial superpower. Tokyo was the world's largest stock market, having eclipsed the New York Stock Exchange in October 1987, eventually to comprise, at ¥611 trillion, 45 percent of the world's equity capitalization. That Japan had concomitantly become the world's richest country was not mere bookkeeping. The paper wealth was translated into economic power. Japanese companies, like IBJ, relied on the strength of the stock market, as well as on their undoubted operational ability, to beat back foreign competition.

The TSE would seem to have found the alchemist's formula for turning base metal into gold. In the 1980s, companies issued massive amounts of new shares and instruments linked to equities in order to finance rationalization, expansion and takeovers. Japan's stock market was milked for all its worth by car manufacturers, steel companies, construction firms, and financial institutions. Moreover, the cost of these financings was absurdly low, tantamount to a dividend

Share of World Stock Market Capitalization

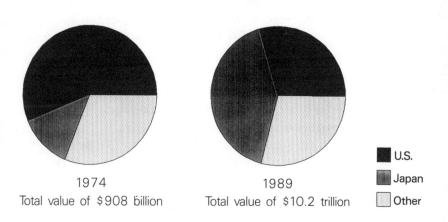

1974
Total value of $908 billion

1989
Total value of $10.2 trillion

■ U.S.

▨ Japan

▫ Other

yield that averaged 0.6 percent in 1985–87—compared to 3 percent in the United States. Investors were prepared to accept high PERs and minimal dividends, because the capital gains were so large. And this would have continued, as long as share prices kept on rising.

The hegemony of the Tokyo Stock Exchange was brief: on March 20, 1990, amid an alarming bear market, it slipped back into second place behind New York. Tokyo's collapse notwithstanding, the challenge that Japanese corporations pose for foreign businesses has been brought into sharper focus. A prolonged fall in Japanese share prices could blunt the competitive edge of Japanese companies. A stock market revival, on the other hand, would sharpen that edge once again.

Despite its prominence in world finance, the Tokyo Stock Exchange remains an enigma to many investors, both at home and abroad. In outward appearance, it resembles most large stock exchanges around the world. But the way in which it has been able to conjure continuously rising prices where other stock markets have not seems to defy comprehension. What factors have fashioned the stock market into such a powerful tool for business? And what are the risks that Japan takes by relying on ever-rising share prices?

THE BALANCE OF CORPORATE POWER

Stock markets have grown best where the balance of interests between owners and managers is tipped in favor of owners—the shareholders. For this reason, Wall Street and the London Stock Exchange overshadow the French and West German bourses, where big institutional investors are more concerned with strengthening the firms in which they own equity than with earning stort-term gains. Yet a well-developed stock market is not a prerequisite for economic success. If anything, strong economies are characterized by a close identity of interest between the owners and managers, who act in partnership to ensure the success of the firm. This is often achieved by keeping companies private or under tight family control. In West Germany, few companies are actually listed, and in South Korea the giant industrial conglomerates known as *chaebol* tend to be dominated by the founding families.

The Tokyo Stock Exchange, whose building dominates the tightly knit community of Kabutocho, Japan's equivalent of Wall Street, is the exception to the rule that big stock markets need strong shareholding interests. Although it became the world's largest and most actively traded market for a period in the late 1980s, shareholders in Tokyo count for less than in any other large capitalist country. Power is decisively in the hands of the employers of capital and kept away from the owners.

In a 1989 study conducted by the New York-based Investor Responsibility Research Center, shareholders' rights in Japan were judged to be as weak as those in France and West Germany, and far short of those in Anglo-Saxon countries such as the United States and Britain. The survey ranked nine countries (Australia, Canada, France, Italy, Japan, Switzerland, West Germany, United Kingdom, United States) by four yardsticks: disclosure of corporate information, voting rights, the ease with which shareholders could introduce corporate resolutions, and shareholder notification of meetings and proxy votes. The closer to one-share, one-vote, the more points. Scores were calculated using the United States as a standard 100. Japan's score was 48. "Among the markets of the big nine," concluded the Center, "Japan has the least protection for shareholders and the most obstacles to investors' activism.''

From the viewpoint of investors, the Japanese corporation is almost impervious to outside influence. American companies must report their business results on a quarterly basis and provide full information in their annual reports and other documents sent to the Securities and Exchange Commission, which supervises the U.S. stock market. Japanese firms only need report their results every six months and then much less thoroughly. Disclosure of information is so poor that it is assumed that companies routinely manipulate their earnings. Shareholders' meetings are but a formality.

Managers in Japan are able to maintain corporate control because all of the big corporations and most of the smaller ones are majority-owned by other companies which, with the exception of life insurers, are themselves listed. Ownership of the big corporations is dispersed widely enough among other companies to allow managers the freedom to pursue their own objectives unhindered by outsiders, provided they keep out of serious financial trouble. Smaller listed companies, however, often find themselves trapped within the power structure. They are subservient to the big corporations for whose benefit they must act.

The corporate shareholders of a company do not—and need not—behave like portfolio investors elsewhere, maximizing their stock market returns by buying cheap and selling dear. Although corporate executives want a long-term return on their investment, that return is seen more as the sum total of a business relationship with another company, of which the stock's dividend yield and capital gain are only a part. They own shares for strategic and symbolic purposes, such as the cementing of long-term business ties, the winning of new customers, and the warding off of unwelcome outsiders. A company holds the shares of another company, and vice versa, in a mutually binding relationship. In Japan, shares are a ticket of admission as well as a store of value.

Corporate shareholders entrust the voting rights associated with their shares to the company's managers. Managers thus have only themselves to answer to. Directorships are almost always appointed from within the company and are regarded as the rightful goal of managers working their way up the ranks. Boards of directors can therefore be relied upon to act in the best interests of the company, not shareholders.

This structure of share ownership eliminates the potential clash between the company in the guise of the employees and its legal form as a collection of assets owned or disposed of at will by shareholders. Japanese managers can thus pursue their long-term goal of building market share without the burden of reporting high earnings or paying large dividends. They are free to make enormous capital investments and price their products extremely aggressively, giving them a tremendous advantage over rivals that are answerable to less-understanding shareholders.

Contrast this situation to that which currently exists in the United States, where half of all shares is owned by individuals with the remainder largely held by proxies for individuals such as mutual funds, pension funds, and life insurers. Just as in Japan, ownership of companies is dispersed widely, making it difficult for any single shareholder to exercise influence even with his more formidable rights. As a group, however, these shareholders have one common objective: to make as much money in the shortest time possible. They achieve their goals by having managers reduce their time horizons and focus on short-term profits. Companies that fail to heed their demands find their share prices driven down, where they become potential takeover targets.

Managers in the United States thus face a continual conflict of interest between acting for the good of the company and for the good of the shareholders. In many cases, they decide to act for their own good, enriching themselves with high salaries during their tenure with the firm and with "golden parachutes" in case they are forced out. In recent years, managers have resorted to leveraged buyouts to escape from the short-term view of Wall Street and its fickle investors.

How Japan developed its unique system of corporate ownership of companies can be traced to historical events. The current concentration of stock ownership in the hands of Japanese companies is not unlike the structure of holdings that existed before World War II. At that time, a few large family-owned companies known as *zaibatsu* propelled the economy. Although the first stock market appeared in Japan as far back as 1878, it was largely irrelevant to the financing

needs of the *zaibatsu*, which controlled banks and other cash-rich institutions. It was not until after World War II that a share exchange,
such as is understood in the West, got off the ground. Before then
there was little difference in the investor's mind between markets for
stocks and markets for commodities like rice. Both were meant for
speculation rather than for long-term investment, and big companies
went only fitfully to the stock market to raise cash.

The American Occupation forces under General Douglas MacArthur tried to place the economy on a modern, Western footing by
breaking up the *zaibatsu*. The authorities sold off their shares to the
general public, and the Japanese parliament passed the Securities and
Exchange Law in 1948, establishing a formal structure for the TSE
and eight other regional exchanges (one has since closed) as well as a
regulatory framework for the entire industry. This was the one time
in Japan's modern economic history that share ownership can truly
be said to have been democratic in the Anglo-Saxon sense.

This state of affairs proved short-lived. Japanese companies soon
began to reestablish their old ties through what was, in effect, a share
"buy-back," which continues today. Unlike in the United States,
Japanese companies are prohibited by law from buying their own
shares and holding companies are illegal. So they have bought each
other's shares instead. Japanese corporations today hold 70 percent
of all outstanding stock, the same percentage owned by individuals in
1949, in the widespread fashion of cross-shareholding.

A MARKET TO SERVE JAPAN

The degree to which managers in Japan are the de facto owners of
corporations does not explain why the market is so actively traded or
why it has performed so well. If anything, the structure of ownership
should have acted to discourage short-term investors. The objective
of cross-shareholding, after all, was to wrest corporate control from
their hands.

Japan's stock market might have developed along the lines of West
Germany's (where large business groupings were also dismantled by
the U.S. forces after World War II) and other European countries'
where similar corporate-ownership patterns exist and stock markets

are much less robust. But this did not occur because of one important plank in the 1948 legislation which Japan stuck faithfully to: Article 65 of the Securities and Exchange Law kept banks out of the securities business (as in the United States and until recently the United Kingdom). Because German-style universal banking was prevented from taking hold, Japan spawned a powerful group of companies, the securities houses, which have continually pressed for the development of a bigger, stronger stock market.

It was the intention of the United States to establish Japanese brokerages as a constituency that would keep the banks in check. The plan succeeded well beyond expectation. Known as the Big Four, Japan's four largest securities houses—Nomura, Daiwa, Nikko, and Yamaichi—have become the largest brokers in the world. They exert a tight hold on the TSE, where they are responsible for almost 40 percent of all shares traded. Their goal has been to win business from individual investors and companies by keeping stock trading active, by promoting higher share prices, and by facilitating new corporate issues. Supporting their efforts is a massive media effort to generate active investor participation.

The brokerage oligopoly is regarded as a necessary evil in Japan. Issuers are dependent on the Big Four because they can be relied upon to distribute their corporate paper better and at a higher share price than anybody else. Investors follow their recommendations since they create liquidity in a market that has a natural tendency to freeze over due to the large percentage of shares locked away in corporate vaults. When uncertainty pervades the stock market, both issuers and investors depend on the Big Four to stabilize share prices. Although the TSE is too large for the stockbrokers to prop up, the shortage of tradable shares allows it to be pushed higher, or at least supported, at critical moments.

The power of the brokers is further enhanced by the fact that Japan's bureaucrats work closely with the securities firms and other financial institutions to ensure that the market performs to satisfaction. Officials tend to turn a blind eye to the use of the stock exchange by politicians for party fund-raising (done by manipulating share prices for a profit), and the legislators reciprocate by taxing capital gains as lightly as possible. The Securities Bureau of the Finance

Ministry protects the brokers from encroachment by the banks and maintains fixed equity brokerage commissions, the largest source of profit for the securities houses. The Finance Ministry permits financial institutions to operate price cartels so that cash flows continuously into the stock market. But the Finance Ministry is not only a disinterested upholder of Japan Inc.; it also tries to sell government-owned shares in companies like Nippon Telegraph and Telephone and Japan Railways at the highest possible price in an effort to pay off the public sector's debts.

Over the years, the government has intervened to buttress share prices by forming special institutions charged with the task of acquiring stocks that nobody else was prepared to buy. The most recent of these support operations took place in the mid-1960s, the last time the market experienced a prolonged slump.

Because the stock market is made to fit so neatly into the rest of the economy, it has become a powerful tool of Japanese business. This is no happy accident: the entire Japanese economy is galvanized to maximize growth for strategic reasons. Money raised through the stock market is quickly invested in improving efficiency, expanding capacity, developing new products, and taking over foreign rivals. It is hard to understand the remarkable role of the stock market without considering the context in which it operates.

Ever since the 1860s when the country was forcibly opened to Western trade and to the modern era, a strong Japan has meant having a competitive industry. After the Meiji Restoration which abolished the *samurai* system and created a modern state, the aim was to catch up with the West, both militarily and economically, under the slogan "rich country, strong army." When Japan's humiliating defeat in World War II led it to renounce "the right of belligerency," the national focus changed. The country's strength would now come solely from a strong economy.

This focus has shaped Japan's business life. First, companies are geared to growth in output. With few natural resources and a population that now exceeds 120 million, Japan would achieve its objective by the export of manufactured goods to pay for the imports of food, oil, and raw materials. Accordingly, Japan chose to concentrate on capital- and technology-intensive industries, because this was where demand and productivity rise fastest. Industry in turn required an abundant and low cost supply of capital. Until the 1980s, the primary source of capital was bank loans; then it became the stock market.

Second, markets are a means to an end for Japan and not, as they are in the United States, an end in themselves. The stock market, like other markets, is made to work for the benefit of Japan and its goal of national security through economic strength. Over the years, the government has intervened in almost every market. Before World War II, subsidies and other concessions were provided to industry so as to avoid surrendering to the demands of the Western Imperial Powers. After the war, the authority of Japan's bureaucracy was enhanced by its inheriting the sweeping mandate of the U.S. Occupation forces. It used this new authority to orchestrate the country's remarkable postwar development.

MITI, the Ministry of International Trade and Industry, chose what technology to introduce, controlled the flow of foreign exchange, decided what sort of equipment could be bought abroad, and even picked who could have the currency to travel. The domestic market was kept closed to imports of manufactured goods through quotas, duties, and a labyrinthine distribution system. This benefited exporters by allowing them to build economies of scale and to use high domestic prices to subsidize their exports.

The bureaucracy sometimes made bad mistakes, as when Sony was initially refused permission, in 1953, to import a new invention called the transistor that later became the basis for the entire electronics industry. But for the most part, MITI has achieved its goals—so successfully that it has been proposed that the United States establish a similar government department.

The structure of share ownership and the strength of the stock market works to the bureaucrats' own benefit. Since shares are owned by corporations, the bureaucrats need not compete with shareholders in determining whether companies should focus on profits or market share. Market share is the predetermined goal of Japan's managers, and they are thus more receptive to industrial policy than would otherwise be the case. By making certain that the stock market is a ready source of corporate funds, the bureaucrats help Japanese companies maintain their pace of investment. In fact, it can be argued that a strong bureaucracy is necessary in Japan precisely because there are no other checks on the behavior of managers. In the absence of a forthright parliament, strong trade unions, or a consumer movement, officialdom is the sole countervailing force to big business.

FINANCIAL POWER

The tight concentration of stock ownership in the hands of firms which represent the interests of managers rather than shareholders is the essential ingredient of the tremendous financial strength of Japanese companies. There are four elements at work here: low-cost finance, hidden assets, *zaiteku* (financial engineering), and high earnings retention.

Free Money

The stock market gives companies the ability to raise funds cheaply by issuing new shares or equity derivatives such as bonds with warrants at high prices. The cost of issuing new shares averaged less than 1 percent in 1989—against a long-term prime rate in excess of 5 percent. It is no wonder that Japan has been on a capital-spending spree—it has cost virtually nothing to invest!

In theory, equity capital is never cheaper than debt because equity carries more risk for the investor. Debt has to be paid back on time, whereas shares only produce a return if the stock price goes up or if the company chooses to pay a dividend. In the case of Japan, however, companies look at the cost of equity merely in terms of the dividend they need to pay—usually ¥5 per share, the legal minimum for issuing new shares. Companies are able to get away with this because corporate shareholding effectively denies to outside shareholders rights normally associated with shares, including the right to a healthy proportion of the company's earnings or a voice in management. To ensure that this continues to be the case even while issuing more new equity, a company will have its corporate shareholders purchase a majority of these shares.

Companies listed on Japan's stock market issued ¥70 trillion worth of equity and equity-related instruments between 1982 and 1989. In

Manufacturers' Investment and Financing

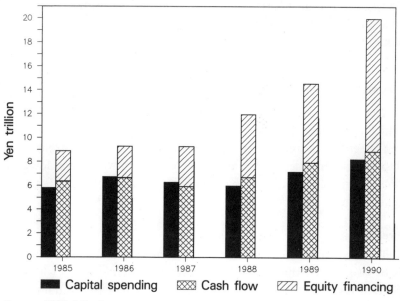

Source: *Nikkei Business*

1989 alone, over ¥25 trillion was raised, equivalent to 6.3 percent of gross domestic product. Much of this amount was raised overseas by issuing warrant bonds (bonds with entitlements to buy common stock at a fixed price within a certain period) in foreign currencies. When the proceeds were swapped back into yen, companies actually ended up paying negative interest rates. Convertible bonds (bonds that can be converted into shares at a fixed price) carried coupons of only 1.5–2 percent a year for blue-chip firms. And if that were not enough, the money raised in 1987–89 so exceeded what listed companies needed for plant and equipment that the surplus was invested in the stock market or in bank accounts. It has also been used to purchase assets, including competing firms, overseas.

In the United States, companies were moving in the opposite direction. Over the same period of 1982–89, companies bought back a net

$495 billion in equities as a result of mergers, leveraged buyouts, and stock-purchase programs. Rather than raising money by issuing shares, corporations were spending their hard-earned cash to buy their own shares from investors. Despite the need for the United States to rebuild its industrial base to compete with Japan, cash was drained out of corporate America.

If the trends in Japan and the United States are taken together, Japanese companies have increased their equity base by $1 trillion relative to their American competitors. U.S. companies experience only the disadvantages of a listing and have to work to minimize the damage on their business. Japanese companies recognize the benefits of a listing and have tried to take full advantage of them while they last.

Thick Cushions

Hidden assets provide another great advantage. Most major Japanese companies today sit on large unrealized capital gains on their equity shareholdings acquired decades earlier at a fraction of their present market value. These hidden assets are a luxury, allowing companies to carry more debt than would otherwise be possible and to command higher credit ratings. These assets can also be drawn on in times of need, either to survive a downturn in demand or to conceal mistakes by management.

Financial Magic

Quick financial gains to bolster company income, a process referred to as *zaiteku*, are another blessing of the stock market. *Zaiteku* earnings were of critical importance in 1986–1987 in helping Japanese exporters weather the impact of the rise in the yen. Under Japanese accounting these earnings are considered "recurring" profits (that is, from continuing operations) even though they usually have nothing to do with a firm's main line of business. The system has become so well entrenched that most companies have established trusts for their excess cash called *tokkin* funds (specified money trusts). These funds permit companies to segregate their long-term corporate shareholdings from their short-term trading account, thereby making them liable to taxation only on those gains from shares in *tokkin* funds. For some companies, gains in the stock market have become a steady and necessary source of profits.

Undistributed Bounties

Finally, because profits or earnings per share are less important to shareholders, Japanese companies need neither report high profits nor pay large dividends. A company is foolish to show higher profits than necessary since this only increases the amount of taxes that it must pay out. Japanese companies thus squirrel away earnings in reserves for times of need and spend heavily on investment in order to increase their depreciation tax shield. A Japanese company can also retain more of the earnings it does report because dividends are usually fixed at a percentage of the face value of the share.

None of these financial advantages that Japanese companies derive from the stock market is enjoyed by U.S. listed companies. Equity in the United States is viewed as expensive compared with debt, because dividends are costly on an after-tax basis and grow over time. American companies have thus repurchased more of their shares than they have issued for the past decade. Since listed companies do not as a rule hold shares in other listed companies, the capital gains resulting from a rising stock market accrue to investors, not companies. For the same reason, shareholdings are not a means for building relations with suppliers and customers. The equivalent of *zaiteku* profits is rare, and when they do occur they are treated as an extraordinary gain that does not contribute to earnings from continuing operations. A listing requires that a company pay attention to its shareholders and that it focus on short-term earnings rather than long-term growth.

DESIGNED TO GO UP NOT DOWN

The competitive advantages that Japanese companies gain from their stock market depend on a single factor: share prices must go up. It is the steady appreciation in share prices that allows the market to function in the way described here. Yet as they have risen at a rapid pace, share prices have gradually lost touch with the fundamental earning power of the companies which they represent. Although continued ascent becomes more difficult, the higher the altitude, the more necessary further rises become.

Whether or not the price rises continue, the structure of the stock market has been designed to promote exactly that. Most stocks are held by strategic investors who are not price-sensitive.

Despite the massive increase in the supply of shares over the years, prices kept on rising, primarily because firms that issued new equity plowed much of the proceeds back into the market. New shares from an issuer were thus willingly accepted, provided that the issuer could be counted upon to do the same for its shareholders when they wanted to sell new shares of their own. This virtuous circle was the flywheel of a veritable money machine.

The cross-shareholding system has also had a critical impact upon the way Japanese share prices behave. Stable shareholders do not sell either when the market tumbles or when it rises sharply. They hold on to the stock because to sell would be a breach of faith with the company whose shares they own. If they did turn those shares into cash, the other company would be released from its obligation to continue holding shares in the seller. Cross-shareholdings are therefore mutually reinforcing, and the steady tightening of these relationships is a continual source of buying pressure.

The Finance Ministry has helped to encourage this by permitting institutional investors—banks, insurance companies, investment trusts, and pension funds—to operate price cartels. With no price competition on investment products, institutions can continue to tie up their assets in low-yielding, long-term shareholdings. This inefficiency is paid for by the beneficiary, whether that person is a depositor, policyholder, or unit-trust holder.

The shortage of tradable shares in the stock market makes it easy for the Big Four to promote higher share prices, which in turn stimulates interest in equity investment and helps companies with their equity financings. Individuals continue to invest in the stock market despite their second-class status, for they too stand to benefit.

Ever higher share prices have made Japan's stock market tolerant of poor management at listed firms. Because shares have performed so well for so long, investors in Japan demand less from a company's management. In such a market, shares tend to move for reasons other than pure fundamentals. Often all that is required is a persuasive market theme. If a company had strong earnings growth, its shares would rise as an "earnings play." If it had weak earnings but large holdings of land or stocks, its shares would rise as a "hidden-asset play." And when the hidden assets were lacking, it would qualify as a "takeover play in need of restructuring." Between 1968 and 1989, the unprofitable, unglamorous stocks of fishery and mining companies performed just as well as the shares of Japan's much-vaunted electronics industry.

Rising share prices also serve to protect companies against hostile takeovers. Few but the richest firms in the world could contemplate buying a corporation whose shares were valued at a PER of 50. A U.S. company could not justify such an acquisition to its shareholders. Yet even poorly performing firms have almost never been brought into play. Not every company is well managed or can have realized the full value of its assets, even in Japan. But weak companies surprisingly tend to carry the highest PERs in the market.

Until recently, it did not matter if Japan's stock market did not follow American precepts of how a stock market should be run or how a share should be valued, because America's standards dominated the investment community around the world. Likewise, Japan's different economic philosophies, though a constant source of friction, could be ignored, because they were insignificant.

The United States is, however, no longer the economic powerhouse it once was, and Wall Street's preeminence among the world's stock markets is challenged by the Tokyo Stock Exchange. The American fear of the competitive challenge from the Japanese economy has developed into a paranoia that the United States will somehow be bought up by firms from Japan. These fears, though exaggerated, do contain a grain of truth—Japanese companies are, indeed, using their greater financial strength to increase their global market share. Because Japan's stock market values its equities in such a special way and treats its companies so differently, every country that has felt the heat of Japanese competition now knows something about the power of Japan's stock market firsthand.

A DESIGN FLAW

Japanese stocks may appear invincible, but they are not crashproof. The Tokyo share market has fallen abruptly, by more than 12 percent on 17 separate occasions since 1949. The two biggest bear markets, which began in 1961 and 1973, were both ushered in by tight money. It took seven years, in the case of the earlier bear market, and six years, in the case of the later, for shares to achieve their earlier peaks. Although the structure of the stock market is intended to promote higher share prices, the TSE remains, despite appearances to the contrary, a real market where prices are determined by buyers and sellers. Investors received a nasty reminder of this in the first three months of 1990 when the Japanese stock market plummeted 29 percent from its high at the end of the previous year.

A number of hypotheses have been put forward to explain the sudden change in direction—a sharp rise in interest rates, the Bank of Japan's actions to control excessive money supply growth, the perception that the economy had peaked—but essentially, it seems that the plunge was a response to a stock market that had ballooned way out of proportion. It was inconceivable that Japanese companies could perform well enough to justify their sky-high share prices. And the rise in interest rates engineered by the central bank triggered the fall.

Without a restoration of confidence in the Japanese stock market, investors only have "fundamentals" as a yardstick by which to value shares. Since dividend yields had dwindled to 0.4 percent and PERs had risen to 60, portfolio investors bought shares solely to make a quick capital gain. Thus, if stock prices failed to rise, they would have to fall to the point where they compare favorably, on a risk-adjusted basis, with other financial instruments before true "value-oriented" investors will step in.

In a bear market, the cross-shareholding network is much less supportive than might be imagined. Strategic investors do not sell when prices fall, but they do not buy either. In the absence of any investor willing to buy, share prices can fall very quickly on little trading volume.

The slump in the early months of 1990 suggests that the spectacular rise in the stock market has begun to undermine a system that has taken corporate Japan four decades to construct. The stock market has become bloated relative to the size of the Japanese economy and it is impossible for share-price growth to continue at its former pace. What is more, the rapid appreciation in wealth in Japan is destabilizing the real economy. Too much affluence is concentrated in the hands of Japanese corporations, leading to high property prices, excessive investment in equipment, and increased trade friction with other countries. And it is turning classless Japan into a country of haves and have nots.

Because corporations have benefited most from the rise of the stock market, they also have most to lose from its fall. Equity financings would be cancelled, unrealized capital gains would shrink, and *zaiteku* profits would turn to losses. Without a recovery of share prices, outstanding convertible bonds and warrants would not be exchanged for equity, and companies would be forced to borrow from banks in order to redeem them. All in all, the impact of a prolonged bear market today would be felt much more keenly than earlier when the stock market was just a sideshow. It now occupies center stage.

A weaker stock market would shake institutional investors out of their complacency. Faced with the prospect of holding poorly performing assets, they would become more vocal in their demands for higher dividends and for a greater say in management. The network of stable shareholdings would disintegrate. The edifice of Japan Inc. could start to crack.

Chapter 2

WHO OWNS JAPAN INC.

In the United States, the primary reason for owning shares is to earn a satisfactory return on investment. In Japan, the ownership of shares serves a different purpose. It is a key that can unlock the door to a very private world—where the decisions of corporate Japan are made. Few are admitted into this inner sanctum—and then only after years of having proved their worth as a reliable supplier of goods and services, or as a loyal customer. But once the honored position of "stable shareholder" is achieved, trust and confidence flow easily, contracts are signed, loans are issued, and technologies are traded.

Understanding this relationship will help to explain the behavior of the Japanese stock market. If a shareholder in the United States believes that the price of his shares will fall, he will sell them to take profits or to cut his losses. When the price of a Japanese stock falls, the stable shareholder will not sell because his relationship with the company whose stock he holds would suffer. Stable shareholding is a long-term business tie which is kept knotted at the bottom of the cycle as well as the top, through thick and thin.

The relationship between the company and the stable shareholder is based on the mutual long-term benefits that both the firm and the shareholder hope to enjoy. In many cases, two firms will own shares in each other to ensure that the stock is in friendly hands. As such, most shares in Japan are owned for strategic rather than pure investment purposes.

This does not mean that the stable shareholder eschews a good

return on his investment, because that is what business is about, East
or West. The return to a stable shareholder, however, is not
calculated simply by looking at dividend income and capital gains,
but rather by taking into account all the financial, commercial and in-
tangible benefits that accrue to the long-term equity holder.

There are investors in Japan who resemble investors in the United
States. Their primary interest is in the maximization of capital gains,
Japanese dividends being too meager to matter much. Invariably
these investors own only a minority of the equity. It is stable
shareholders who predominate, and the fact that they do affects
every important element of the Japanese stock market—capital
issues, dividend yields, shareholder rights, share-price behavior, and,
most important, the value investors place on common stock.

By limiting the supply of actively traded shares, stable shareholding tends to make Japanese shares more illiquid than they
appear. And because stable shareholders are largely indifferent to the
stock price, the number of investors willing to sell does not increase
markedly when the price rises. Stable shareholders also help companies to issue equities, since they will purchase new issues in proportion to their stake in the company.

STABLE SHAREHOLDERS

Each year Japan's stock exchanges report the number of their
shareholders, and each year since 1970 this number has shown an increase. At the end of March 1989, the survey of corporate records
turned up 22.7 million shareholders in Japan—roughly one out of
every six people.

Taken at face value, these figures show an impressive degree of
shareholder democracy in Japan. The true picture, though, is somewhat different. Six shareholders own 25 percent of all listed shares in
the country. These plutocrats are not people but companies.

The top six shareholders in Japan are business groups referred to
as *keiretsu*, literally a "group arranged in order". Four of them are
the postwar successors to the largest holding companies known as
zaibatsu (or financial cliques), which rose to prominence after Japan
began to catch up with the West in the nineteenth century and which

Shareholders of Japan's 1,978 Listed Companies
(March 1989)

	Number of shareholders	Percent of all shares owned
National and local public organizations	1,364	0.7
Financial institutions	114,039	45.6
Long-term, city, regional banks	34,622	16.3
Trust banks	20,978	9.9
(owned by investment trusts)	6,942	3.1
(owned by pension trusts)	3,791	1.0
Life insurance companies	15,079	13.1
Casualty insurance companies	9,246	4.2
Other financial institutions	34,064	2.1
Industrial corporations	703,918	24.9
Securities companies	78,799	2.5
Individuals	21,644,201	22.4
Foreigners	152,597	4.0
TOTAL	22,694,918	100

Source: *Kabushiki Bunpu Jokyo Chosa, FY1988* (Tokyo: Zenkoku Shoken Torihikijo Kyogikai, 1989)

eventually extended their reach into every facet of Japanese business life.

The *zaibatsu* emerged after the Meiji restoration of 1868 when the state wanted to develop the economy as quickly as possible. This development was achieved by working closely with a few families that were especially aggressive in expanding their businesses. Each *zaibatsu* consisted of a privately owned holding company which, before World War II, controlled a number of manufacturers, trading companies, and financial institutions. The holding company owned strategic stakes in its core constituents and often in their satellites, leaving at best only a small quantity of shares available to the public.

Three of the six *keiretsu*—Mitsubishi, Mitsui and Sumitomo— bear the same names they had before the war, while Yasuda changed its name to Fuyo. The other two *keiretsu*, which evolved after 1945, are centered around Sanwa Bank and Dai-Ichi Kangyo Bank (DKB). The workings of these six *keiretsu* have had a significant impact on Japan's business world as well as its stock market.

It is important to note that, unlike the prewar *zaibatsu*, the latter-day *keiretsu* has no holding company at its center. This was the decree of the 1947 Antimonopoly Law, which was promulgated at the urging of the U.S. Occupation forces. The law declares that nonfinancial companies capitalized at more than ¥10 billion, or with net assets in excess of ¥30 billion, cannot own shares in another firm greater in value than their share capital or net worth. Banks are currently prohibited from owning more than 5 percent of the shares in any one company, and insurers from owning more than 10 percent. In the absence of holding companies and with limitations upon the amount that can be owned in another firm, the institution of cross-shareholding was born. It is the corporate equivalent of blood brotherhood.

A good deal more will be said later about these business groups, but at this point it is worth taking a closer look at exactly who are Japan's shareholders. Based on annual reports issued by listed companies and by the life-insurance industry (whose members are unlisted), a breakdown of share ownership shows that one hundred firms owned 40 percent of shares outstanding in March 1989, while listed companies and life insurers own 60 percent. With the inclusion of shares owned indirectly by corporations through trusts and by other unlisted firms, Japan Inc. owns 70 percent of itself.

These numbers indicate a much higher concentration of shareholding than what the stock exchange's survey of corporate records would lead one to expect. This is largely due to multiple counting. For example, while the survey shows over 15,000 life insurance shareholders, in fact Japan has only 25 life insurance companies, but each stake held in a company is counted as that of one shareholder. Japan's largest shareholder, Nippon Life, is counted 1,090 times for the shares it holds (ranking among the top twenty shareholders) in 1,090 companies. Multiple counting also holds true for individual investors. A 1983 survey conducted by the Securities Information Center found that only 4.2 million households owned shares, with individual shareholders numbering 5.9 million. While the actual

Actual Shareholders in Japan
(March 1989)

	Number of shareholders	Percent of all shares owned
LISTED COMPANIES		
City banks	12	9.2
Long-term credit banks	3	2.7
Trust banks	7	2.7
Regional banks	92	3.7
Casualty insurers	14	3.8
Major industrial corporations	250	17.1
Other industrial corporations	1,524	7.2
SUBTOTAL		46.4
UNLISTED INSTITUTIONS		
Major life insurers	8	10.8
Other life insurers	17	1.7
Unlisted casualty insurers	9	0.3
Investment trust management companies	15	3.1
Pension funds	NA	1.0
Tokkin & fund trusts	NA	2.6
Other trusts	NA	0.4
Other financial companies	NA	2.0
Unlisted industrial corporations	NA	4.7
Securities companies	NA	2.3
Public institutions	NA	0.4
SUBTOTAL		29.3
OUTSIDE SHAREHOLDERS		
Individuals	10,000,000	19.9
Foreigners	NA	4.3
SUBTOTAL		24.2
TOTAL		100

number has undoubtedly increased during the recent bull market—particularly after the public sale of shares of Nippon Telegraph and Telephone—it nonetheless remains well below published figures, possibly 10 million people.

The pattern of ownership today is radically different from what it was immediately after World War II. At that time, the Occupation forces under General Douglas MacArthur dissolved the *zaibatsu* as part of an overall plan to remove "all obstacles to the revival and strengthening of democratic tendencies among the Japanese people." Because these family-controlled groupings effectively controlled the economy, their breakup was seen as essential to the liberalization of Japanese society.

The groups targeted for liquidation were, as mentioned earlier, Mitsubishi, Mitsui, Sumitomo, and Yasuda, along with 79 other designated holding companies. Some 53 members of the *zaibatsu* families were also required to turn over their personal securities holdings. Eventually 30 of the holding companies were dissolved while the remainder were drastically restructured. The shares of these companies were sold to their employees, people living in the vicinity of their factories, as well as to the general public in a securities "democratization movement".

Widespread public ownership of corporations has not been a characteristic of Japan. In the years after the TSE was first established in 1878, only a small number of shares was ever traded because so few stocks were listed and the majority of these were owned by a handful of wealthy men. The situation changed a little in the 1930s when the *zaibatsu* needed to sell shares to the public in order to expand their heavy industries. Until this time, the Mitsui, Mitsubishi, and Sumitomo *zaibatsu* companies had relied primarily on their leading shareholders, usually senior executives or members of the controlling family, to provide new capital by borrowing from banks on the security of their shareholdings.

Just before the breakup of the *zaibatsu* in 1945, there were 443 million shares listed on the Tokyo Stock Exchange (TSE) and 1.71 million shareholders, of which 1.67 million were individuals. When the *zaibatsu* were dissolved, these groupings held 155 million shares, of which the controlling families owned 10.5 million. This represented a quarter of the shares listed and unlisted at the time. When the TSE reopened in 1949, individuals owned 69.1 percent of all listed shares, securities houses held 12.6 percent, other financial in-

Structure of Share Ownership

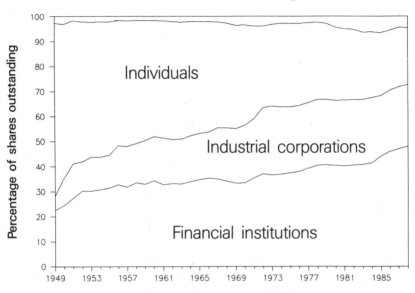

Source: Securities Exchange Association of Japan, FY89

stitutions 9.9 percent, nonfinancial companies 5.6 percent, and the government 2.8 percent.

Today the situation is almost completely reversed. Corporations own 73 percent, individuals 22.4 percent, the government 0.7 percent, and foreigners 4 percent. Thus, for only a brief period in the 1950s was corporate Japan truly owned by "the people." Since then, the percentage of shares outstanding held by individuals has steadily dropped as companies in general and *keiretsu* in particular have built up their own holdings. It is ironic that the six big *keiretsu* today own a quarter of total shares outstanding—the same proportion held by the *zaibatsu* when they were dissolved in 1945.

A decline in individual share ownership has also been seen in the United States. Yet, while individuals' holdings have fallen from 71 percent of the market in 1980 to 59 percent by 1988, most of this decrease has been taken up by proxies for individuals such as mutual funds, pension funds, and insurers. U.S. corporations own few shares in other listed companies, and banks are prohibited by law from doing so.

Why Individuals Sold

Since the relative decline of individual shareholdings in Japan is so important, it is worth understanding why this happened. Japan's defeat in World War II saw the transfer of *zaibatsu* shares to individuals, who began in 1947 to bid up share prices by as much as seven times on the unofficial over-the-counter market as a hedge against rampant inflation. Payment for the purchase of these shares was one of the few ways that access could be gained to bank deposits frozen just after the war. When this inflation was abruptly halted in 1949 by strict fiscal controls advised by American banker Joseph Dodge, shares lost their attraction as a hedge. As soon as the stock market reopened in 1949, many of these shares were sold.

In the 1950s and early 1960s, individuals often had to sell part of their holdings when companies issued a rights offering to their shareholders. This is the right to buy new shares at the standard par value of ¥50 a share. These rights offerings were the only way companies could increase their equity capital, but the drawback was that the rights were not transferable (a restriction lifted in July 1966).

If individuals did not have the money to pay for their shares, they were forced either to sell part of their old shares for cash or to forgo the new shares allotted to them. Because the market price of a share was adjusted downward after the rights issue to reflect the increase in shares outstanding, investors unable to pay for the new issues suffered a capital loss. They thus sold their shares to investors who could afford to pay—conveniently enough, banks and other stable shareholders. After "public" offerings at market price were permitted in 1969, the public was rarely allocated shares. Selected companies received them instead.

The major reason for the decline in individual shareholdings was that as prices rose, individuals chose to realize their gains. These holdings were sold through the stock market and often bought by corporations. Moreover, rampant stock price inflation has put direct investment in equities out of reach of many ordinary people because the minimum order is 1,000 shares. Individuals have, instead, taken to buying investment trusts (mutual funds in U.S. parlance).

The decline of the individual's stake in Japan Inc. has gone unlamented by corporate issuers. From their point of view, individual investors are a headache. As unstable shareholders, they will sell their shares when prices rise or when a fall is anticipated. In addition, they lack the wherewithal enjoyed by banks and insurance companies to buy new issues of shares.

The two bear markets that occurred in 1949–50 and 1961–65 highlighted the apparent fickleness of individual investors. In the first postwar bear market, individuals sold their shares almost immediately after the market reopened in order to pay for daily necessities. At the time of the second bear market, investment trust companies were one of the biggest shareholding institutions, but when individuals rushed to redeem their investment-trust certificates, the sell-off worsened. At their peak in 1964, investment trusts owned 9.5 percent of all shares. That quickly dropped to less than 2 percent and has since stayed close to that level.

In both cases, the government acted to reverse the share slump. In 1951 the Finance Ministry introduced margin trading, raised the limit a bank could own in a company from 5 percent to 10 percent (since reduced to 5 percent in 1987), and reestablished the investment-trust industry. During the second slump, the authorities, banks, insurers, and securities companies set up, in 1964 and 1965, two special institutions for the purpose of buying shares held by the investment trusts and securities companies. Two lessons were learned from these experiences. The first was that it was possible to support share prices by intervening in the market. The second was that prevention—in the form of stable shareholdings—was better than the cure of intervention.

Why Companies Bought

The original motive for stable shareholding was a fear of being taken over. With so many shares in the hands of individuals in the 1950s, a number of takeovers were attempted. The most celebrated of these was the bid for control of Yowa Real Estate, the predecessor to Mitsubishi Estate. This worried the former *zaibatsu* companies, particularly those of the Mitsubishi Group, since Yowa Real Estate owned many of the buildings in which they were head-quartered. When the 1947 Antimonopoly Law was relaxed in the 1950s, *zaibatsu* companies saw stable shareholding as an effective means of takeover protection, and the practice flourished.

Another wave of stable shareholding occurred when Japan became part of the Organization for Economic Cooperation and Development (OECD) in 1964, one requirement of which was capital liberalization. In fear of being bought by foreign companies, almost every company raised its stable shareholding level. This period also saw the establishment of industrial *keiretsu* among assemblers and their parts suppliers.

Stable shareholding was given a boost in 1969 by a change in the way new shares were issued from rights offerings at par value to public offerings at market price. This permitted companies the luxury of issuing fewer shares to raise the same amount of funds and of sell-ing these shares to selected shareholders.

From its roots as a takeover defense, stable shareholding was in-stitutionalized within corporate Japan. Today it is a symbol of part-nership in business.

THE FAVORED FEW

The structure of share ownership in Japan has created two classes of shareholders, the "outsiders" and the "insiders." The outsiders, who are individuals, foreigners, and speculative groups, buy shares purely for investment and, in the issuer's view, contribute nothing to the growth of the company's business. Their main functions are to help the company maintain its listing requirements and to create some liquidity in its shares.

The sole objective of outsiders is to make a capital gain by buying cheap and selling dear. Holding onto shares for the sake of the divi-dend has not been part of investor psychology since the late 1960s, a time when the average yield on the First Section of the TSE exceeded 4 percent. It is now 0.4 percent.

The obsession with capital gains is often attributed to tax laws. Un-til April 1989, capital gains earned on annual transactions of up to

200,000 shares were tax-free. Since then, a capital-gains tax of 1 percent of the value of each sale of shares is levied for individual investors (actually the tax is 20 percent, but capital gains are assumed to be only 5 percent per sale). On dividends, however, investors must pay a 20 percent withholding tax. While the difference in tax should not be ignored, the more critical factor is that outsiders have no alternative but to take a capital gain since they have no power to force managers to increase dividends.

For insiders, who own shares for strategic reasons, the situation is strikingly different. They are a company's partners, whose relationship is both symbolized and insured by stable shareholding. As long as two companies trust each other, the stable shareholder will continue to hold his stake and will remain a silent shareholder. The voting rights to which they are entitled through their shareholdings are entrusted to management, guaranteeing votes for the Board of Directors. Should the stable shareholder be treated poorly, however, it can either sell its holdings or exercise its voting rights against management.

The system does not buy independence, however. No company is completely autonomous because stable shareholding in the company also implies a degree of control. Most companies prefer to have a large number of stable shareholders rather than a few big ones. Yet, 474 out of 1,612 listed companies on the TSE have a single shareholder who owns more than 20 percent of their outstanding shares, making them in essence subsidiaries. The flow of goods and services reflects the pattern of cross-shareholding. This decreases business risk and consummates the relationship between companies. But it also limits free competition and encourages the growth of cartels.

The inside shareholders are the stakeholders in a Japanese company. They consist of customers, suppliers, employees, and banks. Ideally, all stakeholders will be shareholders. To strengthen the common bonds, 91 percent of all listed companies have employee shareholding plans with an average participation rate of 46 percent. The amount of shares employees own, though, is less than 1 percent of the total.

Special privileges are accorded to the inside shareholders. The major shareholders—the 12 city banks—maintain seats on the boards of 597 listed companies and account for 35 presidents and 44 vice-presidents of industrial companies. Until recently a company reported the business results to its main shareholders prior to a public announcement. Formally, at least, this practice was made illegal when Japan's insider-trading regulations were tightened in April 1989.

Although stable shareholders do not invest in shares to make a profit primarily, the share price is important in two respects. First, if it rises above acquisition cost, the unrealized capital gains give hidden strength to the balance sheet. This improves a company's credit rating and enables a borrower to collateralize its shareholdings, thus gaining leverage for further investment. Second, if the share price falls below the acquisition cost, the shareholder must then show a valuation loss on its income statements. Most strategic investors, however, rarely have to face this prospect because the greater part of their holdings was bought before 1970 at prices close to par value (in most cases ¥50) in a market where the average share price at the end of 1989 was ¥1,800.

There is a third group of investors that cannot be categorized as either insiders or outsiders. They include investment trusts, pension trusts, *tokkin* funds ("specified money trusts"), and fund trusts. These funds are not completely stable because they are intended to act as investment instruments for the benefit of individuals (as in investment trusts and pension trusts), or as anonymous vehicles through which stable shareholders can behave like outside investors and trade shares actively (as in *tokkin* funds and fund trusts). Their investment behavior and performance suggests, however, that their objective is not solely to generate the best profit. In fact, most of these trusts have the more modest aim of simply offering a higher return than money-market instruments.

THE *KEIRETSU*

Consider now the ties that bind the constituent members of the big six *keiretsu*. According to *Toyo Keizai*, a leading economic publishing company, these six groups owned 25 percent of all shares

Japan's Major Industrial Groups

	Total companies in group	Total listed companies
Daiei	133	7
Fuji Electric-Fujitsu	172	12
Hitachi	679	24
Ito-Yokado	27	4
Kobe Steel	114	11
MEI	560	12
Mitsubishi Chemical	118	8
Mitsubishi Corp.	459	7
Mitsui & Co.	513	13
NEC	185	9
Nippon Kokan	107	6
Nippon Steel	190	34
Nissan	104	28
NYK	181	5
Seibu Railway, Seibu Saison	50	8
Sekisui Chemical	172	4
Sumitomo Metal Industries	150	12
Tokyu	351	14
Toshiba	246	14
Toyota	259	26
TOTAL LISTED COMPANIES		258

Source: *Kigyo Keiretsu Soran 1990* (Tokyo: Toyo Keizai, 1990)

outstanding as of March 1989, but the six are not the only shareholding groups in Japan. Add to the list 40 other major business groups which have grown up since the war, centered around such companies as Toyota Motor, Nippon Steel, Tokyu Corporation, Matsushita Electric, and Hitachi. These groups control an additional 5 percent of Japanese shares.

Because the big six *keiretsu* employ as little as 4 percent of the Japanese labor force and account for only 14 percent of all corporate sales, the argument has been made that their influence on the economy is exaggerated. But there is no doubt that they dominate the stock market. In the fiscal year ending March 1989, they were responsible for 58 percent of all listed companies' sales (excluding financial institutions), 39 percent of net income, and 35 percent of assets. To date, the core companies of these *keiretsu* have issued 46 percent of all outstanding shares, 18 percent of which is cross-held within the groups.

The best example of a seamless web of cross-shareholdings is the Mitsubishi Group, the most traditional-minded of the *keiretsu*. The original Mitsubishi company was established in 1870 when Yataro Iwasaki, an entrepreneur, started a shipping company by leasing three steamers from a territorial lord. In a short time and with much government help, Iwasaki came to dominate the Japanese shipping industry. The Mitsubishi company gradually expanded into related businesses like trading (Mitsubishi Corporation), casualty insurance (Tokio Marine & Fire Insurance), warehousing (Mitsubishi Warehouse), shipbuilding (Mitsubishi Heavy Industries), and banking (Mitsubishi Bank).

Today the group is centered on a trading company, a bank, and a shipbuilder. The group owns 26.9 percent of its own member companies' shares and 5.4 percent of all shares outstanding in the stock market. Over the past decade, cross-shareholding levels have stayed remarkably steady. It might have been expected that the members of the *keiretsu* would become more independent, but this has not occurred.

The recent activities of the Mitsubishi *keiretsu* show that its companies are improving their own competitive position as well as that of the *keiretsu*. In October 1989, Mitsubishi Estate invested ¥120 billion in the Rockefeller Group to give it a firm position in the New York real estate market. In December 1989, Mitsubishi Corp., Mitsubishi Chemical, and Mitsubishi Paper spent ¥18 billion to bring under their wing a major textile maker, Kojin, that had restructured after going bankrupt in the mid-1970s. In March 1990, Mitsubishi Corp. completed its ¥130 billion takeover of Aristech Chemical, the former chemical division of USX, with financing provided by Mitsubishi Bank and Mitsubishi Trust Bank. It plans to break up Aristech and

Ownership in the Mitsubishi Keiretsu
(March 1989)

	Percent of company held by group	Percent of group owned by company
Mitsubishi Corp.	32	1.90
Mitsubishi Bank	26	3.69
Mitsubishi Heavy Industries	20	2.48
Mitsubishi Trust Bank	28	4.99
Nippon Trust	15	0
Tokio Marine & Fire	24	2.77
Kirin Beer	19	0.39
Mitsubishi Rayon	25	0.13
Mitsubishi Paper	32	0.14
Mitsubishi Kasei	23	0.99
Mitsubishi Gas & Chemical	24	0.22
Mitsubishi Petrochemical	37	0
Mitsubishi Plastic	57	0
Mitsubishi Oil	41	0
Asahi Glass	28	0.94
Mitsubishi Mining & Cement	37	0.44
Mitsubishi Steel	38	0
Mitsubishi Metals	21	0.30
Mitsubishi Cable	48	0.07
Mitsubishi Kakoki	37	0.02
Mitsubishi Electric	17	0.64
Mitsubishi Motors	55	0.11
Nikon	27	0.15
Mitsubishi Estate	25	0.81
Nippon Yusen	25	0.52
Mitsubishi Warehouse	40	0.19
Meiji Life (mutually owned)	—	4.77

Source: *Kigyo Keiretsu Soran 1990* (Tokyo: Toyo Keizai, 1990)
Note: Percent ownership based on top twenty shareholders of company

Japan's Top Shareholders
(March 1989)

	Portfolio value (¥ bn)	Percent of stock market (%)
Nippon Life	15,456	2.99
Dai-Ichi Life	10,585	2.05
Meiji Life	7,413	1.44
Taiyo Kobe Mitsui Bank	6,997	1.36
Sumitomo Life	6,968	1.35
Industrial Bank of Japan	6,587	1.28
Dai-Ichi Kangyo Bank	5,984	1.16
Fuji Bank	5,529	1.07
Mitsubishi Bank	5,390	1.04
Sanwa Bank	5,196	1.01
Asahi Life	5,065	0.98
Long-Term Credit Bank	4,875	0.94
Sumitomo Bank	4,854	0.94
Tokio Marine & Fire	4,527	0.88
Tokai Bank	3,748	0.73
Mitsui Life	3,261	0.63
Mitsui Trust Bank	3,075	0.60
Mitsubishi Trust Bank	3,060	0.59
Yasuda Life	2,932	0.57
Bank of Tokyo	2,730	0.53
TOTAL		22.14

Source: *Kigyo Keiretsu Soran 1990* (Tokyo: Toyo Keizai, 1990)

sell the parts to Mitsubishi Chemical, Mitsubishi Petrochemical, Mitsubishi Gas Chemical, and Mitsubishi Rayon. In the same month, four companies of the Mitsubishi *keiretsu* reached agreement with West Germany's Daimler-Benz Group for a broad range of business tie-ups. Most recently, Mitsubishi Metal and Mitsubishi Mining & Cement agreed to merge in December 1990 to become Japan's largest

producer of nonferrous metals. Both companies were part of Mitsubishi Mining until 1950, when the metals division was spun off as a
separate company.

Note how cash-rich financial companies dominate the holdings of
the Mitsubishi's Group's shares. The top 20 corporate shareholders
in Japan are, in fact, all financial institutions; together they control
22 percent of shares outstanding.

The structure of ownership in a *keiretsu* is different from the single
holding company of the *zaibatsu*. The shareholders of the *zaibatsu*
holding companies were profit-motivated individuals just like the early capitalist families of the United States, the Rockefellers, the
Vanderbilts, and the Mellons. The shareholders of the *keiretsu* are
corporations, creating an economy in Japan that could be described
as corporatism.

The members of the *keiretsu* are more independent than were the
zaibatsu companies, and their shareholding structure is less
vulnerable because there is no single paramount company that can be
targeted. A stone thrown through a *keiretsu* web will make a hole,
but the web can remain intact. Moreover, *keiretsu* have prospered by
being a lot less exclusive than the *zaibatsu*. A Mitsubishi Group company will buy from a Sumitomo firm and borrow from Dai-Ichi
Kangyo Bank. But when the integrity of the group is threatened,
affiliates are expected to rally round to protect the center.

Only six of the former *zaibatsu* dismantled after the war were able
to regroup as *keiretsu*. The Nissan Group, made up of 137 companies
before the war, including Nissan Motors and Hitachi, never restructured. Even so, the ties remain strong, with Hitachi today supplying
most of the electronic parts for Nissan cars.

These two companies have managed to form another type of *keiretsu*, the industrial group, where several companies cluster around a
single large company, usually a long-established manufacturer. Such
groups are born in the following way: a division of the main company is established as a separate company which in turn establishes
other companies in order to increase the rate of growth and diver-
sification. This also helps to decentralize decision making.

Companies often voluntarily join an industrial *keiretsu* to
strengthen their business ties with the main company. The members

Listed Nippon Steel Group Companies

		Percent owned by Nippon Steel
NIPPON STEEL	World's largest steelmaker	
ORE AND MATERIALS		
Nittetsu Mining	Limestone mining	27.8
Japan Metals & Chemicals	Top ferroalloy manufacturer	8.7
Pacific Metals	Largest producer of ferronickels	13.2
Nippon Denko	2nd largest ferroalloy producer	5.8
Kurosaki Refactories	Firebrick maker	44.0
Harima Ceramic	Firebrick maker	45.6
Kyushu Refactories	Firebrick maker	15.0
Shinwa Kaiun	Ore shipping company	13.1
BLAST FURNACE STEELMAKERS		
Nisshin Steel	Blast furnace steelmaker	9.5
Nakayama Steel	Medium-sized integrated steelmaker	—
ELECTRIC FURNACE STEELMAKERS		
Godo Steel	Major electric furnace steelmaker	6.3
Tokai Kogyo	Small electric furnace steelmaker	10.0
Topy Industries	Electric furnace steelmaker	7.8
SPECIALTY STEELS		
Daido Steel	World's largest special steelmaker	10.3
Sanyo Special Steel	Principal maker of special steels	11.9
Aichi Steel Works	Toyota-related special steelmaker	7.7
ROLLED STEEL		
Daido Steel Sheet	Principal maker of galvanized steel	47.8
Toshiba Steel Tube	Small-diameter steel tubes	15.7

Takasago Tekko	Cold-rolled stainless steel hoops	19.2
Nippon Kinzoku	Stainless steel hoops and rims	12.3
STEEL PRODUCTS		
Nichia Steel Works	Thin wire rods and iron sheets	23.8
Suzuki Metal Ind.	Integrated steel wire maker	22.0
Nippon Concrete Ind.	Concrete products	13.0
Tokyo Rope Mfg.	Wire rope manufacturer	—
Nippon Tetrapod	Wave-killing concrete blocks	22.9
Sanko Metal Ind.	Long-span metal roofing	15.7
CHEMICALS		
Nippon Shokubai Kagaku	Leading chemical maker	10.5
Nippon Steel Chemical	Coal-chemistry based chemical co.	58.7
Nihon Parkerizing	Rust preventatives	5.5
CONSTRUCTION		
Fudo Construction	Civil engineering	16.0
Taihei Kogyo	Construction and engineering	43.4
Okazaki Kogyo	Plant engineering and construction	5.2
Chuo Build Ind.	Maker of lightweight scaffolding	6.6

Source: *Japan Company Handbook* (Tokyo: Toyo Keizai, 1990

of such groupings include component suppliers, specialized manufacturers, distributors, and joint ventures in new enterprises. In some cases, the main company of the group is also a member of a bank-centered *keiretsu*, as is the case with Mitsui & Co. and Hitachi.

The number of subsidiaries and affiliated companies in these industrial groups can grow very large. There are 513 companies in the Mitsui Group, 679 companies in the Hitachi Group, and 133 companies in the Daiei Group. Most of these satellite companies are majority-owned and unlisted, though some of the bigger groups have several listed companies of which the main company might own 10–60 percent.

The group centered around Nippon Steel, the world's largest steelmaker, provides the best example of how shareholdings in an industrial *keiretsu* are used to extend the reach of a company. Nippon Steel and its group of 190 companies had combined sales of ¥6.2 trillion in the year ending March 1989. The group is engaged in a broad range of activities including production of ordinary steel, specialty steels, processed steels, chemicals, energy, alloys, ceramics, as well as transport and information services. There is considerably less cross-shareholding among the group than within the six big *keiretsu*. Instead, Nippon Steel holds a stake in all of the companies.

In contrast, the NYK Group, centered on Japan's largest shipping company, has only four listed affiliates. All were independent companies forced to join NYK when the shipping industry was restructured around six core shipping companies by the government in 1964. The remaining 37 consolidated subsidiaries and 181 unconsolidated subsidiaries engage in shipping, marine resorts, harbor transport, trucking, air freight, trading, real estate, and finance.

In the Matsushita Electric Group, many of the listed companies are very large, but they nonetheless remain consolidated subsidiaries of Matsushita Electric. Matsushita owns 50.8 percent of Japan Victor (which had sales of ¥866 billion in the year ending March 1990), 57.5 percent of Matsushita Telecommunications, 57.3 percent of Matsushita Kotobuki Electronics, 51.8 percent of Kyushu Matsushita, and 27.8 percent of Matsushita Electric Works.

In general, financial companies hold the shares of manufacturers, and manufacturers hold shares of financial companies. Financial institutions own 47 percent of the shares of manufacturing companies and 40 percent of the shares of other listed financial companies, while nonfinancial corporations own 22 percent of the shares of manufacturing companies and 42 percent of listed financial companies. The banks are the most important type of shareholder.

Chapter 3

THE BIG INVESTORS

THE BANKS

The banks are at the heart of Japan Inc., owning 18 percent of the nation's equity. The Finance Ministry has divided up the banking industry in order to rule it. There are 1,079 deposit-taking institutions in the country, ranging from agricultural giants to credit cooperatives, but as far as the stock market is concerned, only four categories really count: long-term credit banks, trust banks, city banks, and regional banks. Almost every bank in Japan owns a sizable portfolio of equities, but by far the largest concentration of shares is held by the three long-term credit banks, the six biggest city banks (each of which leads a *keiretsu*), and the seven trust banks.

The three long-term credit banks—Industrial Bank of Japan, Long-Term Credit Bank, and Nippon Credit Bank—have been responsible for much of the long-term lending for industrial investment in Japan since 1945. They therefore have close ties to capital-intensive companies such as electric utilities, steel makers, shipbuilders, petrochemical companies, car manufacturers, and heavy-machinery makers. The banks' links to government are also closer than those of other financial institutions because they are an important tool of industrial policy. With their wider loyalties, the long-term credit banks have transcended *keiretsu* ties in their efforts to promote economic development, and they own a vast array of shares.

The six largest city banks—Sumitomo, Mitsubishi, Taiyo Kobe

Mitsui, Dai-Ichi Kangyo, Sanwa, and Fuji—are the core companies of their own *keiretsu*. When *zaibatsu* holding companies were banned after World War II, these banks came to assume the mantle of chief protector and promoter of their respective groups. They are the main shareholders in each *keiretsu* and provide much of the group companies' borrowing. In the Sanwa group, for example, Sanwa Bank provides 19 percent of the loans of Fujisawa Pharmaceutical, 25 percent of the loans of Hitachi, and 15 percent of the loans of Sekisui House, Japan's largest house builder.

Each trust bank—Sumitomo, Mitsubishi, Mitsui, Yasuda, Chuo, Toyo, and Nippon—is related to one of the city banks. They are the only banks permitted to do trust work. This involves the management of pension funds (a privilege they hold almost exclusively with the life-insurance companies), fund trusts, and other trust assets as well as the administration of *tokkin* funds and investment trusts. Although long regarded as the poor relations of the city banks, the dramatic growth of the Japanese stock market caused a surge in trust banks' assets and profits in 1982–88.

Most of the shares held by the banks are for stable shareholding purposes, not portfolio investment, and were acquired in the 1950s and 1960s. That was a time when stock prices were a fraction of what they are now. Portfolios were accumulated with two aims in mind: first, to rebuild the business ties destroyed when the *zaibatsu* were dissolved; and second, to cement the relationship between a bank and a borrower through cross-shareholdings.

This was critical during the era of double-digit annual economic growth in 1955–72. Money was chronically in short supply. Interest rates were held at artificially low levels by the government, and credit had to be rationed. For the borrower, maintaining a good relationship with a bank was therefore vital to the growth of a company's business. Banks gained from equity participation in growing companies, while stable shareholding enabled firms to be highly leveraged. A share stake in a borrower gave the bank a strong incentive to stand behind the firm if it ran into trouble.

Companies in turn held shares in the banks, and if they found themselves in trouble they could sell these shares to realize a capital gain. When stable shareholders are greatly in need of cash, they do

Companies with Lowest Levels of Individual Ownership
(TSE 1st sec., March 1989)

	Percent of shares owned by individuals
Industrial Bank of Japan	2
Long-Term Credit Bank	3
Nippon Credit Bank	4
Yasuda Trust	4
Mitsubishi Trust	4
Sumitomo Trust	4
Mitsui Trust	5
Showa Shell	5
Japan Housing Loan	5
Koito Manufacturing	5

Source: *Kabushiki Bunpu Jokyo Chosa, FY89* (Tokyo Zenkoku Shoken Torihikijo Kyogikai, 1989)

sell their stocks, but to other stable shareholders. In 1974–75, when industrial profits collapsed due to the soaring cost of oil, many companies did just that. Even now, many of the small troubled shipping companies that are unable to pay interest or principle on their borrowings still maintain large holdings of bank shares. One example of this is Taiyo Kaiun, which has only five ships and 124 employees yet owns more than ¥14 billion-worth of equities.

Despite a big shift from bank financing to equity-linked financing by listed companies since 1975, the banks' appetite for owning shares has not diminished. This can be seen in the rising percentage of total shares outstanding owned by banks. They have continued to be major buyers of new equity issued by corporations, even though the money raised is often used to retire debt owed to the banks.

The reasons why the banks continue to buy shares are, again, strategic. For one thing, a higher shareholding compensates for the loss of influence over a company that would normally follow a reduction in bank borrowing. The banks themselves are now hungry for capital and have repeatedly called on their own stable shareholders to buy their new issues of equity. Companies are more likely to heed them if the banks have done the same for them too.

Although many large companies no longer need to borrow much money, banking is still a matter of relationships. The banks want to earn fee income generated by such activities as foreign-exchange dealing, advice on mergers and acquisitions (M&A), and when permitted, equity underwriting. Stable shareholding opens doors, so banks have an unrivalled information network that customers can draw upon. And with M&A becoming more prevalent in Japan, firms are hoping that banks can help protect them from unwanted corporate suitors. It is estimated that the new strategic investments of the five major city banks amounted to ¥1.1 trillion in fiscal 1988, up sharply from ¥150 billion in 1986, and ¥500 billion in 1987.

These privileges for the banks do not come cheap. The average yield on common stock was 0.4 percent at the end of 1989, while the average cost of funds to the banks was 5 percent. But the banks themselves have been raising a great deal of money in the stock market, and they tend to pay an even smaller dividend than average. Moreover, these yield figures apply only to newly purchased shares. The yield the banks receive on the book value of their holdings is considerably higher than the market's current yield as most of the shares owned by the banks were acquired at prices close to par value. Nonetheless, the acquisition of shares in recent years has led to a steady decline in the average yield on their portfolio to 2–3 percent.

The rising share ownership by the banks and indeed all financial institutions has created a situation similar to what existed during the era of the *zaibatsu*. Companies have come to depend on the banks and other stable shareholders to purchase their shares and on internal sources of finance rather than on funds provided by the public at large, the result of which further tightens the banks' control over the stock market. This is one of the primary reasons that the banks are so keen to enter the securities business, from which they are currently forbidden. Their control of the stock market through share ownership would allow them to dominate corporate underwriting, if the government were, as expected, to remove the wall separating banks from securities houses.

Apart from straightforward share buying in their own names, the banks also purchase shares in two other ways. One is through *tokkin* funds. These are special trusts set up by banks, insurers, and nonfinancial firms to enable them to trade actively in the stock market. The trusts are treated as separate from long-term investment portfolios; when a *tokkin* fund sell shares, the bank is only liable for capital-gains taxes based on the acquisition cost of shares bought by the *tokkin* fund rather than on the average acquisition cost of all the shares the bank owns in a company. Beyond their tax-relief appeal, *tokkin* funds also permit banks to trade in shares anonymously so that corporate relations are not upset.

Tokkin funds are managed by investment advisory companies, usually subsidiaries of banks, insurers, or securities companies, but the fund sponsor has a fair degree of leeway in deciding what is bought or sold. The typical performance target of a *tokkin* fund is an 8 percent annual return. Although illegal, it is common practice for an investment advisory firm to guarantee such a return to its client in order to increase funds under management.

Until March 1989, profits derived by the banks from *tokkin* funds were treated as "other interest income" under bank accounting rules, even though they were actually capital gains. This allowed them to conceal the poor profitability of their banking business. Since then, new rules require them to disclose their *tokkin* profits separately.

The other means of trading in shares is through fund trusts. Managed by trust banks, these offer the same financial benefits of *tokkin* funds. One advantage of fund trusts is that the trust assets can be transferred directly to the sponsor when the term of the trust expires, allowing the sponsor to delay realizing capital gains or losses. *Tokkin* funds must be redeemed in cash.

Banks have become more active traders of shares than has been the case, and their holdings have grown. Is there anything that can stop their growing further? In 1945, General Douglas MacArthur's Occupation administration prevented individual banks from holding more than 5 percent of the shares outstanding in any single company. This was raised to 10 percent by the Finance Ministry in 1951 to permit the banks to support share prices during the bear market of the time. But at the end of 1987, the 5 percent rule was reimposed, compelling many banks to reduce their stakes in companies. Banks will

probably try to find ways to circumvent the limits—through the use
of *tokkin* funds and other types of trusts or through their many leasing, consumer finance, and real estate subsidiaries and affiliates.

In view of the importance of the banks, it is puzzling why the Occupation authorities did not dismantle them as they did the trading
companies. Mitsui Trading and Mitsubishi Trading were completely
dissolved in July 1947, but the banks were largely untouched, except
for the limitation on the number of shares they could own and the
separation of banking from securities underwriting. A couple of
plans were, in fact, considered by U.S. officials to split up each of the
big banks into two or more parts, but after due consideration only
Teikoku Bank got the ax. Teikoku was the largest bank in Japan
before the war, formed from the merger of Mitsui Bank and Dai-Ichi
Bank, which the Mitsui *zaibatsu* had originally established. The bank
was split into its original parts, then in 1972 Dai-Ichi Bank merged
with Nippon Kangyo Bank to form Dai-Ichi Kangyo Bank (now the
world's largest), and in 1990 Mitsui Bank merged with Taiyo Kobe
Bank. The banks were thus able to regroup many of the original
elements of the *zaibatsu* and emerged stronger as a result.

THE INSURERS

Japan's 155 banks held ¥193 trillion worth of personal savings in
June 1989, more than 29 percent of individuals' total savings. The 48
life and casualty insurers held ¥128 trillion. This higher concentration of funds gives the insurance industry a great deal of influence as
an institutional investor. This is particularly true for the big seven life
insurers—Nippon, Dai-Ichi, Asahi, Meiji, Yasuda, Mitsui, and
Sumitomo—which have more than ¥85 trillion in assets. One sign of
this influence is that insurers are allowed to hold up to 10 percent of a
company's stock, double the limit for the banks.

From a company's viewpoint, insurers make ideal shareholders
because they almost never have any reason to sell. They own 16 percent of outstanding stock but account for less than 1 percent of turnover in the stock market. They are forbidden by the Finance
Ministry from paying their annual dividend to policyholders from
capital gains. Better still, they have enormous inflows of cash with

which to buy additional shares, and except for the listed firms, they do not burden companies with issues of their own. Some 15 of the 23 casualty insurers are listed, while all 25 life insurers are unquoted. Most of the latter are mutual companies, belonging to their policyholders.

Realized capital gains either offset capital losses or are placed in special reserves, which can then be drawn upon to pay a special dividend when a life-insurance policy matures or the holder dies. With little need to sell their shareholdings, the life insurers have accumulated unrealized capital gains of ¥36 trillion as of March 1990. Since most life insurers are mutually owned by their policyholders, these gains are legally the policyholders' property although in practice they are not.

Some of the companies suggest that they could not pay out these gains even if they were permitted to do so, because they do not know how much belongs to current policyholders and how much to deceased ones. The listed casualty insurers make a similar case. They say that it is impossible to determine how to divide their hidden assets between policyholders and shareholders, so they have decided not to apportion them at all. As policyholders do not receive the benefits of the buildup of these capital gains, insurance premiums are much higher in Japan than they ought to be, judging by their investment returns.

If outside investors are constantly searching for capital gains, insurers are always on the lookout for higher yields to pay policyholders. Accordingly, the life insurers have invested heavily in high-yielding U.S. treasury bonds, even though they suffered currency losses of ¥4.3 trillion in the three years to March 1988 due to the drop in the dollar. This is no small sum considering that total securities investments abroad in that period was ¥13.1 trillion. The life insurers can be reckless with their investments, because the cushion of hidden assets allows them to conceal their mistakes. When Drexel Burnham Lambert went bankrupt in early 1990, its largest unsecured creditor was Taiyo Life and its fourth largest was Sumitomo Life.

Investment in equities made accounting sense in the 1950s and early 1960s when dividend yields went as high as 11.9 percent, but that rationale disappeared as dividend yields fell significantly below Japanese government bond yields. Nippon Life—the world's largest nongovernment insurer—owns 3 percent of the entire Tokyo stock market. It earned a yield of 1.94 percent on its stock portfolio in the year ending March 1989, a quarter of its return on bonds. But Nippon Life and the insurers continue to be steady buyers.

Why do insurance companies bother? One reason is that the government allows them to use *tokkin* accounts to skirt the problem of not being able to pay policyholders from capital gains. In January 1988, in order to restore confidence in the stock market following the crash, the ceiling on *tokkin* investment was lifted from 3 percent of their total assets to 5 percent. Such accounts were needed to pay variable life policies, where the proceeds fluctuate depending on the performance of the funds. These policies were first introduced in 1986.

The main reason for buying shares, though, is the same as for the banks—strategic necessity. Since 1945, insurers have performed a service similar to that of the banks—making long-term loans to industry. A quarter of a century later, 68 percent of the life insurers' assets were still in the form of loans. But by 1988 this proportion had fallen to 36 percent, again for the same reason as with the banks: major companies no longer need to borrow. As a result, the proportion of their assets held in securities has doubled during the same 18-year period to 44 percent.

Insurers buy shares to maintain good ties with their borrowers, to sell group insurance, and to gain entry to a firm's premises during working hours to solicit contracts from employees. And they are bound to the *keiretsu* almost as tightly as the banks are. Nippon Life is affiliated to the Sanwa *keiretsu*, Meiji Life to the Mitsubishi *keiretsu*, and Sumitomo Life to the Sumitomo *keiretsu*. In another, more unusual example of vertical integration, Chiyoda Fire and Marine, a medium-sized casualty insurer, is particularly strong in car insurance—not surprising, given Toyota's 40.6 percent ownership of the company.

Insurers are becoming choosier, nonetheless, about the companies in which they are willing to become a stable shareholder. Unless a company has a pension fund to be managed or a large number of employees for group insurance, it is very difficult to procure a life in-surer as a stable shareholder. Dai-Ichi Life earmarks ¥300 billion a year for strategic holdings, yet receives requests totalling ¥1 trillion from its sales department. Life insurers are no longer the shareholder of last resort they once were.

Even if there were no strategic reasons for buying shares, Japan's insurers have too much money and too few alternative investment op-portunities to stop purchasing, given their tremendous inflow of funds. Life insurers' assets grew from ¥46 trillion in March 1985 to ¥112 trillion in March 1990, and are expected to grow rapidly for the next twenty years. Casualty insurance firms are increasing at a similar rate, albeit from a much smaller base of ¥22 trillion worth of assets as of March 1990.

Such forecasts could well prove conservative for one reason—that Japan's population is aging rapidly. The proportion of people over the age of 65 will more than double to 25 percent between 1990 and 2020. That is roughly the same proportion as in other developed coun-tries, but the rate of change is twice as fast as in the West. So the population is preparing for that day by saving for old age. The Japanese people now face the same problem as the life insurance com-panies in that there are not enough instruments to invest in. Life in-surance has a virtual monopoly on the management of long-term sav-ings, while they and the trust banks control virtually all the country's private pension funds.

Furthermore, the premiums that insurers charge their customers is fixed by the life and casualty industry cartels so that companies do not need to compete on investment performance. Interest rates on savings products offered by the casualty insurers are kept slightly above the rate on bank deposits, while the top five life insurers pay an identical annual dividend to their policyholders (6.5 percent a year in March 1989). Little wonder that insurers are among Japan's most profitable companies.

In exchange for protection from price competition, the industry's investment policy is tightly regulated by the Finance Ministry. Almost all the premiums received by the life insurance companies, whatever the source, is put into a general account. Companies can in-vest no more than 30 percent of their general account in equities, no more than 30 percent in foreign securities, and no more than 20 percent in real estate. Their loan portfolio is controlled as well. Three different laws keep them out of banking and securities dealing and prevent them from competing directly with casualty insurers.

The insurance industry may have significant investment power, but their influence within the Finance Ministry is considerably weaker than that of the banks. The insurers aspire to be major players in international finance, particularly investment banking, but the law prevents them from setting up their own banking institutions in overseas markets, let alone domestic ones; Japanese banks, on the other hand, have securities subsidiaries abroad. As an alternative, insurers have acquired strategic stakes in foreign investment banks and fund managers, notably Nippon Life's 13 percent acquisition of Shearson Lehman Hutton. At home, Nippon Life and Sumitomo Life together have sizable stakes in eight stockbrokers.

What may seem puzzling is why insurance firms do not use their influence to demand higher dividends from issuing companies. In fact, the association of insurers publishes an annual list of companies that fail to meet the promised ratio of dividend payout to net profit, threatening refusal to subscribe to future public offerings from these companies. Yet the embarrassment has little effect on the offenders even as the payout ratio continues to fall. The muted reaction to such broken promises might be due to the insurers' desire to avoid alienating too many companies lest the authorities suggest a lowering of the ceiling on their corporate shareholding. All those insurance funds have to go somewhere. And the more the insurers press their demands as investors, the fewer benefits they will receive as stable shareholders.

PENSION FUNDS

Japan's life insurers already play an important role in the stock market. It is a role that can be expected to expand further because life insurers share, with the trust banks and Daiwa Bank (the only city bank allowed to conduct trust business), the right to manage all private pension funds. The only exception is a small amount of employees' pensions, which were opened in 1990 to investment advisory firms, including foreign firms. Pension assets totalled ¥123 trillion in March 1989 and are predicted to grow by 15 percent a year well into the next century. Of this amount, ¥92 trillion is in government hands, part of which is passed to the insurers and trust banks. Guidelines for investments are tight here, too. Up to 30 percent of the total portfolio is allowed for equities and the same proportion for foreign-currency securities.

Until now, pension management had been about as cozy as the insurance business. Under the guidance of the Finance Ministry, insurers got away with paying more or less uniform rates of return (about 9 percent in 1988) and with avoiding the public disclosure of the exact amount of their returns. The trust banks have made disclosures only since 1986. Investors could see how management had performed—from an average return of 12.6 percent in 1988 for Chuo Trust to 5.7 percent for Daiwa Bank. Even so, performance relative to returns from the stock market is abysmal. The average corporate pension fund returned 9.5 percent in fiscal 1986, 9.2 percent in 1987, and 8.5 percent in 1988, while the stock market was up 5.3 percent, 17 percent, and 25 percent respectively.

Companies rarely choose pension fund managers on the basis of performance, however. The purchase of a computer system or the extension of a loan may be sufficient to win the rights to manage a pension fund, but the determining factor is more fundamental—stable shareholding. In October 1989, when Japan's five largest steel companies (Nippon, NKK, Kawasaki, Sumitomo, and Kobe) announced they were establishing pension funds, they stipulated that any interested trust bank or life insurer should be prepared to buy at least 10 million shares of a company. If they wanted to handle the lucrative administrative work for these funds, they would have to buy 50 million shares. This meant a purchase of 600–700 million shares in all. Why the strong-arm tactics? The steel companies, which had just completed equity-linked financings, found their share prices slumping soon after as investors began worrying that steel profits had peaked. Since further financings would be required to improve their balance sheet, their shares had to be rescued.

Such coercion may become a thing of the past, if and when performance-based competition among pension-fund managers heats up. The decision by the government in 1990 to open the industry to outside managers was a small step in this direction. The liberalization affects employees' pension funds of ¥19.6 trillion, which are growing by 15 percent a year. Up to ¥1.5 trillion annually will be open to outside investment advisors to compete for. Eventually, this amount will be 30 percent of total pension assets.

INVESTMENT TRUSTS

At the end of 1989 the average price of a share on the Japanese stock market was ¥1,867 with a minimum trading order of 1,000 shares for a ¥50 par-value stock. If paid for in full, a single transaction would cost the average office worker the equivalent of three months' salary. Investment trusts are therefore one of the more affordable ways for small investors to play the stock market, apart from margin trading. The return these trusts have achieved has been dismal. In the 12 months to July 1989, 27 percent of 903 funds surveyed returned less than 5 percent to the investor during a period in which the average return on common stock was 20 percent. More than four-fifths of the trusts delivered less than 10 percent, and through the 1980s when the market appreciated 21 percent annually, the average return was 3.8 percent on an equity investment trust.

Investment-trust management firms in Japan say that the objective of most funds is not to outperform a stockmarket index, but to provide a better return than that of a bank deposit—hardly a challenge. It should be noted that "equity" funds invest less than 40 percent of their total assets in the stock market. An average of 20 percent of funds are kept in call loans (overnight loans to banks) and 30 percent in bonds, including convertible bonds. It is a testament to the hard work of the investment-trust sales force—and to the lack of saver choice—that the amount invested in investment trusts rose eightfold to ¥57 trillion in 1981–89. About three quarters of the 3,000 funds on offer are for stock investment, and they held 3.4 percent of all equities at the end of 1989. This underestimates their importance, because they accounted for almost 8 percent of total stock market transactions that year.

The disparity between share of ownership and share of turnover

Investment Trust Assets

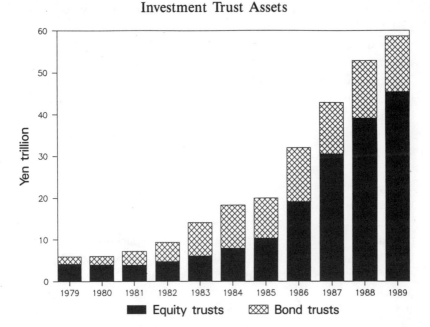

Source: "Monthly Report of Investment Trusts," no. 352 (Tokyo: The Investment
Trust Association, 1990)

would indicate that investment trusts are churned mercilessly, at an
average rate of 2.5 times a year. The reason for the high turnover and
the poor performance is the same: they are managed by a small cartel
of Japanese stockbrokers' affiliates. Competition has been virtually
nonexistent. Until 1990, only 15 companies had licenses to offer investment trusts in a market of the same size as that of the United
States, which has 350 firms. The four largest investment-trust
management firms in Japan—which are tied to Nomura, Daiwa,
Nikko, and Yamaichi—control three-quarters of the industry and
usually turn in the worst performances.

Brokers receive a lot of business from investment trusts. When a
new fund is launched, the broker selling the investment trust certificate earns a sales commission. When the investment trusts buy or
sell stocks and bonds, the broker also earns a commission. And
because brokers own the investment-trust management companies,
the annual management fee comes to them as well. The trusts, which

are both closed and open-ended, usually cannot be redeemed for the first two years of their five-year life. But unit-trust holders come under intense pressure from salesmen to cash out of funds and to reinvest in new ones as soon as it is legally possible.

Paradoxically, the better the fund performs, the higher the redemption rate. Investors are keen to take their profits as soon as they can, because so many trusts do badly. The trusts claim that this need to meet redemptions accounts for the high ratio of funds invested in cash. Even so, a 30–40 percent allocation to cash seems excessive.

The trust managers' choice of stocks is poor, because they have no choice. Securities companies tend to foist low-quality shares onto the fund managers to support the stock price of a corporate client or to dump new issues that have not been taken up by other investors. At the end of 1985, when the stronger yen was sparking investors' interest in domestic stocks and bank shares, the trusts had 34 percent of their portfolio in export-oriented electricals and only 4 percent in financials.

Japanese investment trusts have never benefited the subscribers much. In November 1941, Nomura Securities launched Japan's first investment trust, and even while the war worsened for Japan, new investment trusts continued to appear.

The government allowed sales of investment trusts to resume in July 1951 in order to help absorb excess shares from the market, which had slumped following its reopening in June 1949. By 1952, investment trusts owned more shares than the life insurers. The growth of the investment trusts was the most important factor in the growth of securities companies. The Big Four dominated the business, their sales accounting for 90 percent of all trusts established in 1958.

The trusts were managed by a department of the securities houses, despite the conflict of interest. When setting up trusts, stock departments would buy shares and then sell them to the trusts at the highest possible prices. Their brokerage business was helped by the trusts holding shares which would then be sold to clients; after the share prices had risen, the trusts would buy them back to allow clients to get out at a profit. As the abuses grew more severe, the Ministry of Finance in 1959 urged the separation of the investment trust business from the other activities of the securities companies. Investment trusts were reorganized into affiliated sales and management companies. This did not end the conflict of interest.

By autumn 1961, the stock market began to falter, but the trusts went on investing in stocks to protect the value of the brokers' own large stock inventories, and by 1962 they held 8.6 percent of all shares. As the bear market worsened, trust holders began to redeem their certificates, exacerbating the slump. Eventually the Bank of Japan helped set up a special institution to buy the shares held by the investment trusts.

In the October 1987 crash, investment trusts bought heavily in order to restore confidence in the market. The subsequent rebound in the market proved the decision was correct, but investment trust holders scarcely benefited, judging by the poor returns of the trusts in 1987–89. And when the stock market fell 29 percent in the first quarter of 1990, the investment trusts were net buyers of ¥1.4 trillion worth of shares.

Competition in the industry may intensify in 1990 when a handful of foreign investment-trust managers are allowed to start selling domestic funds. This measure is intended by the Finance Ministry to give the old cartel a run for its money, but little more than that. New firms must create a network for the distribution of their investment trusts throughout Japan. Since it is too costly to establish a large branch network, the new firms are forced to rely on Japanese brokers to whom they must pay generous brokerage commissions. With their large branch networks, Japan's banks would provide a more formidable challenge to the brokers, which is why they are being kept out of the investment-trust industry.

FOREIGN INVESTORS

If individual investors are unreliable as far as Japanese firms are concerned, foreign investors are an outright threat. One of the strongest incentives for building up cross-shareholdings in the mid-1960s was to prevent takeovers by foreign companies. In 1972, the government in principle allowed the possibility of a foreign takeover, causing corporate share ownership to jump up.

There have been no successful hostile takeovers of a Japanese company by a foreign concern (and only a handful of failed attempts). There have not been many friendly acquisitions either. Such takeovers usually occur when the targeted company is so weak that no other Japanese company would buy it. One example is Sansui Electric, a loss-making manufacturer of audio equipment, which was acquired by Polly Peck International, a British firm, in October 1989 for ¥15.6 billion. Another was Banyu Pharmaceutical, taken over by Merck of the United States in 1983.

Japanese law specifically limits foreign ownership in 21 "strategic" companies. Foreigners are not permitted to own shares in Nippon Telegraph and Telephone (NTT) or Kokusai Denshin Denwa (KDD), respectively the domestic and international telephone companies. When shares of Katakura Industries, a small silk spinner, were being acquired by a Hong Kong group in 1978–79, the government stepped in to prevent foreigners taking more than 25 percent of the firm.

Foreign investors have been active in Japan's stock market since the early 1960s. For a while they were the trend setters, their every move eagerly followed by small, local investors. But as share prices climbed, foreigners grew wary and sold off their holdings in 1983–89. By the end of the decade, they owned only 4 percent of Japan's total equity against 6.3 percent in 1983. Because of foreigners' tendency to sell at the first sign of trouble, a high foreign ownership ratio is today regarded as a liability by domestic investors (as well as by issuing companies).

The largest foreign shareholders in the market are U.S. automakers and oil companies. General Motors owns 0.1 percent of the Japanese stock market through a 40 percent share of Isuzu and a 3.6 percent stake in Suzuki Motors. Ford owns 24 percent of Mazda, and Chrysler 10.2 percent of Mitsubishi Motors. Esso Eastern, Shell Petroleum, Mobil Oil, Caltex, and the Kuwaiti and Saudi Arabian governments all have major stakes in Japanese oil refiners and oil-exploration companies. However, these major foreign shareholders do not seem to understand the purpose of equity holding in Japan and treat it rather like a portfolio investment. General Electric once owned 10 percent of Toshiba but sold its holdings in the early 1980s. Getty Oil owned 50 percent of Mitsubishi Oil but sold its shares to

Firms Where Foreign Ownership Is Restricted

	Maximum %age share ownership allowed
Arabian Oil	25
All Nippon Airlines	33.3
Asahi Broadcasting	20
Chubu Broadcasting	20
Fuji Electric	25
General Oil	49
Hitachi	25
Japan Air Lines	33.3
Katakura Industries	25
KDD	0
Mainichi Broadcasting	20
Mitsubishi Oil	50
Nippon Air Systems	33.3
Nippon Television	20
NTT	0
Sankyo	25
Showa Shell	50
Toa Sekiyu	50
Tokyo Broadcasting	20
Tokyo Keiki	25
Tonen	50

Source: Nihon Keizai Shimbun

the Mitsubishi Group for $210 million in mid-1984. At the end of 1989, these Mitsubishi Oil shares would have been worth $1.7 billion. Chrysler reduced its stake in its Japanese partner in late 1989 in order to raise cash.

GOVERNMENT

The Ministry of Finance is also a big shareholder, though in recent years it has been selling its holdings to the public as it privatizes industry. It is currently in the process of selling its shares in NTT and will later sell off the former Japan National Railways. The way the government sold part of its holdings in NTT says much about its attitude towards investors.

The plan involved selling half NTT's shares to the public in four tranches while keeping the rest in state ownership. The first tranche, it was decided, would be sold in two stages: first, 200,000 shares in October 1986 at a public auction to big investors on whom the government could rely to set a "fair" price, and second, the remaining 1,650,000 shares later at a price based on the average bid at the auction. The early bids may have even surpassed Finance Ministry expectations if the resulting initial public offering price was any indication: an extraordinarily high ¥1,197,000, or 77 times prospective March 1988 earnings. When the remaining shares were sold in single units by lottery in February 1987, more than 10 million Japanese applied. The lucky ones saw NTT's stock open for trading at ¥1,600,000; from there it soared to ¥3,180,000 nine weeks later. At its peak, the entire telephone company was valued at ¥50 trillion with a prospective PER of 204.

NTT's share price then began a relentless decline. It was only with great effort on the part of stock brokers that NTT's share price could be stabilized around ¥2,600,000 in October 1987, the time of the crash, to set the stage for the sale of the second tranche the following month. Individuals did not want the shares, and so the tranche was forced into the hands of institutions and companies that did business with NTT. NTT's share price subsequently fell to below its initial public offering price (a decline allegedly tied to the expectation of the break-up of NTT into three companies).

The problems with NTT scared the government so much that when if offered shares of Okinawa Electric Power to the public in September 1989, the asking price was less than 10 times earnings and only slightly more than book value. The Finance Ministry is even more worried about listing the companies formed after the dissolution of Japan National Railways, the word's most heavily indebted corporation. By March 1991, JNR will have accumulated a deficit of ¥28 trillion. To cover this, the government would like to raise ¥15 trillion from the sale of stock to the public, with the remainder provided by the sale of former JNR landholdings, such as freight yards.

THE HERETICS

Japanese companies' desire to ensure that their shares are held by stable shareholders has ironically helped speculator groups, of which there are about 40 of note. These groups are not aiming for control of a corporate target; they know it would be almost impossible to achieve. Instead they try to embarrass the company into asking a stable shareholder to buy their shares back at a profit, often by exchanging the shares for land. Alternatively they try to corner all the floating shares of a company to lift the price. Another way is to reduce the number of freely traded shares to a point where a company faces delisting. This is easier to achieve than in most Western countries because there are so few floating shares.

An official study conducted between April 1987 and March 1989 found 128 cases of share cornering by speculator groups. Targeted companies included Konica and Kokusai Kogyo. In 1988 alone there were 95 such cases as compared with 25 targeted firms five years earlier. The impact of this buying on share prices is dramatic. In 32 cases, share prices rose by four to six times, and in nine cases the share price increased over 10 times. Janome Machine, the number two sewing machine maker in Japan, saw its share price rise from ¥346 in December 1985 to ¥4,280 in July 1988. Its three major current shareholders are Koshin, a speculator group that gained control of Kokusai Kogyo, Daiei Real Estate, and Toa Finance; together they hold a combined 29.6 percent of the company's shares.

Because of the intimate relationship between a company and its stable shareholders, the annual general meeting is a formality, lasting 45 minutes on average in 1989. It is the job of another variety of heretic, the *sokaiya*, to ensure that proceedings do not go smoothly.

Sokaiya literally means somebody whose business is to attend stockholders' meetings. Before World War II, *sokaiya* were freelancers who made certain these gatherings went smoothly and received a small honorarium from the company in return. Their activities later became a kind of protection racket, aimed at forcing companies to pay money to avoid embarrassment and at intimidating anybody else from asking awkward questions.

By the 1960s, *sokaiya* were moving into one another's territory, and bodyguards had to be hired in the event of violence. These toughs were often members of the *yakuza*, as the organized crime syndicates began to take an interest in the *sokaiya*'s business. Tokyo's Metropolitan Police Department knew of 908 *sokaiya* who were operating in its jurisdiction at the end of 1988. A third of them belonged to 24 different groups, while 220 were members of extreme right-wing organizations. In the rest of Japan, there were another 423 *sokaiya*. The police say that the *sokaiya* problem has declined since Japan's commercial law was amended in 1982 to make it a crime for companies to pay off extortionists, but no special law against *sokaiya* exists because of the difficulty of distinguishing between them and bona fide shareholders.

The Metropolitan Tokyo Special Violence Countermeasures Federation, a group of 1,420 firms trying to stamp out *sokaiya*, contend that the extortionists' activities "are becoming more complex, more diverse, and are spreading." What seems clear is that stockholders' meetings are now less popular for *sokaiya*. In Tokyo in 1988, there were only 93 who showed up, of whom 34 asked questions or made speeches.

Gone are the days when *sokaiya* could keep a shareholders' meeting going for more than 13 hours by continuously asking questions, as happened to Sony in January 1984. Instead, *sokaiya* are diversifying into the publishing business, burrowing for dirt on the private lives of company presidents or on dubious business practices. The firms concerned are then asked to pay large sums of money for a "subscription" to the publication.

But companies are not taking any chances. On June 29, 1989, 694 listed companies held their annual shareholders' meetings at the same time to try to prevent an individual *sokaiya* from attending more than one of them.

A CHINK IN THE ARMOR

Such investors as banks and insurers, which should be concerned about earning a good return on their holdings, are among the most docile shareholders and continue to be avid buyers of shares. They, like all financial institutions in Japan, have been heavily insulated from competition by bureaucratic regulation that has rigidly segmented the industry. Price cartels have been fostered and foreign firms kept out. Deregulation and the internationalization of Japan's financial markets could, however, force banks and insurance companies to reassess their investment policy and emphasize higher returns at the expense of their long-term business relationships.

In 1990, the market for investment trusts and pensions was opened to international competitors for the first time. Bank deposit rates are being liberalized, and new international rules for capital-asset ratios have been instituted. Moreover, as the population ages, the call for higher returns on investment will increase. With these changes in prospect, financial institutions may be forced to compete harder, and some of the indifference to returns may disappear.

In order to assess the impact of these factors on Japan, consider once more the predicament of the life insurance companies. They are taking in more premium income than they know what to do with. Their difficulty is investing the money wisely. For the first time in 14 years, they have been asked by the Finance Ministry to disclose the actual gains and losses on their equity, bond, and other investments starting in March 1990. This puts the insurers on notice that they will no longer be able to hide behind their status as mutual institutions. Yet pressure on the insurers for greater disclosure, embarrassing them into performing better, is likely to remain weak.

The big issue is whether the Finance Ministry will ever change its guidelines and allow insurers to realize more of those paper profits from their stockholdings to pay their policyholders. Again, this is likely to be gradual. Even if they were permitted to realize their gains, a sudden increase in equity sales by the life insurance companies would jeopardize their business ties as well as the general level of share prices. Fiercer competition among fund managers of a different stripe might actually place a higher premium on those long-term relationships. This applies to all institutional investors in Japan. It is not a simple trade-off between performance and long-standing business ties.

This is illustrated by the nine foreign trust banks that were allowed to open in Japan from October 1985. In the four years since then, these banks were able to attract only 0.19 percent of the ¥19.3 trillion pension assets held by all 17 trust banks in Japan, despite the wealth of experience and skills brought from abroad. Without business contacts, the only way a newcomer can break into Japan's fund-management market is to offer high performance. Even then, Japanese institutions and individuals are wary about entrusting their funds to an outsider. It may take the whole of the 1990s for the concept of performance to seep through, and that is how the Ministry of Finance prefers it. A free-for-all among institutional investors on the U.S. model is anathema to Japan's mandarins.

Chapter 4

THE STOCK TRADERS

The purpose of a stock market is to provide a means by which investors can buy and sell shares and companies can raise capital. Japan's stock market performs this function, but this does not fully describe what else it does. A fuller encapsulation would be to describe it as an inadequately regulated exchange controlled by a cartel of brokers and run for the benefit of listed companies. Whereas in the U.S. stock market, the emphasis is on investor protection achieved through strict regulation, the aim in Japan is to strike a balance between control over the market and a high level of trading activity. Control over the market to some degree is deemed necessary given the important role the market plays within the Japanese economy. But it cannot become too pervasive, for investors would be driven away. Liquidity would dry up, making it imposible for firms to raise capital. The high concentration of stock in the hands of stable shareholders tends to cause liquidity in Japan's stock market to evaporate.

It is possible to manage the stock market because the Ministry of Finance, listed companies, and the securities firms tend to view the market from the same perspective. The Ministry of Finance protects the individual investor from outright fraud, but it is also a promoter of Japanese industry. It has structured the securities industry in the same way that it has structured the banking and insurance industries: to minimize internal competition and to channel funds to industry. Listed companies support a controlled market because they derive

Composition of Trading by Customer Accounts
(Percentage of customer orders)

	1981	82	83	84	85	86	87	88	89
Insurance companies	1	1	1	1	1	1	1	1	1
Banks*	4	4	3	4	9	15	20	24	24
Investment trusts	6	5	5	4	5	5	5	6	11
Industrial companies	11	9	10	11	12	15	17	18	14
Individuals	59	61	61	55	50	42	37	36	32
Foreigners	13	13	15	19	17	15	14	9	12
Other	6	6	6	5	6	6	6	6	6
TOTAL	100	100	100	100	100	100	100	100	100

Source: *Annual Securities Statistics* (Tokyo: Tokyo Stock Exchange, 1990)

*including *tokkin* and fund trusts

tremendous financial benefits from it, both in terms of raising capital and of building hidden assets. As a result of this arrangement, the securities industry makes large profits and in return strives to maintain a high level of investor interest and to ensure the successful sale of new financings.

The individual investor should not to be disregarded. He (often she) is the single most important trader of shares and the ultimate source of new cash for the stock market. In 1989, individuals accounted for 23 percent of the ¥673 trillion in turnover of the largest securities companies and for 30 percent of commissioned trades. Individuals thus set the tone of the market and strongly influence whether it goes up or down. Their concept of what makes a company's shares attractive sets the standards of value which all other investors must heed.

Active trading by individuals allows the brokers to run the market in a way which would not be possible if institutional investors were bigger traders themselves. While banks and insurance companies, by virtue of their holdings, could easily dominate the market, they choose not to exert influence by trading their investment portfolios. These institutions hold shares mostly for strategic purposes. Any trading that they do engage in is conducted primarily through *tokkin* funds and fund trusts. Stable shareholders do not actively determine share price movements except when they occasionally intervene to buy shares. Their role is to constrain the supply of tradable shares by not selling.

POWER OVER THE TSE

The securities industry and the Ministry of Finance share a tight relationship in that brokers are given a lucrative franchise in exchange for ensuring that the market behaves as the ministry would like it to. Four brokers—Nomura, Daiwa, Nikko, and Yamaichi—account for 36 percent of all equity transactions. Even this understates their influence, because 34 smaller brokers are affiliated with the so-called Big Four; if their trades were included, these stock market *keiretsu* account for 54 percent of total turnover.

In other areas of investment and corporate finance, the situation is even more lopsided. The Big Four account for 33 percent of over-the-counter bond dealing, 53 percent of listed convertible bond trading, 74 percent of equity underwriting, 78 percent of funds under management in investment trusts, and 99 percent of all Eurodollar warrant-bond issues by Japanese companies.

Stockbrokers have a strong incentive to keep trading active. Income derived from equity brokerage commissions accounted for 38 percent of the Big Four's total revenues of ¥2.8 trillion in the year ending March 1990, while underwriting provided an additional 14 percent and investment-trust-related activities contributed 15 percent. If they were part of universal banks, as brokers are in West Germany, other considerations such as corporate control and lending would take precedence over brokerage income and underwriting. But in Japan, the Securities and Exchange Law separates banks and brokers. It is one of the few written rules which stock players strictly follow.

The 1980s' equity boom made the securities industry the most profitable business in Japan, with a return on equity that averaged 21 percent in 1985–89. Nomura Securities had the highest profits of any company in Japan in 1987, and ranked second to Toyota in 1989.

Big Four Brokerage *Keiretsu*

	Percent owned by group	FY89 TSE share (%)	Group share of market (%)
NOMURA BROKERAGE KEIRETSU			
Nomura Securities		10.40	
ACE Securities	36	0.36	
Ichiyoshi Securities	10	0.70	
Ishizuka Securities	78	0.01	
Kokusai Securities	35	3.36	
Maruhachi Securities	43	0.12	
Marukin Securities	11	0.07	
Nichiei Securities	12	0.47	
Sanyo Securities	8	3.29	
Takagi Securities	39	0.45	
World Securities	49	0.52	
GROUP MARKET SHARE			19.8
NIKKO BROKERAGE KEIRETSU			
Nikko Securities		8.56	
Kaisei Securities	38	0.42	
Kaneju Securities	15	0.27	
Narusei Securities	25	0.11	
Nippon Securities	41	0.27	
Sanka Securities	48	0.29	
Tokyo Securities	34	1.38	
GROUP MARKET SHARE			11.3
DAIWA BROKERAGE KEIRETSU			
Daiwa Securities		8.50	
Century Securities	14	0.35	
Dojima Securities	8	0.03	
Hinode Securities	34	0.40	
Kaneyoshi Securities	71	0.06	
Universal Securities	32	1.25	
GROUP MARKET SHARE			10.6
YAMAICHI BROKERAGE KEIRETSU			
Yamaichi Securities		8.60	
Chuo Securities	44	0.36	

Daichu Securities	28	0.08	
Ogawa Securities	40	0.05	
Kyoritsu Securities	39	0.27	
Maruko Securities	27	0.21	
Naigai Securities	48	0.54	
Naito Securities	52	0.24	
Taiheiyo Securities	39	1.39	
Utsumiya Securities	5	0.25	
Yamagen Securities	10	0.10	
Yamamaru Securities	70	0.18	
Yutaka Securities	8	0.13	
GROUP MARKET SHARE			12.4
BIG FOUR KEIRETSU TOTAL			54.1

Source: *Nikkei Kinyu Menpo* (Tokyo: Nihon Koshasai Kenkyusho, 1990)

Profits would probably be much lower if the fixed scale of commissions were removed as it was in the United States in 1975 and in London in 1986. Instead, the Tokyo Stock Exchange has slowly lowered the scale of brokerage commissions.

The Finance Ministry's guardianship of the securities market dates from the years immediately after World War II. The American Occupation authorities split up the financial industry (so that brokers might act as a counterweight to the major banks, which were central members of the *zaibatsu*). Until the stock market boom of the 1980s, securities houses had always been subservient to the banks, but today competition from the big brokers threatens the banks.

The Ministry of Finance protected the brokerage cartel from foreign competition until the threat of retaliation against Japanese securities houses operating overseas forced the TSE to grant membership to six European and American stockbrokers in 1986. By early 1990, a total of 24 foreign brokers had been granted seats out of a total of 114. Their share of turnover has steadily increased to an average of 6 percent of TSE volume in 1989.

Since the removal of barriers to entry, the main device for preserving the brokerage oligopoly is the existence of fixed brokerage commissions. Ostensibly, fixed commissions serve to protect the

livelihood of the 246 unlisted brokers which would suffer if price competition were introduced. This is probably true, but it should be
noted that fixed brokerage commissions also maintain relative
market shares. Price is, after all, the natural basis for competition in
a business like securities broking. The rate structure benefits the individual investor in the sense that deregulation of commissions
would probably result in lower dealing costs for institutional buyers
and higher costs for individuals. The individual investor plays too important a role in the market to be lightly discarded.

The Big Four use their influence over the stock market to ensure
that equity offerings by corporations are well received. Promoting
share prices prior to an issue is common in Japan; indeed, it is expected. Companies usually choose an underwriter based on how
much support it has given to a company's shares in the months prior
to an issue.

The responsibility of an underwriter does not end with the issue. It
must also support the share price after the sale by recommending the
stock. This is done to please investors and to encourage the exchange
of convertible bonds for shares and the exercise of warrants. This
task is made easier for the Big Four by their influence over the market
and their control of the largest investment trusts. Share price
manipulation is illegal in Japan, although securities companies are
permitted to stabilize share prices of companies for 20 days until the
final pay-in date for public offerings or for convertible bonds. From
April to October 1989, there were 54 cases of such stabilizing operations for companies whose issues lacked investor appeal.

In almost all stock markets, securities firms face a conflict of interest between the operations of their brokerage and their underwriting departments. Issuers want a high price for their shares while
investors want a low price. This is particularly so in Japan where the
Big Four are responsible for three-quarters of all equity underwriting
business. This gives them access to a great deal of corporate information, but makes their brokerage advice hard to trust.

For years, stockbroking was not the kind of profession respectable
people wanted their sons to enter. The once-dubious reputation of
the securities industry dates back to its origins after the Meiji Restoration of 1868. Those who became stock brokers when the Tokyo

Stock Exchange opened in 1878 were small money changers (like Nomura), rice dealers, and pawnbrokers. The big trading houses like Mitsui and Sumitomo entered the more refined world of banking instead.

From the outset, the division in status between banks and brokers had a self-fulfilling quality to it. As far as the government and the public were concerned, the stock market deserved its speculative reputation, because shares were traded no differently from commodities. For more than 200 years before the introduction of shares and joint-stock companies into Japan, the country had traded commodities such as rice. Rice was a staple in the diet and also a means of paying taxes, fines, and tributes. Trading in rice futures allowed a buyer or seller to hedge against price fluctuations. Feudal lords were thus able to raise money by selling rice bills against the next harvest.

Accordingly, the regulations adopted for the stock exchange in 1878 were largely based on the Rice Exchange Regulations of 1876: a term of one month for settlement and a three-month system for futures transactions. Spot transactions did not necessitate actual delivery; a transaction could be offset by an opposite transaction during the same day and only the balance paid. In 1893 the exchange law was again revised, and the new law governed both stock and commodity exchanges, with only minor changes, until 1943.

Before World War II, the Tokyo Stock Exchange itself was a shareholder-owned company run for profit, initially by taking two-thirds of the commissions earned by brokers. Its regulations were lax in order to permit participation by poorly capitalized brokers. Most stock transactions were speculative, involving no actual transfer of stock. Shares in the exchange itself were also listed, and for much of the prewar period they were the most actively traded. One listing on today's TSE is Heiwa Real Estate, which owns the stock exchange building and whose rental income is linked to transaction volume.

Officials in the Ministry of Finance are only now being troubled by the conflicts of interest within the securities industry. This state of affairs has arisen as the ministry's responsibilities have become more divided. First, these officials are the regulators, which in Japan means a position of unrivaled authority. Their writ runs across the board. Second, they are protectors of the securities industry, in particular against its invasion by the Japanese banks. Third, these officials function as the largest issuers of all, not only of massive amounts of government bonds but also of equity. A high-priced stock market is required in order to sell off government-owned firms at the highest price possible.

Many other governments in the world face similar conflicts of interest. The solution is often to establish an organization, independent of government, to oversee the conduct of the securities industry in the public interest. Not in Japan. Control remains centralized in the hands of the Finance Ministry, the most powerful department of state whose prestige is as high as the brokers' is low.

It is in the interest of the Ministry of Finance to avoid a repetition of the financial problems the industry faced in the early 1960s. At that time, the brokerage industry generated more than half of its profits from trading on its own account, and Yamaichi Securities, then the nation's biggest broker, held large positions in Second Section stocks that it had recently underwritten. When the market slumped in 1962–65, the entire industry was hurt badly, Yamaichi in particular.

Enter the Ministry of Finance. It placed a moratorium on Yamaichi's interest payments and offered it a loan of ¥28 billion from the Bank of Japan, the central government bank. It then forced the merger of a number of securities companies and placed restrictions on a broker's exposure to equities. In those five years, mergers and bankruptcies reduced the number of securities dealers from 600 to 284.

Officials in the securities bureau of the Ministry of Finance have a tradition of being highly protective of the companies in their charge. It is a tradition often attributed to the practice, widespread among all ministries, of *amakudari*. At the retirement age of 55, bureaucrats "descend from heaven" to a well-paid sinecure in the private sector. It is a reward for a prestigious but poorly paid civil-service job, minimizing in the meantime the lure of petty temptations. Officials in the ministries thus have good reason to keep an eye on the progress of various companies through the old boy network—and vice versa. As convenient as this is, the distinction between public and private service is thereby blurred, rendering the Ministry of Finance a ministry for banks and securities companies.

Such conflicts of interest were not always the case. Under the guidance of the American Occupation authorities, Japan did create a Securities Exchange Commission (SEC) through the Securities and Exchange Law of 1948, which largely mimicked U.S. securities regulations. Japan's SEC was made up of three commissioners, appointed by the prime minister, with their own staff, charged with regulating the stock market. However, when the Americans left in August 1951, the SEC was abolished, its powers and personnel absorbed by the Ministry of Finance. "The value of the commission as an independent agency, above politics and internal bureaucratic influences and pressures, has not been appreciated," wrote T.F.M. Adams, a financial historian who helped reopen the country's stock exchanges after the war. Perhaps the role of an autonomous SEC was understood all too well.

WHEN MARKETS CRASH

Three important elements work to control Japan's stock market: the extraordinarily high proportion of equity brokerage and underwriting in the hands of the Big Four, the very tight concentration of share ownership, and the existence of a regulatory organization that works independently of neither the securities industry nor the government. In virtually all Japanese industries, government and business cooperate to enhance economic growth, but in the context of the stock market, this intimacy is increasingly awkward now that capital markets are becoming internationalized.

The combination of these three elements is best seen in the crash of October 1987, when major stock markets around the world dropped further and faster than ever before. Although overpriced Tokyo was expected to trigger such a crash, the world stock market collapse was led by panic in New York. Tokyo followed it down, but only part of the way. The TSE shed 21 percent of its value in the first month after the crash, but this was considerably less than the 32 percent drop in the Dow Jones Industrial Average.

An examination of how the two markets behaved at that time sheds light on the different philosophies of share trading in the United States and Japan. In Tokyo, a combination of regulatory, technical, and organizational factors cushioned the damage, although it is impossible to say which took precedence. For one thing, Japanese share prices cannot go into free fall. Unlike New York, there is a daily limit that averages plus or minus 15 percent of the price movement of individual shares. On October 20, 1987, the day after Wall Street's fall, only 55 stocks out of more than 1,800 TSE listings were traded until the close because the imbalance between would-be sellers and buyers was too great. On the morning of the crash itself, only 10 million shares changed hands, with most of the remaining 475 million conducted at the close. That was half the daily average turnover.

Officials of the TSE, who are empowered to indicate a special quotation on shares, lowered prices incrementally on untraded stocks. Even then, buyers could not be found until shares reached their limit for the day, where they remained until the close when buy and sell orders were matched. Although this mechanism essentially denied investors the ability to sell their shares, it also gave the Ministry of Finance, the securities companies, and major institutions time to plan a counterstrategy.

The prevailing pattern of share ownership in the TSE helped prevent a rout. In the first two or three weeks after the crash, only foreigners were big sellers. Japanese companies did not sell because they had no need to, and physically they could not. Individual investors, meanwhile, were looking for bargains and were heavy net buyers on the day after the crash when the market rebounded 10 percent.

Behind the scenes, the Finance Ministry called on the institutions to support the market. In the month following the crash, three support operations took place. The first occurred on October 20, when the market fell 15 percent, its largest decline in a single day. The Big Four were asked by the ministry to create a market in shares of NTT, the largest issue on the TSE and one scheduled to have a ¥4.9 trillion share issue for the government on November 10, 1987. It was vital for fiscal policy as well as for investor psychology to prevent NTT's share price from collapsing. At the time of Tokyo's crash, NTT was one of the shares which had frozen untraded at the bottom of its daily limit. As a result of the brokers' intervention, 20,000 shares changed hands that afternoon at a price of ¥2.65 million. This was slightly above the bottom and a shade higher than what the market regarded as the minimum price acceptable to the Finance Ministry for its share sale.

On October 27, when morale sagged again, the Finance Ministry held a meeting with executives in charge of securities dealing at Japan's three largest trust banks and three largest life insurers. The firms were consulted on the prospects for shares and not formally asked to support the market. Yet news of the meeting was enough to steady people's nerves.

A few days later, a sharp fall in the U.S. dollar alarmed investors with the prospect that the economy would slow down again as had occurred in 1986. On November 11, the Nikkei Average fell 1,000 points, breaching 21,000, a level at which a large number of investors would begin to receive margin calls. This time it was the turn of the Big Four to stage what appeared to be a coordinated purchase of shares, thereby pushing the index back above 21,000.

By contrast, the New York Stock Exchange (NYSE) saw a record volume of 608 million shares on the day of the crash, four times the daily average. New York trading was frenzied, while Tokyo was eerily quiet. In the U.S. stock market there were no circuit breakers of the kind that limited the daily movement of shares in Japan. Stock-index futures and options markets in the United States magnified the see-saw, while mutual funds saw massive redemption orders and were forced to sell shares to pay off investors. At that time, the only index-futures contract in Japanese stocks was in Singapore, besides an experimental operation in Osaka. The lack of technical sophistication in Japan was an asset.

The organization of the NYSE was strained to the limit. Specialists, the more than 50 firms required by the rules of the exchange to make a market in assigned stocks, were overwhelmed by sell orders and faced the prospect of bankruptcy. Their capital, much of it in equities, was almost wiped out in the turmoil, intensifying the alarm in the rest of the market. The specialists' equivalent in Tokyo, the 12 *saitori* match buy and sell orders and are not allowed to trade on their own accounts. They are brokers' brokers and could stand firm during the crash.

The type of support that Japan's government and the financial industry gave the market during this critical period is not new. Since the market was established, there have been numerous precedents for active involvement to support and control share prices. In 1931, the life insurers established the Life Insurance Securities Company to buy shares, while in 1937, following a panic on the exchange, the Great Japan Securities Investment Company was founded for the same purposes. Another stock purchaser, the Japan Securities Investment Company was founded in 1940 to be replaced by Japan Joint Securities a year later. A Stock Price Ordinance gave the government authority to fix minimum prices of shares from August 1941, but this had to be amended to include maximum share prices as well due to the market's jubilant response following the attack on Pearl Harbor.

The government continued to support share prices when the stock market reopened after the war on May 16, 1949. The market peaked by September 1949, and prices fell until June 1950 due to an excessive supply of shares, when the Nikkei Average reached ¥86 compared with ¥176 when the exchange opened. To prop up the market, the government permitted trading on margin in 1951 and reestablished the investment-trust industry. The government also allowed city banks to increase their holding of shares.

In January 1964 when the effects of the early 1960s' bear market were most severe, major banks and the Big Four founded the Japan Joint Securities Co., which bought ¥189 billion worth of stocks in 190 different issues, or 3 percent of the market. A year later, 57 securities companies established the Japan Securities Holding Association to buy the Second Section stocks held by brokers and investment trusts. By July, it had taken over stocks worth ¥182 billion from investment trusts and ¥50 billion from securities companies.

The actions taken to control the stock market during these times of crisis are not meant to determine the level of share prices, but are intended to minimize the damage. Despite all their confidence-building measures, the market fell by 23 percent between October 14, 1987, and January 4, 1988. In the 18 months before the crash, the stock market had climbed 120 percent, thanks to falling interest rates. When rates began to rise again as Japan's economic growth accelerated from May 1987, the stock market began to fall. Although triggered by New York, the crash on the TSE reflected the fact that interest rates had more than doubled to 6 percent by October 1987.

The share slump in the first quarter of 1990 demonstrates that the stock market could not be controlled indefinitely. Concerned about excessive money supply growth, the Bank of Japan began to raise the Official Discount Rate in mid-1989. Rumors were circulating as early as September 1989 that the Bank of Japan wanted to see the stock market fall by 30 percent to defuse the speculative bubble in land and stock prices.

When the stock market finally collapsed in the early months of 1990, the government took similar actions to those seen after the October 1987 crash. The amount of cash required to buy on margin was lowered from 60 percent to 40 percent in February. The "30 percent rule" imposed by the authorities in 1989, whereby a major broker could not account for more than 30 percent of trading in any stock in any single month, was temporarily lifted. Investment trusts were net buyers and in fact had raised their weighting in equities to 49 percent of their portfolio, a bull market high, in December 1989. Securities companies declared a moratorium on all new equity-linked issues to stop new shares from coming onto the market. Meetings were held among major institutions and the Finance Ministry, and pronouncements were made (at ever lower prices) that the bottom had been reached.

While these actions restored confidence somewhat, Japan's stock market was simply obeying the same rules that govern investment everywhere else in the world. The illiquidity of the stock market only made the decline sharper.

ON THE WAY UP

The three elements that aim to support the Japanese stock market when an emergency strikes—the brokerage oligopoly, the concentration of ownership, and the role of the Finance Ministry—also influence the way the market behaves on a day-to-day basis.

Because of their size and marketing power, the Big Four can influence which sectors and companies will be in the spotlight and which will not. Whether or not investors agree with their choices depends largely on how strong a case can be made for an improvement in the outlook for a company, an industry, or the economy. Although it is true that the TSE is a speculative market, much of this speculation concerns corporate profitability and long-term growth—two fundamental factors. Yet because their earnings are directly related to trading volume, the brokers tend to promote shares beyond what fundamentals alone would imply.

Similarly, the concentration of ownership of shares greatly affects liquidity and patterns of trading. The preponderance of stable shareholders that keeps sellers out of the market during bad times keeps them out of the market in good times as well. This creates a chronic shortage of stock for trading in the market. This is a double-edged sword for the brokers. On the positive side, as prices rise, few additional shares come onto the market since supply is relatively price-inelastic. Thus, share prices can rise far and fast on a small sign of buyer interest. This enhances the power of the Big Four among investors who want to know who is buying rather than why. On the negative side, lack of tradable shares makes trading difficult and thus limits the number of investors that can trade in a single issue at the same time.

Traders of Japan Inc.

The active traders of shares behave in a very different fashion from stable shareholders, who are passive long-term investors. The benefits that they derive from ownership are often unrelated to the actual gains on their investment. Active traders, on the other hand, turn over their portfolios at a rapid pace since their only objective is to make a quick return on their investment.

Active traders of shares are the various types of outside shareholders described earlier: individuals, foreigners, speculative groups, *tokkin* funds, investment trusts, and small unlisted companies. Capital gains are all they can expect, and the volatility of share price movements encourages quick profit taking. Indeed, share prices can quickly reflect earnings prospects as much as ten years into the future. Once share prices discount these future earnings, there is no incentive to wait to see if they materialize. If they do, all that will be shown is that the price appreciation was justified. If these earnings do not materialize, then an investor faces the prospect of losing his gains.

Active trading is also encouraged by the short-term objectives of most investors. *Tokkin* funds, for example, aim to earn at least an 8 percent return each year. Many companies established *tokkin* funds because interest rates on bank deposits and yields on bonds had fallen below this level during the 1980s. Sponsors of these funds often do not want a return higher than 8 percent since too much profit will lay the company open to charges of stock speculation. Indeed, at the end of accounting periods, managers of successful funds are often forced to give up some of their gains, either by deliberately losing money or carrying over the profits into the next fiscal year. Investment trusts are also active traders, turning over their portfolios to generate commissions for their sponsoring brokers.

The speculative groups are least interested in fundamentals. Their sole objective is to corner the tradable shares in a stock, to push up the share price, and then to sell out. Individuals seek capital gains as well. The individual investor plays a vital role in the stock market by accounting for one-third of all commissioned trades and magnifying the impact that the brokers have on the market. Before Japanese institutional investors began actively trading shares in 1985, the role of the individual was greater. In 1981 they accounted for 41 percent of total turnover and 58 percent of commissioned trades. Although their importance is declining on the First Section of the TSE, they continue to predominate on the smaller Second Section. Here, 96 percent of all trading is commissioned, 57 percent of which is done by individuals. The securities companies provide little liquidity to the Second Section since its market capitalization is only 3 percent of the size of the First Section.

All securities companies in Japan depend upon small investors and employ large sales forces. Nomura Securities, has 5,000 salespeople and derives 40 percent of its equity brokerage commissions from individuals' orders, the lowest proportion in the industry. Although brokerage commissions are fixed, the scale of fees in Japan is tilted in favor of the individual as opposed to the institutional investor. Commissions on a transaction below ¥3 million average only 1.1 percent.

Individual investors sometimes have an advantage over institutions. First, their order sizes are so small that they can invest in illiquid stocks without boosting the price. Second, the individual investor can, if he so chooses, take a long-term view rather than having to meet the (admittedly low) performance targets set for investment-trust managers. Third, the individual can buy and sell shares quickly to take advantage of the abundant investment information available—data which are of the same quality and timeliness as that received by institutions.

Individuals are encouraged to buy and sell on margin to promote active trading. Introduced by the American Occupation forces to popularize the stock market, margin buying involves paying between 30 percent and 70 percent of the value of a transaction in cash (or collateralizing with securities) and then borrowing the rest from a broker or a securities finance company. Selling on margin involves putting up collateral and then borrowing and selling shares in the hope that their price will fall. Margin trading accounted for an average of 17 percent of all trading on the TSE in 1989 and about 35 percent of individuals' trades.

The outstanding margin balance is thus a fair barometer of the sentiment of the small investor. A high margin-buying position indicates bullish prospects but selling pressure within six months, the maximum period that margin positions can be held. A high ratio of sell orders to buys indicates the opposite. The size of the net margin position has been used to signify whether the market is overheated, with 2 percent regarded as a warning signal. The TSE can try to dampen or to encourage speculation by changing the margin collateral requirement.

Foreign investors are unique in that they are one of the few groups interested in outperforming the market, that is, earning a better return than achieved by the indices. Theoretically, this would seem to be easy since other investors have different objectives in mind. But it is actually more difficult than it appears. The 70 percent of shares locked away in the vaults of stable shareholders are the equivalent of index funds that deliver average market performance. This means that active players are competing against each other, as well as providing the securities companies with all of their brokerage commissions.

Water Everywhere but Not a Drop to Drink

On the face of it, claiming that Japan's stock market is illiquid is nonsense. The value of daily turnover on the TSE has grown from ¥191 billion in 1983 to over ¥1 trillion in 1988 and 1989. A total of 222 billion shares were traded in 1989 in a market with 314 billion shares outstanding. But the shares that are traded are turned over at a frantic pace—almost three times a year—because almost three-quarters of all shares are locked away. Moreover, this trading is not evenly distributed throughout the market but tends to cluster in a few industries or companies for short periods. Many shares of companies listed on the TSE with market capitalizations of more than ¥50 billion can spend days without changing hands. This kind of thinness creates volatility.

For example, the Industrial Bank of Japan, saw its share price rise 8 percent on August 7, 1989, creating $7 billion in shareholder wealth on a mere $25 million worth of trading. Only 3.7 percent of its 2.3 billion shares outstanding are considered floating shares, that is, shares held in units of less than 50,000.

The thinness of the market creates a dilemma for institutional investors. For one thing, it is almost impossible for them to buy a large position without causing the share price to move up quickly or to sell a large position without causing the share price to tumble. Institutional investors must therefore choose either, first, to follow the herd and invest in the most actively traded shares or, second, to accumulate a position slowly and risk becoming trapped in an illiquid stock. With little need or desire for risk, most institutional investors tend to buy the few stocks that are heavily traded at any given moment.

Due to the lack of liquidity in many shares, particularly the ones with a small capitalization, large institutional investors cannot easily outperform the market. Share prices of illiquid issues can move a long way in thin trading and thereby have a disproportionate effect on the stock market index.

The illiquidity is reflected in the two major indices of the Tokyo Stock Exchange: the Tokyo Stock Price Index (TOPIX), established in 1968, and the Nikkei Average, begun two decades earlier at the

Brokers Trading on Own Account

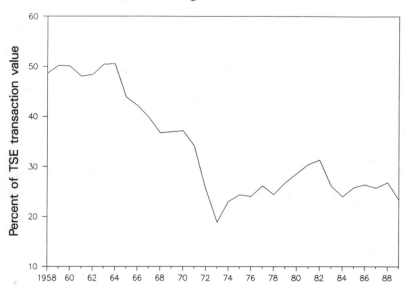

Source: Annual Securities Statistics (Tokyo: Tokyo Stock Exchange, 1989)

start of postwar share trading in Japan. TOPIX is the more representative of the two because it includes all shares listed on the First Section of the TSE, each weighted according to its market capitalization. The trouble is that the thinly traded bank shares comprise 20
percent of TOPIX. The more widely watched is the Nikkei Average,
which is made up of 225 shares and compiled simply by summing the
¥50 par-value equivalent prices of the constituent issues and dividing
by an adjustment factor. In this way, ¥50 par-value shares with a
high price have a much bigger weighting than large-capitalization
stocks with a low price.

As a result, thinly traded stocks have an influence on the Nikkei Index far out of proportion to their capitalization. Department store
Matsuzakaya has the second-heaviest weight in the index and can
move very erratically. Korakuen Stadium, an amusement ground,
comes in fourth. Brokers say that on quiet days it only requires a
trade of 1,000 shares in each of 20 issues to move the Nikkei Average
by 300 points or almost 1 percent.

Securities companies are often responsible for creating liquidity by trading for their own account, buying and selling blocks of shares to insitutions, or promoting certain issues heavily to create demand. If the securities companies did not do this, liquidity in the market would dry up and their brokerage commissions would plummet. Securities companies' own account trading sometimes comprises more than 40 percent of turnover on a given day. In the past five years they have accounted for 27 percent of trading.

Brokers make very little profit from stock trading, a fact which suggests that their main purpose is to boost liquidity. In the six months between April and September 1989, when the stock market rose 9.5 percent, Nomura Securities traded ¥10.2 trillion worth of stocks on its own account and lost ¥4.9 billion in the process. Yamaichi and Nikko fared just as badly.

Excess Liquidity in the 1980s

The phenomenon of excess liquidity seen in the 1980s played into the hands of the brokers. Excess liquidity does not refer to the existence of too many tradable shares but too few of them in relation to the amount of money looking for a home. This situation existed through much of the later 1980s for a number of reasons: slack capital investment, weak loan demand, a large current-account surplus, and the revaluation of the yen. Owing to a dearth of alternative investments and low interest rates, the stock market appeared the best place in which to put the spare cash.

Between 1972 and 1982, average daily trading value increased from ¥69 billion to ¥123 billion. By 1985, it had doubled to ¥264 billion, and in 1986, it doubled again. At the end of the decade, average daily turnover reached ¥1.3 trillion.

The growth in liquidity made life easier for the brokers. They did not have to create demand for shares artificially; they just had to direct the flow. The percentage of the total turnover made by trading for their own account dropped from 33 percent in 1982 to 23 percent in 1989.

Companies with the largest market capitalizations might be expected to be the most active stocks when the market as a whole was at its busiest. On the contrary, the popularity of a stock as a trading

TSE Annual Trading Volume

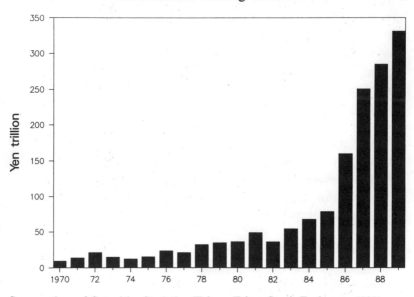

Source: Annual Securities Statistics (Tokyo: Tokyo Stock Exchange, 1989)

counter depends on the proportion of shares held in stable hands. Among the large capital issues, the most illiquid are financial firms, particularly the largest banks, whose shares change hands once every ten years on average. Financials represented 20 percent of market capitalization in 1982, but they only accounted for 3.5 percent of turnover. While the financial sector performed better than most when liquidity was at its peak, reaching 32 percent of the market's total capitalization by 1987, it nonetheless accounted for only 9.5 percent of turnover that year.

Most of the turnover was concentrated instead in cyclical industries such as steel and chemicals. These companies have the greatest number of shares outstanding, relatively low levels of stable shareholding, and low stock prices. In 1988, steel firms accounted for 18 percent of trading and only 4 percent of market capitalization. Their shares changed hands every four months. High turnover ratios were also seen in paper and pulp, chemicals, and nonferrous metals.

THE INVESTMENT DECISION

In some respects, the TSE fully deserves its speculative reputation. Share prices of many companies are out of line with their fundamental value, shares are ramped, and margin trading is common.

Two other factors promote speculation in shares. The first is the rapid way in which corporate information is disseminated. This information is unfailingly bullish and is fostered by the Big Four which emphasize investment on market themes. These are simple reasons for buying a category of shares as quickly as possible. And investors take the cue.

The second is simply the fact that no theory of how a share should be valued has taken root in Japan. Without a standard, it is difficult for an investor to say when a stock is fairly priced. This stems in part from the preponderance of stable shareholders and a corresponding lack of professional fund managers. The United States and the United Kingdom have fund managers who have developed theories of investment. There are no such people in Japan. Despite its size, the TSE is still immature.

Information Junkies

Japanese investors are deluged with news, rumors and tips on the stock market, and the information is circulated so rapidly that it is very difficult for one group of investors to learn something new before everybody else hears about it. The fact that trading in many stocks is so thin actually helps news gatherers. Any sudden buying or selling is immediately translated into a noticeable share-price movement. It may be difficult to discern exactly who is doing the trading because of the widespread use of nominee accounts, but an army of newspaper reporters is quickly on the scent.

The most important source of information is the *Nihon Keizai Shimbun*, which owns the rights to the name of the Nikkei Average. To describe it as the *Wall Street Journal* or the *Financial Times* of Japan does not quite do it justice, because economic news is regarded as more indispensable than in the West. The *Nikkei* has a daily circulation of 2.8 million and is required reading for every manager in the country. Naturally, this newspaper provides news about markets, companies, industries, and the economy. It also conducts opinion surveys and uses its in-house database to forecast economic trends.

The *Nikkei* differs from Western financial newspapers in another respect: it is not expected to be accurate. The government unashamedly uses it to test public reaction to possible changes in policies, and companies use it in the same way when they want to change course. The *Nikkei* is regarded as a business tool to shape reality rather than a strict source of news and comment for businessmen.

The newspaper has 1,000 full-time journalists, most of whom compete for space in five morning and four evening editions daily, each averaging 35 pages. In contrast, the *Financial Times* has 300 journalists to fill 80 pages. News gathering in Japan is a highly competitive business with reporters working frantically to make it into print. Under such circumstances, it is common for mistakes and speculative reportage to creep in, but this is tolerated to a greater degree than in the West.

Due to its dominance in supply of economic news, the *Nikkei* receives preferential access to corporate information. Its forecasts of a firm's earnings almost always come directly from management. The newspaper, for example, releases its "estimates" for the results of the banking industry one week before the firms themselves reveal them. The *Nikkei*'s forecasts of bank results for the year ending March 1990 were uncannily accurate, and would have been regarded in many other countries as inside information.

Nikkei Estimates and Actual Results
(Net income in ¥ bn for year ending March 1989)

	17 May 89 Nikkei	29 May 89 results
Sumitomo Bank	198.5	198.3
Dai-Ichi Kangyo Bank	179.5	179.8
Fuji Bank	172.0	172.0
Mitsubishi Bank	167.5	167.4
Sanwa Bank	155.5	155.5

Source: *Nihon Keizai Shimbun*, company reports

The *Nikkei* itself has spun off a number of daily newspapers and magazines, of which the most important for the stock market is *Nikkei Kinyu* (*Financial Daily*). Each of the main Japanese industries, too, has its own daily newspaper. For the individual investor, there are six daily newspapers, available at most newsstands, dealing entirely with .he goings-on in the stock market. Their names all incorporate basic investment terms such as stock (*kabushiki*), investment (*toshi*), and securities (*shoken*). Hence: *Kabushiki Shimbun, Nikkan Toshi Shimbun, Kabushiki Shijo Shimbun, Nihon Shoken Shimbun, Shoken Shinpo* and *Shoken Nikkan Shimbun.*

All have a similar format consisting of a long article highlighting a sector or theme, the economic background to it, and then smaller articles featuring a number of stock recommendations for the day. A typical selection of articles from these papers will give an impression of their somewhat breathless style:

SUMITOMO GROUP stocks, including Sumitomo Realty, Sumitomo Construction, and Sumitomo Warehouse have picked up recently. Brokers are trying to increase trading volume to become the underwriters for a financing. (*Kabushiki Shimbun*, June 27, 1989)

NIPPON SANSO. European investors are buying the stock. The company is related to all the current market themes (environment, linear motor trains, capital spending, consumption). Developed sprays using oxygen instead of fluorocarbon gases. Has largest share in liquid helium to be used for linear motor trains. Planning to build laboratory for superconductivity research. Financing highly likely. (*Kabushiki Shimbun*, June 27, 1989)

HANKYU REAL ESTATE. Hidden assets are estimated to be over ¥6,000 per share. Redevelopment projects in Osaka's central business district will start soon, and Hankyu owns substantial areas there. (*Kabushiki Shijo Shimbun*, August 2, 1989)

NIPPON OIL & FATS. Has been developing fuels for rockets. Strengthening aerospace development. The drug EPA, which has anti-cholesterol properties, is likely to be approved as a functional food. Diversifying into real estate and house refurbishing. (*Kabushiki Shijo Shimbun*, August 4, 1989)

KONICA. Nippon Tochi, an unlisted real estate company, seems to have acquired about 10 percent of its outstanding shares under different names. The company is rumored to be trying to buy back the shares at a high price. (*Kabushiki Shimbun*, August 7, 1989)

NIPPON MEAT PACKERS. Discovered anti-AIDS agent from chicken bile. Likely to hit record high earnings this fiscal year. Low PER of 43. (*Kabushiki Shijo Shimbun*, August 8, 1989)

NIPPON MEAT PACKERS. Likely to benefit from the deregulation of beef imports from 1991. Acquired cattle ranch and meat processing plants in Australia and New Zealand. Also strengthening sales networks. Price target is ¥2,620. (*Nikkan Toshi Shimbun*, August 21, 1989)

KYUSHU DENKIKOJI. At current share price, its PER is only 36. Political funds appear to be buying with an eye towards a general election next year. Also the speculator who reportedly bought Ichida and Sankyo Seiko is aggressively buying. The company celebrates its 45th anniversary this year. Also commemorative dividend hike likely. (*Kabushiki Shimbun*, October 20, 1989)

IHI. Starting to develop 300,000 square meters of land in Toyosu (Tokyo Bay) into office buildings and housing. After completion of construction in September 1992, more than ¥300 billion in rental income is expected. Total sales to reach ¥1 trillion by 1994 due to growth of aerospace-related business and strong ship demand. (*Kabushiki Shimbun* and *Nikkan Toshi Shimbun*, November 1, 1989)

ALL NIPPON AIRWAYS. The share price is about to take off. Needs large amounts of capital to pay for new aircraft and hotel business. Further rise in share price, followed by financing, is expected. (*Kabushiki Shimbun*, December 1, 1989)

It is a mistake to dismiss these stock market newspapers as rumor-ridden rags. First, stockbrokers themselves are the primary source of most of the articles. The reports are intended to generate interest in market themes and specific stocks often because many of their clients have already invested in them. If one considers that the Big Four are shareholders in many of these papers and that "planting" stories in stock market dailies is extremely easy for stock brokers, then the stories give an indication of where the market is moving, even if some of the move has often already occurred.

Second, these papers are widely read. *Kabushiki Shimbun* alone has a daily circulation of 120,000. In total, over 400,000 copies of the stock market newspapers are circulated every day. The reports should not be ignored since they are read by individual shareholders who are the most important short-term investors. A skim through the stock market dailies is essential to keep in touch with the stock market. Institutional investors also read these papers closely, and the market response to some of the reports and rumors can be so fast that pausing to check certain points often means missing out on the entire upward movement of the share price.

The investment media in Japan is rich and diverse, ranging from electronic information services such as JiJi Press and Quick to the authoritative *Weekly Toyo Keizai*. The weekly business magazines occupy a special place in the canon of news sources. Japanese business leaders are lionized almost like movie stars in the United States. Much of the weekly financial literature is devoted to personality profiles of the plutocrats, some of which is libelous gossip. These articles coexist with reports that are often more accurate and analytical than anything that appears in the dailies (or in brokerage reports). And then there are the private research organizations, the largest being the Teikoku Data Bank, whose 1,200 professionals conduct a million pieces of business research a year.

No survey of Japan's providers of financial information would be complete without a look at the two most widely used sources, the *Shikiho*, literally quarterly report, published by Toyo Keizai, in both Japanese and English (*Japan Company Handbook*) versions, and *Kaisha Joho* (literally, company information), published by Nikkei. These quarterly paperbacks contain basic financial information on all firms listed and traded over the counter. They include a brief description of the company, its earnings outlook, business developments, an abbreviated balance sheet, recent financings, the top ten shareholders, the number of floating shares, the directors, main banks, and underwriters.

The *Shikiho* has been published in virtually the same format since the market reopened in 1949, so it is easy to trace the long-term performance of a company. In the 1968 edition, only sales, profits, and the percentage of par value that a company would pay as dividends were reported. A table allowed investors to translate share prices and

Nippon Lace

3521
日本レース

Est.: December, 1926   Fiscal (Half) Year Ended: September
Head Office & Factory: Kasugacho, Nishinokyo, Nakagyoku, Kyoto
Tel.: 075-811-8151   Telex: 05422175   604

Tokyo Branch: Tel. 03-663-9471
President: Tohei Murata
Reference(s): Daiwa, Nippon Trust, Kyoto

Capital Change:

Month & Year	Allotment Ratio	New Capital (¥ mil.)
('49-June	SE	47)
'55-Feb.	1:1G	282
'57-Feb.	1:2	423
'63-May	7:10G4	719
'66-Sept.	2:5PO	1,010
*	N	

Capital: (¥50 par value)	1,010
Total Assets: (Sept. '73)	9,710
Stockholders' Equity: (Sept. '73)	1,972
Employees: (Sept. '73)	476
Average Age: (Sept. '73)	29
Monthly Starting Pay: (1973)	59,000
No. Shares Out.: (Sept. '73)	20,200
No. Stockholders: (Sept. '73)	5,101

Major Stockholders: (1,000)   %
Ueda Construction   1,315 (6.5)
Ibuki Construction   1,218 (6.0)
Seiji Iwai   800 (4.0)
Dai-ichi M. Life Ins.   740 (3.7)
Jotaro Iwai   570 (2.8)
Daiwa Real Estate   539 (2.7)
Foreign Ownership   64 (0.3)

Listed: Osaka, Tokyo, Kyoto
Overseas Listed: —
Underwriter(s): Yamaichi

Sales Breakdown in %: (Sept., 1973)
Laces (93), bowling alleys (7) Export
Ratio: 6%

Business Results: (¥ mil.)   († one-year settlement)

	Sales	Current Profit	Profit	Earnings Per Share	Dividend Per Share	Equity Per Share
1970-Sept.	2,702	(—)17	(—)16	¥(—)0.8	¥—	¥93.7
1971-Mar.	1,165	24	2	0.1	—	93.7
Sept.	1,342	10	(—)15	(—)0.7	—	93.0
1972-Mar.	1,185	54	28	1.4	—	94.4
Sept.	4,581	117	33	1.6	—	96.0
1973-Sept.†	3,355	99	51	2.5	—	97.1
1974-Sept.*	4,500	180	70	3.5	3	

Characteristics: Japan's largest manufacturer of laces. However, moving to diversify its business front by taking to real estate and leisure industry lines, such as bowling alleys.

Remarks: Sales are anticipated up 20% in the September, 1974 period because of the favorable tone of the lace market. Also plans ¥1 billion real estate sales to push revenues up sharply. Its subsidiary, Kohoku Nippon Race put into operation from Sept., 1973. Good chance of ¥3 dividend revive. With bowling alleys doing poorly, company is studying the switch to office buildings, etc.

NIPPON LACE
3521
日本レース

Largest lace manufacturer, based in Kyoto. Diversifying into cosmetics and formal wear. Lineup of major stockholders changing rapidly. Current management under control of Toho Mutual Life Insurance-affiliated Toho Kikaku. Stress on development of new market for apparel. Considering advance into new fields.

Outlook: Laces recovering sharply thanks to increasing trend toward high-quality products and rising demand. Laces div turning black for first time in 5 years. Among apparel, new brands and black formal wear performing well. But marine products div worsening again due to bearish market prices for tuna and reduced purchases. Maintains net profit by selling own land. Plans review of marine products div in and after Mar '91 term, incl possibility of pull-out from marine products business.

Income (¥mil)	Sales	Operating Profit	Current Profit	Net Profit	Earnings per sh	Dividend per sh	Equity per sh
Sep '87	2,381	(-)375	(-)375	(-)382	¥(-)18.9	¥0	¥108.4
Sep '88	2,353	(-)344	(-)371	(-)394	(-)19.5	0	88.9
‡Mar '89	2,493	(-)47	(-)58	(-)76	(-)3.8	0	85.1
Mar '90*	3,330	(-)120	(-)160	90	4.5	0	
Mar '91*	4,000	100	50	20	1.0	0	
•Sep '89	1,535	(-)155	(-)188	68	3.4	–	88.5
•Sep '90*	1,850	(-)50	(-)80	(-)80	(-)4.0	–	
□Sep '88	2,356	(-)282	(-)336	(-)379	(-)18.8		91.9
□Mar '89	2,493	6	(-)15	(-)59	(-)2.9		88.9
□Mar '90*	3,330	(-)70	(-)120	110	5.4		

TYO   PER – ~ –

1100 ¥
900
700
5.7
mil
1.9
0
'85 '86 '87 '88 '89

Sales Breakdown	(Sep '89, %)
Laces	42
Textile Products	14
Cosmetics	19
Marine Products	25
Others	1
Export Ratio	**0**

Prices	High		Low	G/L(%)
~'86	1600 ('83)		35 ('71)	
'87	950 (Mar)		524 (Apr)	(-)8.3
'88	795 (May)		585 (Jan)	5.1
'89	980 (Dec)		641 (Mar)	38.5
⚡'90	930 (Jan)		890 (Jan)	0.0

Finance	(000shs)
May '49 1:1(¥50)	940
Feb '52 1:2 Gratis	2,820
Feb '55 1:1 Gratis	5,640
Feb '57 2:1(¥50)	8,460
May '63 10:7(¥46)	14,382
Sep '66 5:2(¥50)	20,200

Stocks (¥50 par value, 1000 per unit)
Shares Out. (Nov 30 '89 000shs) 20,200
No. of Shareholders (Sep 30 '89) 2,626

Major Holders(%)		Foreign Owners	0.5
Japan Securities		Sanyo Kosan	1.5
Clearing	27.3	Toho Life Ins.	1.4
Kaike Service	24.1	Akihide Yamano	0.9
Yamano Beauty		Toho Kikaku	0.8
Mate	3.7	Okasan Securities	0.7

Financial Data(¥mil)	•Sep '89	□Mar '89
Total Assets	3,923	3,994
Fixed Assets	1,177	1,527
Current Assets	2,745	2,466
Current Liabilities	552	2,134
Working Capital	2,193	332
Bank Borrowings	1,598	1,615
Capital Stock	1,010	1,010
Capital Surplus	4	4
Shareholders' Equity	1,788	1,794
Equity Ratio(%)	45.6	44.9
Interest & Dividend Net	(-)36	–

Facility Investment(¥mil)
Mar '90* 77 (Mar '89 0)
R&D Expenditure(¥mil)
Mar '90* 0 (Mar '89 0)
Highest in Current Profit(¥mil)
Sep '82 216
References: Fuji, Mitsui, Chuo Trust, Shiga, Kyoto Kyoei
Exchanges: TYO, OSA
Underwriters: Yamaichi
Est: Dec 1926 **Listed:** Aug 1949
Employees (Age) 56(39)
Chairman: –
President: Masahiko Takeda
Overseas Offices None

Principal Office Tel: 075-255-1201
689-1, Takanna-cho, Karasumashijo-Agaru, Nakagyo-ku, Kyoto 604 **Fax:** 075-231-4522

Sources: Japan Company Handbook, First Section (Tokyo: Toyo Keizai, first quarter 1974, spring 1990); reprinted by permission of the publisher

dividend rates into the yield on the stock. For banks, only bonds, deposits, loans, securities and the dividend rate were given, with no profit figure. Nor was the number of shares outstanding of a company reported, making determination of earnings per share and PERs more difficult. In the 1970s, however, recurring profits and dividends were added, and in 1975 earnings per share, dividends per share, and the book value per share were included. And in 1977, the concept of consolidated earnings was introduced as a new way of valuing companies.

The *Kaisha Joho* recently changed its format by including a picture of a facial expression to depict, at a glance, how a company was faring.

Face Analysis

Amount of hair: growth rate of recurring profits

Angle of eyebrows: operating profit growth (/ means profits growing more than 10%; \ means profits falling more than 10%)

Roundness of eyes: earnings per share (the higher EPS, the rounder the eyes)

Width of face: level of recurring profits to sales for the current fiscal year, compared to the average ratio for the past five years

Position of pupil: sales growth (straight ahead— high growth; looking left—low growth)

Length of face: sales volume

Mouth: recurring profits to sales (smile indicates profit margin improving by 10% or more; frown indicates profit margin declining by 10% or more)

Source: Kaisha Joho (Tokyo: Nihon Keizai Shimbun, 1990 spring edition supplement); reprinted by permission of the publisher.

FUJI SEITO

2111
フジ製糖

Medium-ranking sugar refiner, based in Shizuoka Pref. Affiliated with Nissho Iwai Corp. Trying to expand nonsugar businesses, incl production of maitake mushrooms, bulbs using tissue culture, cut-flower activator and natural antioxidant extracted from tea leaves. Earning power increasing.

Outlook: Despite rising shipments, liquid sugar sales slipping down due to abolition of sugar consumption tax. Refined sugar market continuing bearish below administered sugar price. Profit falling due in part to higher costs stemming from purchase of raw sugar at premium in preceding term. Launching improved cut flower activators. Developed small packaged sugar "Mini Pack" for gift items. Nonsugar lines chalking up ¥350 mil sales(up 21%) in Feb '90 term.

Income (¥mil)	Sales	Operating Profit	Current Profit	Net Profit	Earnings per sh	Dividend per sh	Equity per sh
Feb '85	13,687	952	634	1,837	¥122.5	¥0	¥18.3
Feb '86	12,988	723	755	792	52.9	0	71.1
Feb '87	12,415	430	503	503	33.6	0	104.6
Feb '88	12,055	437	498	350	23.4	3	128.0
Feb '89	12,580	549	622	316	21.1	3	145.9
Feb '90*	12,500	180	200	80	5.3	3	
Feb '91*	12,500	180	200	80	5.3	3	
·Aug '88	6,185	258	286	126	8.4	0	133.2
·Aug '89	6,239	79	110	30	2.1	0	144.6
·Aug '90*	6,300	80	110	30	2.0	0	

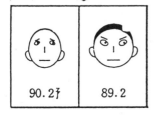

90.2予　89.2

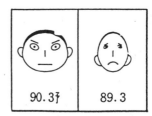

90.3予　89.3

Namura Shipbuilding

7014
名村造船所

Medium-standing shipbuilder affiliated with Sanwa Bank. Closely related to Mitsubishi Heavy Industries in tech field. Ships account for some 70% of entire sales, but diversifying into steel structures, incl bridges and floodgates. Keen on construction of facilities for ocean thermal power generation.

Outlook: In 2nd half, new shipbuilding orders for 5 ships expected. Unit price improving. Consecutive construction starts of seven 95,000-ton tankers yielding substantial operating effect. Land machinery, mainly bridges, turning into black. Current account turning into black thanks to windfall dividend income of ¥500 mil from overseas sub. Plans to wipe out cumulative loss of ¥3.2 bil by eating into separate fund reserve by end of Mar '90 term, helped by unexpectedly sharp recovery.

Income (¥mil)	Sales	Operating Profit	Current Profit	Net Profit	Earnings per sh	Dividend per sh	Equity per sh
Mar '85	26,788	1,913	1,651	1,667	¥55.6	¥3	¥227.0
Mar '86	34,236	4,430	3,899	524	17.5	3	240.7
Mar '87	21,281	(-)1,215	(-)902	(-)1,139	(-)38.0	0	199.2
Mar '88	14,219	(-)2,284	(-)2,355	(-)1,461	(-)48.7	0	150.5
Mar '89	13,441	(-)1,806	(-)1,674	(-)1,447	(-)48.2	0	102.2
Mar '90*	22,200	600	600	600	20.0	0	
Mar '91*	30,000	1,100	600	600	20.0	0~4	
·Sep '88	4,066	(-)787	(-)601	(-)601	(-)20.0	0	130.4
·Sep '89	7,748	(-)515	(-)707	(-)707	(-)23.6	0	78.6
·Sep '90*	13,000	400	200	200	6.7	0	

Sources: Japan Company Handbook, Second Section (Tokyo: Toyo Keizai, spring 1990); *Kaisha Joho* (Tokyo: Nihon Keizai Shimbun, spring 1990); reprinted by permission of the publisher

The most important function of both publications is that they give an estimate of earnings for the current fiscal year and the following one. These forecasts are usually made, unofficially, by the companies themselves and form the basis for what is known as the street estimates. An earnings surprise for a company can be discerned simply by comparing the actual figures that appear in the latest edition with the forecast in the previous one.

Japanese companies feel obliged to meet their profit forecasts, so the estimates that appear are remarkably dependable. By looking at the growth rates in recurring profits, it is also possible to find the most rapidly expanding companies and industries and to know, with reasonable accuracy, which sectors investors will pay attention to over the coming year or two. All this makes life untaxing for securities analysts in Japan. If they so chose, they could simply use the forecasts that appear in the two information books, adding or subtracting a little here and there to reflect their own expectations for a company's earnings.

In order to supplement this voluminous diet, stock-chart books are widely read, in particular the weekly *Golden Chart* and *Toshi Radar*. These contain historical two-year charts of the share price of every listed company. They are mainly used to determine the risk of making an investment or the likely degree to which new information may have been discounted already in the share price.

A glance at the twenty-year chart of Meiji Shipping shows that investor interest in the stock picked up in 1985. Its share price increased 54 times over the next five years despite the fact that it has only 109 employees and has not turned a profit since 1986. A speculator group was allegedly cornering its shares.

Share price charts are useful in Tokyo due to the shallowness of trading and the fact that they are so closely watched. The lack of liquidity causes shares to respond to the slightest pickup in trading activity. The share price of Taiyo Kobe Bank rose sharply in the two months prior to the announcement, on August 29, 1989, that it was to merge with Mitsui Bank to form one of the largest banks in the world. From the chart, it was clear something was going on, since Taiyo Kobe's share behavior was out of line with that of the rest of the banking sector. When its merger with Mitsui Bank was formally

Meiji Shipping

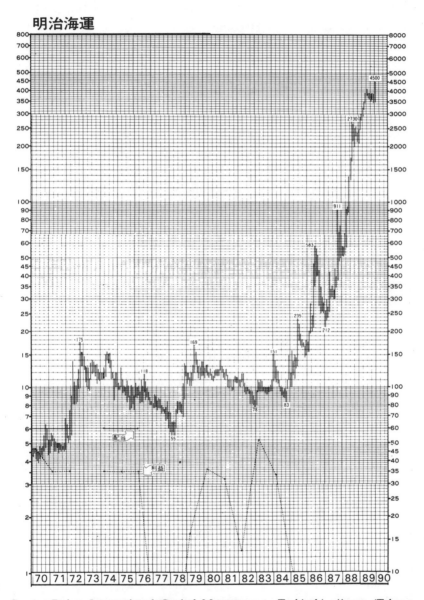

Source: Daiwa International Capital Management, *Tsukiashi nijunen* (Tokyo: Jitsu Nichi Research Center, 1990), 628; logarithm graph reprinted by permission of the publisher

announced, Taiyo Kobe's share price rose untraded from ¥1,600 to ¥2,090 to account for the fact that 1,000 shares of Taiyo Kobe Bank would be exchanged for 800 shares of Mitsui Bank, then priced at ¥2,400. In its investigation, the Ministry of Finance discovered that the main broker during this period was Shinyei Ishino Securities, in which Taiyo Kobe Bank owned a 5 percent stake. No violation of insider trading was found as Shinyei claimed it was acting independently. Rumors circulated, however, that Taiyo Kobe's share price was being pushed up to make the exchange rate of shares more favorable to Taiyo Kobe.

The pattern of Japan's bull markets shows how useful charts are. At least a year before it happened, many technical analysts predicted the end of Japan's bull market. The charts also noted that every ma-

Taiyo Kobe Bank

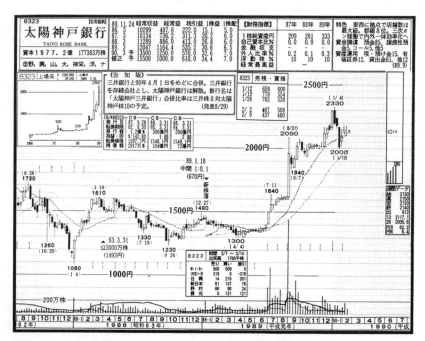

Source: First Section Chart Book, no. 727 (Tokyo: Toshi Radar, February 19, 1990); reprinted by permission of the publisher

Bull and bear markets in Japan

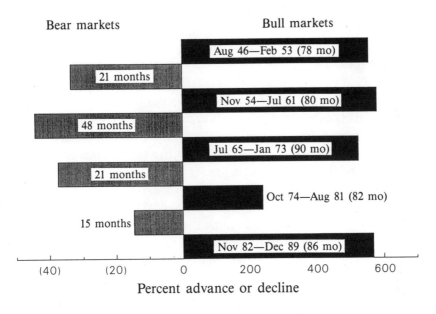

Bear markets   Bull markets

Aug 46—Feb 53 (78 mo)

21 months

Nov 54—Jul 61 (80 mo)

48 months

Jul 65—Jan 73 (90 mo)

21 months

Oct 74—Aug 81 (82 mo)

15 months

Nov 82—Dec 89 (86 mo)

(40)   (20)   0   200   400   600

Percent advance or decline

jor postwar bull market had lasted between 78 and 90 months, and that the Nikkei Average in each case had risen 5.25–5.80 times (with the exception of the bull market after the first oil shock when the market only rose 2.4 times). In actuality, the 1980s' bull market lasted 87 months, during which the Nikkei rose 5.68 times between October 1982 and December 1989.

Armed with a welter of information, individual investors are just as well off as institutional investors. The stock analysis provided by Japanese brokerages for large clients offers little more insight than what is available every day in the press. Their securities analysts are often salesmen-in-waiting, newly hired employees who are learning how the stock market works.

MARKET THEMES

Faced with an illiquid stock market lacking a consistent method of valuing shares, Japanese brokers need a basis for recommending stocks that can appeal to investors and thus generate business. This problem is solved through the use of market themes, which are usually related to the improvement of a company's business. These themes provide the rationale for buying a collection of stocks, which may have a wide variation in PERs and quality. For stockbrokers, the best themes are those that are easy to understand and will take several years to bear fruit. Investors will have less reason, therefore, to concern themselves with short-term corporate performance.

One further advantage of themes is that they help to build consensus, particularly among small investors, as to which industries and companies are in favor. This is important in a shallow market. When there are few themes, the market tends to lack direction and trading volumes decline.

Themes make life easy for the brokers. They can recommend shares without worrying how much the shares are really "worth." They merely have to find a plausible story to support their recommendations. There must be some underlying logic, though, since Japanese investors place great store in the shares of companies with improving fundamentals. The difficulty lies in working out how much to pay.

The Big Four tend to use a top-down approach in creating a theme. After a careful analysis of the economy, a picture of the future is created. All of Japan's large brokerage houses operate large research organizations to help them do this. Herewith, two examples:

Tokyo Bay Redevelopment

Tokyo Bay Redevelopment was the major stock market theme of 1986–87 and encompassed eleven urban redevelopment projects proposed by the government in 1986. These projects stemmed from the September 1985 agreement by the world's major industrial countries to revalue the yen to curb Japan's excessive trade surplus. As part of this agreement, Japan promised to turn its economy away from exports to rely more on growth in domestic demand.

Redevelopment of the heavily industrialized area around the bay would be the means by which Japan could show the world it was working hard to stimulate domestic demand. Redevelopment of the area was also needed to ease transport bottlenecks and relieve the chronic shortage of office space in central Tokyo.

Most of the land around Tokyo Bay had been reclaimed in earlier decades. There was a great increase in reclamation projects after World War II, when local governments attracted heavy industrial developments to the cheap, plentiful reclaimed land within easy reach of booming Tokyo. Only energy, heavy industrial, and transport companies were allowed in. These artificial islands sit only a few miles from Ginza, which boasts the most expensive real estate in the world. The main property owners are the government and industrial companies which had located their aging industrial facilities there.

These projects could be self-financed and thus required no money from the government. While the price of commercial real estate has reached the level where yields on developments employing newly purchased prime land are minimal, in the case of land already owned, the returns on newly invested funds are vastly higher.

As a stock market theme, Tokyo Bay Redevelopment fitted perfectly for several reasons. First, the need for redevelopment was obvious as well as part of government policy. Second, the projects would affect a large number of out-of-favor companies, which happened to have cheap share prices and a domestic orientation. This was an important factor for investors since exporters, the previous market leaders, were then suffering from the effects of the strong yen. Out-of-favor firms also had a large number of shares outstanding, allowing them to absorb the excess liquidity of the stock market. Third, these companies would see their net worth increase substantially due to the rezoning of their landholdings from industrial to commercial use. Fourth, since the value of these companies was based on their landholdings, rather than on their slim earnings, investors did not have to worry about high PERs.

The key factor was the value of the landholdings relative to the market value of the company. In fact, the closer a company was to bankruptcy the more attractive it became: the turnaround would be spectacular and the necessity to redevelop the greater. Finally, the fundamentals of the companies were actually improving due to the fact their domestic businesses were picking up. Tokyo Bay may have been the catalyst, but other positive factors were at work.

The list of beneficiaries were numerous, including Mitsubishi Steel, whose share price rose from ¥540 in late 1987 to ¥3,520 a year later, IHI, Tokyo Gas, and Onoda Cement. By mid-1988, however, Tokyo Bay began to fade as a market theme. Share prices had risen to a point where they had largely discounted the potential impact of redevelopment on the value of the value of their landholdings. Thus, the fact that full-scale redevelopment never took place, owing to a variety of problems, did not matter to the investor.

Most importantly, however, the domestic economy began to expand at a rapid pace. The companies that owned Tokyo Bay land saw their basic businesses of steel, cement, warehousing, and chemicals recover so much they were reluctant to relocate their facilities. Rather than hidden assets, the focus was on earnings.

The landholdings in Tokyo Bay remain. Some redevelopment plans have gone forward; most have not. Should the stock market once again demand it, plans for Tokyo Bay Redevelopment might be dusted off and put on the table again.

Linear Motor Trains

Linear Motor Trains is a theme which has been gradually emerging since 1987 and is likely to continue throughout the 1990s. Unlike conventional trains, linear motor trains are propelled by means of electromagnetic attraction and repulsion. Magnets are housed in both the train and in the tracks, and trains are magnetically levitated one-to-ten centimeters above the tracks.

Linear motor trains offer a number of advantages over conventional trains. They can be designed to travel at speeds of up to 500 kilometers per hour, which can give airliners a run for their money. For Japan, this means that the train time between Tokyo and Osaka could be reduced from three hours currently to one hour. And since these trains can climb steep gradients and pass through smaller tunnels, they would be suitable for Japan's mountainous terrain.

Linear motor trains also have strategic and national implications. Superconducting magnets would consume less energy to create powerful magnetic fields, and development of the trains would bring Japan to the forefront of superconductivity technology. It would be a strategic national investment, helping also to ease the crowding around Tokyo. (West Germany may be close to putting their linear motor trains into service, beating Japan to the punch.)

Support for the trains comes from a number of interests; the Ministry of Transport; JR Tokai, the former national railway company spinoff that operates between Tokyo and Osaka; local politicians; and of course the companies that would receive part of the ¥1 trillion worth of construction and machinery orders. A 50-kilometer test track between Tokyo and the land-locked city of Kofu in Yamanashi Prefecture has been proposed.

As with Tokyo Bay, linear motor trains have a number of attractions as a theme. First, it is a big project, meaning that the benefits for a company are considerable. Second, there is a very long-term payoff, since the proposed link between Tokyo and Osaka would take over a decade to complete. Third, linear motor trains as high technology are attractive to investors. Heary electrical companies (Hitachi, Mitsubishi Electric, and Toshiba), cable companies (Hitachi Cable, Furukawa Electric, and Sumitomo Electric), railway car makers (Tokyu Car), construction companies, even local banks (the share price of the local Kofu bank doubled in 1988) have ridden with the theme.

But compared to the Tokyo Bay Redevelopment theme, where companies owned valuable land irrespective of its development, linear motor trains have so far had less of an impact on the market. For linear motor trains, companies have to receive actual orders. Delays and technical problems with the rail project make it hard to judge the outcome. There is the fear that passengers will suffer ill effects from the electromagnetic radiation. Nevertheless, if the JR companies are listed, linear motor trains will probably feature prominently as a market theme.

SHARE VALUATIONS

Japan's high share prices can be partly justified by the country's economic performance and by the structure of the market, topics discussed later. What is more difficult to understand is the inconsistency with which individual companies are valued. Conventional standards for valuing companies do not seem to apply to the TSE.

Sector Comparison
(Ending 1989)

	Share price appreciation 1968–89 (x)	PER (x)	Average share price (¥)
Electric power & gas	15.7	61	656
Foods	17.1	66	1,719
Textiles	17.4	103	1,529
Marine transportation	18.2	276	1,441
Fishery & forestry	18.4	319	1,221
Transportation equipment	18.6	75	1,432
Machinery	19.1	82	1,790
Iron & steel	21.9	48	1,482
Pulp & paper	22.0	59	1,382
Commerce	22.5	79	2,441
Nonferrous metals	22.7	98	1,319
Glass & ceramics	22.8	72	1,717
Rubber products	23.3	72	1,462
Real estate	23.6	78	2,266
Mining	23.7	99	1,623
Electric appliances	23.8	66	2,099
Precision instruments	25.3	76	1,522
Metal products	26.0	58	2,116
Services	26.3	112	2,939
Chemicals	27.3	68	1,627
Other products	29.5	67	2,499
Construction	31.9	71	1,849
Oil & coal products	32.3	55	1,575
Land transport	34.5	173	1,999
Air transport	34.9	126	2,005
Warehousing	38.7	98	1,720
Communications	39.5	67	2,628
Finance & insurance	100.3	50	1,850

Source: *Annual Securities Statistics* (Tokyo: Tokyo Stock Exchange, 1989)

There are two ways in which Japanese shares defy fundamentals. The first is the distribution of PERs by industry sector. Assuming that all Japanese companies follow similar accounting standards and operate in the same economic environment, companies with a good outlook ought to have higher PERs than companies with a poor outlook. Often the opposite is the case: the poorest industries have the highest PERs.

The second is the share-price performance of industries over a long period of time. Industries have performed roughly the same on the stock market since the late 1960s, regardless of differences in earnings growth. An investor would have made just as much profit investing in mines and fisheries as in Japan's much-vaunted electrical companies. Share prices appear to have gone up regardless of earnings.

The Illiquidity Factor

The mispricing of shares may simply be the result of an illiquid market in which themes dominate. Few questions are raised as to whether the shares are worth the asking price when the brokers shine the spotlight on a single stock or industry sector. This is particularly so when a specific industry is in vogue. The stock prices of all companies in the same field tend to move in concert, irrespective of their individual circumstances. Those that fail to move up during the initial buying wave are picked up eventually. Finding the right sector is often more important than picking the best stock. Yet over the past 20 years, there is little difference between one sector and another.

Japanese companies in the same industries will compete in the same markets and follow virtually the same strategies. If there is a reason to buy Sumitomo Bank, Toyota, or Hitachi, then the same factors are likely to apply to Mitsubishi Bank, Nissan, or Toshiba. The coordinated movement of share prices is also a reflection of Japan's hierarchical society. Companies try hard to maintain their market shares, earnings, dividends, and share prices relative to their competitors. This rank consciousness is reinforced by the media, which is continually publishing rankings of Japanese companies in terms of sales and earnings. A high share price is a status symbol to a Japanese company.

There is evidence to suggest that Japanese investors may value

Hierarchy of Share Prices
(Ending 1989)

	Sales rank	Share price (¥)	PER
SYNTHETIC FIBERS			
Asahi Chemical Industry	1	1,260	44
Toray	2	1,010	35
Teijin	3	958	40
Mitsubishi Rayon	4	893	85
HEAVY ELECTRICALS			
Hitachi	1	1,520	22
Toshiba	2	1,270	29
Mitsubishi Electric	3	1,100	37
BROKERAGES			
Nomura Securities	1	3,440	28
Daiwa Securities	2	2,350	18
Nikko Securities	3	1,920	22
Yamaichi Securities	4	1,930	20
ELECTRIC POWER COMPANIES			
Tokyo Electric Power	1	6,190	90
Kansai Electric Power	2	5,020	79
Chubu Electric Power	3	4,970	80
Tohoku Electric Power	4	4,230	73
Kyushu Electric Power	5	4,130	76
SHIPPING COMPANIES			
Nippon Yusen	1	1,170	191
Mitsui O.S.K. Lines	2	1,130	197
Kawasaki Kisen	3	1,120	131
COMMUNICATIONS EQUIPMENT			
NEC	1	1,870	35
Fujitsu	2	1,510	27
Oki Electric Industry	3	1,200	33

RAILWAYS

Seibu Railway	1	7,620	734
Tokyu Corp.	2	2,700	326
Odakyu Electric Railway	3	1,780	193
Tobu Railway	4	1,700	223

shares solely on the basis of their sales ranking rather than on their level of earnings per share. The stock of an industry leader will often carry the highest price but the lowest PER. Because it is the investors' perception of rank that determines the share prices, the resulting PERs may or may not be out of line with the industry leader. Some argue that higher PERs for the followers is justified by the fact that profits are more likely to recover. The trend across industries, however, shows that the performance gap between the leaders and the followers has usually been widening.

The automobile industry is a good example. Without doubt, Toyota is the finest automaker in Japan. The company is the most profitable, has the best growth prospects, and faces the least financial risk. Isuzu and Fuji Heavy Industries (maker of Subaru cars) are in the opposite situation. If the highest PER were accorded the best company in the industry, then Toyota should have it; yet it carries the lowest. By contrast, Toyota has the highest share prices among auto companies while Fuji Heavy Industries has the lowest.

The Liquidity Trap

Herds of buyers cause share prices to overshoot their appropriate level. When an industry falls out of favor, however, the opposite does not necessarily happen. Prices do not decline immediately because the sudden absence of buyers traps would-be sellers. Rather than throw away their gains by cashing in immediately, these investors slowly unwind their positions in a process than can take several years. But when panic selling occurs, prices can fall sharply on thin volume.

The pharmaceutical sector was caught in this liquidity trap in the late 1980s. Drug stocks caught the eye of investors in 1984–85 on pros-

Mochida Pharmaceutical

持田製薬

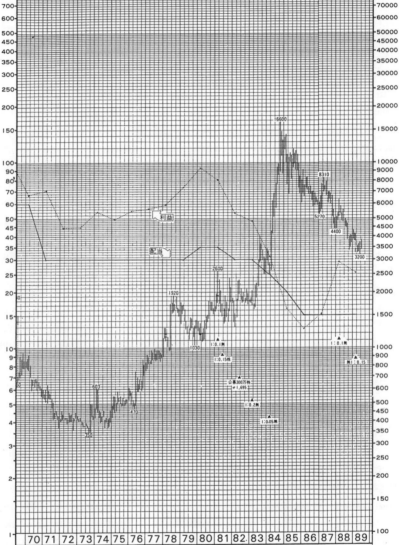

Source: Daiwa International Capital Management, *Tsuikiashi nijunen* (Tokyo:
    Jitsu Nichi Research Center, 1989), 184; logarithm graph reprinted by
    permission of the publisher

pects of new drug launches, and their share prices rose sharply. Share prices then drifted down for four years. Mochida Pharmaceutical was the best performing drug stock during this boom. Its share price rose from ¥1,600 in 1983 to ¥16,600 by the end of 1984 on speculation that it had discovered a cure for cancer. At its peak, Mochida had a market capitalization of ¥1.3 trillion and a PER of 1,020. No miracle drug was forthcoming, and Mochida's share price steadily fell the following four years, bottoming at ¥3,200 in the middle of 1989.

The Heated OTC Market

If the mighty TSE can overreach itself, so too can the humble Over-the-Counter market. In late 1989 and early 1990, Over-the-Counter stocks gained attention for their good growth prospects, relatively low PERs, and the launching of a number of OTC stock funds. Between September 1989 and March 1990, the average share price soared by 90 percent.

The OTC market is even more illiquid than the TSE, with the top ten shareholders controlling in many cases 80–90 percent of shares outstanding. Moreover, placing orders is difficult since they are all handled by the Japan Over-the-Counter Securities Company, which has only 14 telephones for taking orders. The market was overwhelmed by the surge in demand from investors. Heiwa, Japan's top maker of pachinko (a popular pinball game) machines, saw its share price quadruple to ¥31,700 by April 1990, giving it a PER of 215 and a market capitalization of nearly ¥2 trillion or 35 times its annual sales. At that price, the shareholdings owned by the president of the company, Kenkichi Nakajima, were worth close to ¥1.4 trillion.

The cheapest stock on the OTC market was Hokkaido Colliery and Steamship, a former coal mining company that now trades in coal. Founded in 1889, this company was once a core member of the Mitsui Group and one of the original 225 companies in the Nikkei Average. For decades it lost money, the result of a decision to remain in coal mining rather than to diversify. From a work force of over 10,000 employees in the 1950s, it now has a staff of 20. Despite a negative net worth of ¥115 billion, or ¥822 per share, and an expected loss of ¥3 per share in the year ending March 1990, its share price rose

175 percent in the first few weeks of 1990. It even surpassed by ¥2 its peak price of ¥278 reached in 1949, giving it a market capitalization of ¥39 billion. Once it reached this level it fell ¥80 the next day.

Mispricing among Low-Priced Shares

The tendency for mispricing is particularly strong for companies with share prices that are low, ¥400 or ¥600. Such stocks are commonly found among mature companies that raised capital in the equity market during the 1950s and 1960s when all new shares had to be sold for ¥50; examples are the textile, shipping, and steel industries. Due to their large size and limited growth prospects, it is difficult for these companies to raise their earnings per share because they have so many shares outstanding relative to their level of profits and shareholders' equity. This situation cannot be rectified since under the commercial code a company cannot buy back its own shares.

Nevertheless, investors have bid prices to ever higher levels. Every

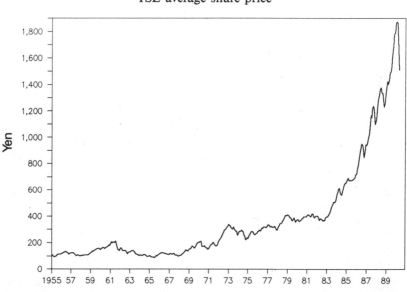

Share Price Inflation
TSE average share price

Source: Annual Securities Statistics (Tokyo: Tokyo Stock Exchange, 1989)

cyclical industry in Japan saw a strong recovery in its earnings in
1988 and 1989 due to strong domestic demand and severe cost reduction. In addition, many of these companies grew·quite wealthy due to
the sharp appreciation of stock and real estate prices. Since they have
been around for a long time, they had more opportunities to purchase land and shares at much lower prices than exist today.

Individuals often buy shares in companies with low prices for no
other reason than that they can afford them. Share-price inflation has
put many companies out of the reach of the small investor, since the
smallest tradable unit is one thousand shares. The average price of a
listed share rose from ¥271 in 1972 to ¥381 by 1982 and then to
¥1,867 by the end of 1989. In 1984, 44 percent of all shares was priced
below ¥400, but by the end of 1989 only 10 percent of shares could be
found below ¥1,000.

There is a greater demand for shares at low prices than there is at
high prices because of the high proportion of turnover by individuals. The phenomenon of cheap stocks catching up with expensive ones is known as *kasa-age*, which is a description of what happens when an umbrella opens—the lower spokes rise faster than the
top.

Many Japanese investors search for the worst-performing companies with low prices because they are confident that the share price
will not fall below a certain level. Stable shareholders are unlikely to
sell their holdings, and the firm's main bank can usually be relied on
to stand by the company and help it restructure.

The Example of NEC and Sumitomo Coal Mining

The popularity of share price charts reflects a belief that share
prices have taken into account all known information. This is what is
called efficient market theory. Investors assume that any unexpected,
positive news will push up the share price, regardless of their current
level. The weaker the company, the greater the potential for a plea-
sant surprise.

Compare the performance of NEC and Sumitomo Coal Mining,
which are both members of the Sumitomo *keiretsu*. NEC was
founded in 1899 as a joint venture to produce telecommunications
equipment by two Japanese entrepreneurs and Western Electric.

Sumitomo Coal Mining was founded in 1927 to mine coal in Hokkaido, Japan's northernmost island. Once a major export industry for Japan, coal mining has lost money since the 1950s.

In the year ending March 1974, NEC reported net income of ¥10 billion on sales of ¥343 billion. It earned ¥13 per share, had a net worth of ¥106 per share and a share price of around ¥200. It was described in that year's edition of the *Japan Company Handbook* as a "top manufacturer of telecommunications and electronic machines within [the] Sumitomo Group; positively advancing overseas in [the] telecommunication equipment field." Meanwhile, Sumitomo Coal Mining had earned ¥1 per share, had not paid a dividend in years, and had a negative net worth close to ¥70 per share. Its shares were priced around ¥100, against ¥16 in 1971. The *Japan Company Handbook* described it as follows: "belongs to the Sumitomo Group; mining coal in Hokkaido; diversifying business on basis of civil engineering and supermarket management; plans to separate coal division."

By 1981, the descriptions of the two firms in the *Japan Company Handbook* read this way:

NEC

Characteristics: Major manufacturer of telecommunications and electronic computers. Belongs to Sumitomo Group. Positively advancing overseas in telecommunications equipment fields.
Remarks: Active market continues for semiconductors, and large-scale and other computers doing well. Communications equipment also firm. Earnings sharply up. Major profit increase offsetting yen appreciation and higher interest with rationalization and advantages of mass production. Following US satellite communications equipment plant with new Scotland IC center.

SUMITOMO COAL MINING

Characteristics: Belongs to Sumitomo Group. Diversifying business to supermarket management and so on. Absorbed real estate subsidiary to keep market listing. Separated coal mining as subsidiary.
Remarks: May dip into accumulated reserves to eliminate losses carried over of ¥4.3 billion, since now firmly in black. Medium-term strategy centers on overseas coal development, expansion of building rental, and strengthening of mining operations. Negotiatings with Majors for coal imports through farming in their concessions in payment for mining technology in Australia and Canada.

By 1990 both companies had essentially achieved what they had set out to do in the early 1970s: NEC built a commanding position in the world's electronics industry and Sumitomo Coal Mining escaped bankruptcy by diversifying out of coal mining. By the beginning of 1990, NEC's consolidated sales had reached ¥3.4 trillion and its profits ¥85 billion. Sumitomo Coal Mining, at the same time, had accomplished its long-term recovery, reporting net earnings of ¥1 billion or ¥13 per share and finally restored its dividend of ¥5. The *Japan Company Handbook* again:

NEC

Characteristics: One of nation's representative high-tech enterprises. Globally known for "NEC" brand, involved in "C&C Strategy", designed for integration of communications and computers by taking advantage of world's largest production of semiconductors. Licensed computer tech to Honeywell (US). Overseas loans and investment high. Outlook: Communications equipment, computers, information terminals, and electronic devices all steady. Among ICs, memory chip prices softening, but ASIC prices firm. Profit to rise, absorbing heavier R&D and depreciation burden. Commemorative dividend likely for 90th anniversary of founding. Plans expansion of IC production capacity at UK plant to 10 million pieces/month, while setting up research lab in US for advanced switching systems. Reinforcing PC assembly plant in UK.

SUMITOMO COAL MINING

Coal distributor of Sumitomo Group. Akabira Mine separated as subsidiary. Diversified into quarrying, building materials, supermarket operations and real estate. Source of earnings is building rental utilizing idle land. Profitability gradually improving. Made capital participation in Australia's Wambo Mining. Outlook: Domestic coal decreasing, but imported coal increasing, mainly for steel industry. Building and machinery parts materials doing strong in Tokyo and Hokkaido. Contributions coming from real estate operations. Profit ratio improving. Current profit projection revised upward. Plans to construct rental building in Hokkaido in fiscal 1990 and golf course in fiscal 1992, to expand profitable real estate operations. Slated to open 2 supermarkets in fiscal 1991.

Despite NEC's preeminence, investment in the much smaller mining company's shares would have been preferable. At the end of February 1990, NEC's share price was ¥1,860, against ¥200 in 1974.

Sumitomo Coal Mining was priced at ¥1,270 against ¥100 in 1974. NEC carried a prospective PER of 31 while Sumitomo Coal Mining sold at 97 times earnings and nine times book value.

Valuations over Time

The apparent lack of consistency among share prices is probably one of the reasons why Japan has never been able to develop a theory of share price valuation comparable to that of the United States. None of the numerous stock market books available attempt to deal with this issue. Instead, they devote their attention to share price charts and vague long-term prospects in an age of "new materials" or "leisure resort society." PERs are not mentioned with regard to whether or not the share is cheap in comparison to that of earnings, but to whether or not it is cheap in comparison to the PERs of other companies in the market.

In the past 40 years, the Tokyo stock market has passed through different methods of valuation. But no theory has held sway for any length of time because prices have risen remorselessly, confounding each hypothesis in turn.

In the decade or so after the stock market reopened in 1949, the TSE was very cheap by most standards, with PERs of 8, dividend yields of 7 percent, and an average annual total return of 20 percent. The standard measure of value was dividend yield, or more precisely, dividends paid as a percentage of par value, which is normally ¥50. Companies having an equity issue were the most attractive. New shares were sold at par value to current shareholders and carried the same dividend rate as old shares, often 8–10 percent of par. Since the market price of a stock was much higher than par, new issues effectively raised the yield on an investor's shares and boosted the share price. A company which was expected to have frequent equity financings was called a "growth stock."

In the late 1950s, this thinking began to break down as companies increased the size of their financings at par value but failed to maintain their increasingly onerous dividend rates. The market was strained to the breaking point when bank credit was tightened. This prompted companies to raise even more money from equity issues in order to keep up with demand for their goods. Share prices fell in response to the increased supply, and the market slump lasted four years.

In the midst of this chaos, foreign investors started buying Japanese shares, lured by an average PER half that in the United States even though the Japanese economy was expanding at three times the rate. They brought with them such concepts as earnings per share and the PER, which were adopted with alacrity by the Japanese, particularly since dividend yields were falling. The shift to new issues at market prices in 1969 made the standard of the 1950s meaningless. The *Shikiho* began to publish companies' earnings per shares as well as dividends per share. These were forms of measurement that had never been needed before.

The imported theories started to look distinctly threadbare just before the first oil crisis when share prices appeared to be overvalued according to these conventional measures of value. In 1972, the TSE's average PER exceeded 25, and stayed close to that figure as Japan recovered from commodity inflation a couple of years later. Even so, foreign investors hung on by searching for cheap shares among the fast-growing companies powering the country's export boom, companies like Sony, Honda, and Hitachi. But by 1984, even these shares were looking overpriced. Foreigners became heavy net sellers.

Like beauty, the value of a shares is in the eye of the beholder. What appeared too expensive to the foreigner looked cheap to the Japanese, who based their valuation on the view that companies were undervalued relative to the true worth of the land and shares that they owned. It did not matter how much a company earned; the important factor was where its headquarters and factories were located.

By the late 1980s, however, "hidden asset" plays receded as the economy started to recover from the recession caused by the revaluation of the yen. Investors shifted their focus in 1988 first to companies seeing an earnings recovery, and then in 1989 to small growth stocks on the Second Section and the OTC market.

By the beginning of 1990, however, the market ran out of issues to buy. While the hidden assets were still there, nobody appeared to care. In fact, as the market began to crash, newspaper and magazine articles talked of Japan's "bubble economy." In the future, investors may flirt with fundamentals, but it is doubtful that only a few months of turbulence will cause investors to give up a lifetime of speculation.

OUTSIDER TRADING

As stock markets around the world grow increasingly interrelated, the TSE has come under pressure to conform to international standards, or at least to Anglo-Saxon ones. At a meeting in Stockholm in 1988, David Ruder, then-chairman of the U.S. Securities and Exchange Commission, urged stock market regulators around the world to adopt compatible legislation to govern the industry. "It's essential that we have a similar level of antifraud laws," he said. "That means laws against market manipulation, against insider trading, and against rumor mongering or misrepresentation of information to the markets." Japan has some elements of all three, but the mix is different from elsewhere. Insider trading is usually considered the most serious offence of the three.

The TSE's thin liquidity and the flood of information make insider trading difficult to achieve and easy to detect. Difficult, that is, but not impossible. It is impossible, though, to say how difficult, because the rules on insider trading have never been invoked in a criminal prosecution in Japan, despite being modeled almost exactly on U.S. law. While the United States built a thick body of case law to flesh out the statutes on insider trading and related offenses, Japan never did.

The most notorious case of alleged insider trading was that of Tateho Chemical Industries in September 1987 in which one of the firm's financiers, Keihanshin Sogo Bank, sold 337,000 shares one day before the company announced a ¥23 billion loss from government-bond futures trading. The bank sold at a price of ¥1,700 per share right before it plummeted to ¥439 per share. After an investigation by the Osaka Securities Exchange, the authorities determined that no specific evidence was found to prove that the law on insider trading had been violated.

At the time of the Tateho affair, the Securities and Exchange Law targeted insider trading in three ways. First, any officer or main shareholder of a company who used inside information "unfairly" could be ordered to pay back to the company any profit made on stock transactions that occurred within six months from the date of buying or selling the stock. Second, stockbrokers were prohibited from trading securities on the basis of "special information" regarding the transactions of their clients. The third forbade the use of any fraudulent device for share transactions. Apparently, the evidence in the Tateho case failed to meet these three criteria, and the case was closed.

Immediately afterwards, the Finance Ministry set to work to revise the legislation, proposing amendments which were passed by the Diet in May 1988. The aim was to specify as precisely as possible what was meant by "inside information" and to determine exactly who would be liable for prosecution. Stronger surveillance powers were adopted and criminal provisions took effect in April 1989.

Even though the rules have been tightened, the question of enforcement is, and always has been, the decisive factor. The TSE's monitoring staff numbers 31 and the Japan Securities Dealers Association, which administers the Over-the-Counter share market, only has six people for the job. The Finance Ministry's entire Securities Bureau has fewer than 150. In contrast, the Securities Exchange Commission in New York has a staff of 2,000.

The lack of personnel in Japan is one reason why it took a year, from the time the criminal provisions went into effect, before police investigated their first case of insider trading. The main suspect was a former president of a finance company who was alleged to have bought 7,000 shares in Nisshin Steamship in June 1989, one day before the firm announced it was entering the hotel business. Shares in Nisshin rose by 50 percent soon after.

This criminal investigation raises the question of whether the securities industry should regulate itself. The Finance Ministry is clinging to the belief that it can. Officials wield a potent weapon that they believe renders the courts unnecessary: the withdrawal of a broker's license. It is a far worse fate than the maximum ¥3 million fine which can be imposed under the law.

True to the spirit of self-regulation, the Big Four have chosen to separate their underwriting and trading departments by so-called "Chinese walls." These were designed to prevent inside information such as upcoming share issues from being passed—routinely by tradition—from one department to the other. Nikko Securities, whose offices were raided by the Finance Ministry in March 1988 on suspicion of ramping the price of new shares in an electrical firm, later banned directors from personally dealing in all securities except government bonds. Banks and insurance companies now also quarantine departments that have access to privileged information.

Nonfinancial firms have changed in-house rules to prevent the disclosure of corporate data. At one point, in August 1988, the TSE had grown so anxious about insider trading that it asked Canon, the camera and office-equipment maker, to reveal its half-year results eleven days early, immediately after the company privately told the exchange that it would raise its dividend. Rumors of an early announcement alone were enough to send Canon's shares soaring. The company soon after decided to stop the practice of revealing its financial results to big shareholders a few hours before the public received them.

The Tateho case, and the subsequent scramble to tighten up trading procedures, demonstrated how inside information circulates in Japan. Bankers, brokers, favored customers, and large shareholders have traditionally had privileged access to corporate information in a country where long-term relationships are the key to profits. Within this charmed circle, business information is routinely passed around. This does not mean that trading by a select few on the basis of information inevitably follows, but it does create an atmosphere where insider trading, as understood in the West, could easily occur.

The most obvious manifestation is in the new issue of shares, convertible bonds, or warrants. In the West, the price of already listed shares tends to fall because of the anticipated dilution of their earnings by the offer of more equity, but in Japan the opposite will happen. Underwriters are meant to support the share price prior to the issue. Periodicals provide information to investors on which companies plan to issue securities or make gratis issues over the coming year.

The underwriter must be careful not to push the price too high, however. The Finance Ministry will not allow a new issue to proceed if the share price exhibits unusual movement or rises more than 30 percent in the six weeks before a firm files an application, although this rule was relaxed slightly in 1988. Brokers deny that shares are ramped before an issue and, of course, manipulation is difficult to prove. In any case, the power of the underwriters is such that when news emerges that one of the Big Four is managing an issue, the share price rises almost of its own accord. Companies "under financing," as it is known, have come to represent a risk-free way for speculators to make money.

Nissan's stock jumped sharply between July and October 1987 on rumors that the auto maker was about to announce a public offering. Sure enough, Nissan issued domestic convertible bonds in December and decided the following month to issue warrant bonds in the Eurodollar market. Similarly Toyota's shares surged in July 1988 before a big convertible bond issue. In the case of a $500 million warrant-bond issue by Sumitomo Metal Industries a month later, the Finance Ministry only gave the go-ahead at the last moment, as the firm's shares had surged by more than 30 percent in the three months before the announcement.

If the antics of Tateho spurred the Finance Ministry into rethinking its policies on insider trading, it was the Recruit Cosmos incident that made insider trading a pressing political issue. In July 1988, it was publicly revealed that a real estate firm called Recruit Cosmos had sold its stock cheaply in 1984–86 prior to its flotation on the Over-the-Counter market. While there was nothing new or illegal in allocating shares to a favored few before a public offering, what outraged the country was that among the 76 people who bought Recruit shares were the personal secretaries to Prime Minister Noboru Takeshita, to Finance Minister Kiichi Miyazawa, and to at least six other cabinet members. The incident was sufficient to cause the resignation of the prime minister and the suicide of his personal secretary.

Even shares that are offered to the "public" go into select hands. In the initial public offering (IPO) for Mitsubishi Motors, the largest industrial firm to be newly listed in many years, for example, securities companies began offering shares as soon as Mitsubishi Motors submitted its required documentation to the Finance Ministry on October 28, 1989. Yet, the public was not informed of the public offer price in the newspapers until November 7. Because IPOs in Japan have tended to shoot up as soon as they are listed, securities companies allocate shares to clients with losses on their investments as well as to buyers of investment trusts.

The privileged distribution of inside information has traditionally been respectable in Japan because it is seen as a way of lubricating corporate relationships. In contrast, individual insider trading on the scale of Ivan Boesky, who was successfully prosecuted in the United States in November 1986 for massive share fraud, is unheard of in Japan. Put another way, nobody has ever been caught.

In the absence of hard news, rumors abound as to which issues are "political" stocks—those said to be owned by politicians seeking to finance their campaigns—and which are "ambulance" shares—the certain winners offered to console clients who have recently lost heavily in the market. Some of the rumors can be deliberately misleading. An electronics company called Meidenko supposedly leaked a story about a possible a tie-up with two construction companies in 1984–86. The rumor turned out to be false, but not before Meidenko's owner, Isao Nakaseko, had made alleged profits of ¥2.5 billion from a range of share deals. He was said to have used 270 different names with 31 brokers to conceal his activities. Nakaseko was later charged with tax evasion.

Probably the greatest check on insider trading is the fact that much of the corporate information (such as half-yearly earnings or expansion plans) that insiders are told about is often uninteresting to the stock market. Whether a company earns ¥30 or ¥31 per share or raises its dividend by ¥1 does not carry the same significance as a Wall Street analyst cutting an earnings forecast. Moreover, the rapid dissemination of information and the quick response to rumors by individual investors makes acting on inside information difficult. The TSE may turn out to be as transparent as the New York market. It is just that the window looks out onto a different view.

An example of this is the issue of corporate disclosure. In the United States, the pressure for more information comes, unremittingly, from shareholders. In Japan, the inside shareholders already know what is going on and the outside ones do not care. Instead, the drive for greater disclosure has to come from the Finance Ministry, with whom all financial reports are lodged, or from overseas.

Accountant audits are required only for the 2,250 publicly traded companies and a few big, unquoted ones. The other 1.8 million firms in Japan make an annual financial statement attested to by a statutory auditor, who usually has no formal accounting qualifications at all. As one might expect, most companies follow the practice of closing their accounts at the same time, March 31, the end of the fiscal year. International accounting firms usually offer the same package of audit services wherever they are in the world. Demand for their services is not very strong in Japan, because firms simply do not need, nor do they want, an exhaustive examination of their books.

It was only in 1989 that companies began to issue their consolidated results simultaneously with their parent figures, but the amount of information about the subsidiaries remains extremely thin. Disclosure requirements are negligible. This adds to the speculative flavor of the stock market since speculation hinges on the existence of some unknown bit of information. If companies disclosed information to the same extent as their U.S. counterparts, including, for example, the market values of their landholdings or the true level of their profits, Japan's stock market would probably become as dull as other markets appear to be from the Japanese perspective.

CHANGING PATTERNS

The close relationship between the Finance Ministry, the securities industry, and the listed companies appears to have served the stock market and investors well. But the relationship is showing its first signs of strain. The rapid expansion of the stock market and the volume of trading has made it difficult for the Big Four to exercise the control they are accustomed to. Their share of equity turnover on the TSE has fallen almost steadily from its peak of 54 percent in 1981 to a low of 34 percent in the six months leading to September 1989, when Nomura's share fell below 10 percent for the first time in 20 years.

The most immediate reason for the decline has been a shift in investment patterns from a market driven by excess liquidity to a market more interested in earnings growth and smaller companies. In 1989, the Big Four failed to find a theme by which to ignite the market, but there were other reasons of a more lasting nature that have created pressure to change the system.

In response to charges by the Brady Commission, appointed by President Ronald Reagan to investigate the causes of the October 1987 crash, that the Big Four manipulated share prices, the Ministry of Finance has prohibited any one broker from accounting for more than 30 percent of the trading volume in any given stock. (This rule was lifted in early 1990 to help support the market.) After similar complaints were voiced in Japan as regards the Recruit Cosmos scandal, the Ministry of Finance formally asked the Securities and Exchange Council, an official advisory body, to make recommendations as to how the Big Four's grip on the market could be loosened. The decline in their share of turnover may simply be the result of practicing self-restraint and giving more business to their brokerage affiliates.

The Ministry of Finance would come under stronger pressure to tighten its supervision of the stock exchange if institutional investors expressed unhappiness with the status quo. The banks are frustrated, of course, because they envy the brokers, but as they issue so many shares themselves, they need Nomura's placing power. As investors, banks have behaved like other corporate shareholders in Japan, thinking of the long term and enjoying the rapid growth in their unrealized capital gains.

Other institutional investors have until very recently been passive investors in the stock market. Most of their shareholdings were acquired at a fraction of their current price, and their sale would result in a large capital gains tax liability. In any case, there would be few buyers even if they did choose to sell the shares they owned: nothing would scare Japanese investors more than the news that corporations were bailing out. Because listed companies own almost half of all shares, it would be tantamount to corporations selling themselves. Japan's biggest shareholders are prisoners in a gilded cage.

Since 1987 there has, nevertheless, been a sharp increase in trading by financial institutions. Banks have been selling shares from their investment portfolio to boost their profits and raise their equity base to meet international guidelines for capital adequacy. For the most part, however, shares thus sold are soon repurchased so that relationships do not suffer. Insurance companies, as well, have become more active with the introduction of variable return policies. Increased investment by both financial and nonfinancial companies through *tokkin* and fund trusts have also had a big impact on the pattern of turnover.

Japanese investors have also started to put more of their money into stock-index funds. The introduction of these funds by the investment-trust industry came in response to a shortage of experienced fund managers and the poor performance of managed funds. As stock-index funds grow in popularity, the concentrated share buying that characterizes the Japanese stock market will be radically altered and broker commissions will fall. Daiwa Investment Trust and Kokusai Investment Trust launched their first index funds in June 1985; in April 1989, they offered spot-type index funds. Daiwa claims that 18.6 percent of its funds is now indexed. Another example is Mitsui Life, which has put one-quarter of its *tokkin*-fund investment—¥200 billion—into index funds.

The biggest incentive to change how the stock market behaves may in fact come as a result of the bear market in Japan in early 1990. Few complained when it was so easy to make a profit. The complaints will come if the goose stops laying golden eggs.

Chapter 5

SHARE PRICE INFLATION

Japanese share prices soared in apparent defiance of the laws of gravity between 1975 and 1989. Even after a sharp correction in early 1990, Japanese shares remained expensive by every conventional yardstick of value, whether the price is compared with a company's sales per share, cash flow, or book value. By the most common measure of value, the price-earnings ratio (PER) of all firms quoted on the First Section of the TSE was 48 at the end of April 1990, compared with a PER of 13 for New York. Almost every Japanese company's share price is higher, relative to earnings, and its dividend yield lower, than that of its American counterpart.

Japanese stock prices have not always been so imposing. Although they rose almost continuously from the time the TSE reopened in 1949, share prices only started moving out of line with PERs in the mid-1970s. Even then, the rise was not remorseless. As recently as the end of 1981, the average PER on the First Section of the TSE was 21, which is not far from the level seen in North America and Europe. Since then, however, the gap between share prices in Japan and in the United States has widened considerably. Although Japanese companies have been very successful, their future outlook hardly justifies so high a rating compared with their U.S. counterparts.

No single explanation for Japan's high share prices has proven satisfactory to foreign investors—or to Japanese investors for that matter. In fact, it would be almost impossible to find one all-encompassing theory to show why the stock market has boomed. Instead,

Relative Valuations
(May 31, 1990)

U.S. company	PER	Yield	Japanese counterpart	PER	Yield
Aetna Life	9.6	5.2	Tokio Marine & Fire	59.2	0.5
American Express	39.2	3.1	Nippon Shinpan	32.1	0.9
AT&T	15.3	3.1	NTT	76.7	0.4
BankAmerica	6.3	3.3	Mitsui Bank	56.4	0.4
Bethlehem Steel	9.8	2.3	Kawasaki Steel	33.2	0.8
Caterpillar	15.3	1.8	Komatsu	35.7	0.7
Chrysler	10.4	7.7	Isuzu	80.6	0.5
Coca-Cola	23.1	1.8	Mikuni Coca-Cola	35.0	0.5
Delta Airlines	9.9	1.6	JAL	129.6	0.3
E.I. Du Pont	11.1	4.0	Mitsubishi Kasei	42.9	0.7
Exxon	12.1	5.0	Nippon Oil	56.5	0.5
General Electric	14.3	2.7	Hitachi	22.5	0.7
General Motors	8.2	6.1	Toyota	19.6	0.8
IBM	12.3	4.0	Fujitsu	24.1	0.6
JC Penney	9.9	4.0	Isetan	95.4	0.3
K mart	8.8	4.9	Ito-Yokado	27.6	0.6
McDonald's	15.7	1.0	Denny's Japan	31.1	0.6
Merck	18.3	2.2	Banyu Pharm.	55.2	0.6
Merrill Lynch	16.1	4.1	Nomura Securities	23.6	0.6
NCR	11.9	2.0	NCR Japan	43.5	0.7
Procter & Gamble	18.6	2.2	Kao Corp.	40.9	0.5
Xerox	7.0	6.5	Ricoh	39.4	0.9

Source: Standard & Poor's; *Shikiho* (Tokyo: Toyo Keizai, summer 1990)
Note: PER and yield based on forecasted earnings

there are four factors that stand out in explaining the market's performance: structural, accounting, macroeconomic, and psychological.
Japan's stock market behaves essentially like any other exchange
where prices are agreed upon by a willing buyer and a willing seller,
and the interaction of supply and demand produces a market price.
What sets Japan apart is the imbalance between supply in the secondary market and the demand for shares.

U.S. and Japanese PERs

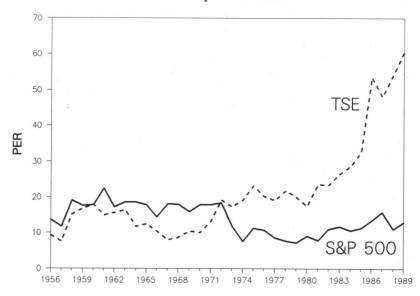

A DIFFERENT STRUCTURE

Stable Shareholding and Higher Share Prices

The most important of the four factors behind the disparity of share prices is the structure of Japan's stock market—that is to say, share ownership and liquidity. Stable shareholders buy because they are obliged to do so, and they do not sell whatever the share price. This has steadily reduced the supply of tradable shares in the market, feeding demand at the same time.

Companies were largely indifferent to their share price until 1969, when there was a public offering of shares at market price by Nippon Gakki, now known as Yamaha, the maker of musical instruments. This showed the importance of a high share price to an issuer, since the higher the share price the lower the apparent cost of equity capital. Cross-shareholdings became the main method of achieving these higher prices.

Before that, the standard measure of value was the par value of a stock, not its market price. Firms issued new shares in the form of rights offerings at par value (normally ¥50) and fixed their dividends as a percentage of par (10 percent or ¥5). From their perspective, it did not matter whether investors bid up their shares to ¥1,000 or left them at ¥100. The stock market was an arena for speculators, and if speculators wanted to pay ¥500 for a certificate with a face value of ¥50, then that was their affair. Stable shareholders increased their stake by subscribing to the rights offerings and received a solid 10 percent yield on their investment.

This practice of rights offerings at par value denied the stock market one of its two primary functions, the efficient allocation of capital. All companies received the same price for their shares and had equal access to equity financing, regardless of differences in their profitability and growth prospects. The only constraint was that a company had to be profitable enough to afford the high dividend yield, a bias that favored high-growth companies. Equity issues were little different from fixed-rate debt.

Even so, the stock market fulfilled its other function, that of determining a price for shares among investors. Share prices determined the cost of access to a company's future rights offerings. A profitable, rapidly expanding company had the need and the ability to make more frequent rights offerings than an unprofitable company. Investors therefore bid up the price of the profitable company. It did not matter much to investors what price a company issued new shares at, since their ownership of the company was not diluted. The main determinant of share prices in the 1950s was the dividend yield.

The system broke down in 1961 when a tightening of credit led to a surge in new rights offerings by companies unable to maintain their dividend rate. New issues meant lower yields, leading outside investors to dump their holdings. As the stock market recovered after 1965, it was proposed that companies issue shares at market price rather than par value. This would allow a company to raise the same amount of funds with fewer shares and thus bear a lighter burden of dividend payments. Issuers, of course, were fully in favor of the changes, as were the brokers at the prospect of underwriting public offerings.

Banks and insurers vigorously opposed the change. Their earnings as financial institutions depended on the yield of their assets, which would be lowered by issues at market price. Moreover, both banks and insurers did not want competition from the equity market since their primáry business was making corporate loans. The life insurers also argued that since share prices incorporated investors' expectations of rights offerings at par value, a shift to issues at market price would lead to a collapse of the market. If a change were to be made, then it should also be that companies based their dividend policy on earnings instead of par value.

A compromise was reached. Companies were urged to return 20 percent of the unearned premium (the difference between the issue price and par value) to shareholders either in the form of gratis issues or higher dividends and to maintain a minimum payout ratio of earnings. Starting in August 1971, companies would report earnings per share and dividends per share. The number of companies which could issue at market price was restricted to the top few hundred listings on the TSE. Finally, companies had to pay a dividend of at least ¥5 a share to qualify for issuing shares at market prices, and new issues at market could not exceed 10 percent of existing capital.

Share Prices Become Relevant

If the story had ended here, Japan's stock market would have probably developed along the lines of the U.S. stock market, for the radical change to issues at market price has been common to most important bourses. Banks and insurers that wanted higher dividends from companies could have bid up the share prices of companies that paid out more and sold the shares of companies that did not, thereby imposing stock market discipline on firms. Reliance on the marketplace to decide prices is a rather un-Japanese approach, however. Japanese firms chose instead to constrain the supply of shares to boost their share prices, and they achieved this largely through stable shareholdings.

Share prices became relevant—the higher the value the lower the cost of capital—but Japanese firms did not want to have to shoulder the burdens borne by their American counterparts. As long as new issues were at par and the dividend was maintained at 10 percent of this, company managers were free to pursue their own objectives without concern for profits, share prices, or investors. But if issues were at market price, consistently higher earnings and bigger dividends would be needed to satisfy shareholders.

Finding stable shareholders was a more attractive alternative for managers, as it freed a company from the demands of, and responsibility to, outside investors. The obvious choice for such a role was other listed companies, whose managers found themselves in a similar predicament. A company's existing shareholders, who already held a large portfolio of stocks at a low acquisition cost, were thus asked to increase their holdings. Additional purchases at market prices would not significantly increase their average acquisition cost per share.

Stable shareholders were also to be found among the members of a firm's former *zaibatsu*, which would not object to rebuilding old ties. A third group of stable shareholders were business partners, with which a company could build a cross-shareholding relationship. As listed companies, they too wanted to enjoy the benefits of higher share prices without bearing the responsibility.

Stable shareholders did not make Japanese managers entirely unaccountable, however. Companies shared responsibility with their underwriters for maintaining a high share price for their stockholders. If their shares fell below the issue price, the firm could not ask its stable shareholders to buy more shares in the future.

These long-term shareholdings were orchestrated by the big securities companies, which stood to benefit greatly from the new arrangement. When new issues came in the form of rights offerings, the brokers played no real role in corporate finance. They merely peddled hot stocks to Japanese housewives. With the switch to public offerings, the brokers gained access to corporate boardrooms. They underwrote the equity financings and promoted the issuer's shares vigorously. Stable shareholding reduced the brokers' risk of underwriting new shares since it also guaranteed a willing group of buyers. Their brokerage business likewise increased because companies wished to accumulate shares in other companies.

Statistics demonstrate how stable shareholdings worked. At the end of 1964 when the bear market touched bottom, banks and insurers owned 22 percent of outstanding shares. By 1972, they owned

34 percent, having absorbed much of the shares previously owned by the investment trusts and securities companies. Nonfinancial corporations owned 19 percent of the market in 1966, 23 percent by 1970, and 28 percent—their peak—by 1974. Individuals, though, saw their ownership fall from 46 percent in 1964 to 37 percent by 1971 and then to 33 percent a year later.

During this rapid transition, Japanese companies bought heavily as issues of shares were offered to select, stable shareholders. Private placements of shares went from ¥4.4 billion in 1970 to ¥90 billion in 1972. Public offerings rose from ¥54 billion in 1969 to ¥637 billion in 1972. Convertible bond issues increased from ¥4.5 billion in 1969 to ¥526 billion in 1973.

In a market controlled by companies, the growth of stable shareholdings had an immediate, ratchet-like effect on share prices. Prices did not fall as much as might have been expected after the first oil crisis, when inflation went as high as 25 percent, interest rates reached 10 percent, and the economy recorded negative growth for the first time since 1949. The market, at its lowest in 1974, was still 40 percent higher than its 1972 level. Average earnings per share for all listed companies fell from a peak of ¥19.6 in 1973 to ¥7.2 in 1976, but PERs rose from 13.3 in 1973 to 46.3 in 1976. Companies, in fact, took advantage of high share prices to cover their losses; those that needed cash sold part of their shareholdings through their main bank to other stable shareholders, with the understanding that the bank would protect the buyers from losses.

Merely limiting the supply of shares in the stock market does not guarantee higher share prices. In theory there is no reason why stable shareholding should affect share prices at all since shares must be owned by someone, stable or not. The only outcome should be increased volatility. However, in the face of demand for shares stimulated by the brokers, stable shareholding allows share prices to rise further for longer periods of time since supply is artificially constrained. Increased corporate ownership of shares and a steady inflow of investable funds, largely channelled through banks and insurers, have helped the TSE perform well since 1975.

The rise of corporate share ownership has also affected valuations. Stock prices were set by dividends, earnings growth, and interest rates when individuals owned most of the shares. Price is often irrelevant now that corporations are big buyers. When a stable shareholder purchases an additional ¥1 billion worth of shares, it does not question the dividend policy of the company or its earnings outlook. Rather, it wants to know how much its own sales will increase as a result, and an agreement between issuer and stable shareholder is often reached to that effect. Or the stable shareholder wants to know how much of its own shares an issuer will purchase.

Furthermore, since one of the main reasons for companies to swap shares is to raise capital, almost all companies have the right to call on their stable shareholders to buy shares as long as they return the favor. The only exception is that a company cannot have an equity financing if its net worth per share is below ¥60 and it does not pay a dividend.

This leads to one interpretation as to why weak companies carry such high PERs: their share prices have been lifted to facilitate equity financings among listed companies. Many companies can only buy the new issues of other companies if they themselves have an equity financing, as regulations prohibit a company from owning stock in excess of its net worth. There would be an imbalance in the flow of dividends, assuming a similar amount of funds were raised, if one company sells its shares at a significantly lower price than what it pays for the shares of other companies. Thus share prices of weak companies have to rise prior to an issue to a level approaching the average share price in the stock market in order to maintain harmony and equality within Japan Inc.

The *Shikiho* regularly reports on the percentage of shares outstanding owned by the top ten stockholders and the percentage of equity owned in blocks of shares of 50,000 or less. The first figure indicates the degree of shares in stable hands, and the second, the amount of shares assumed to be freely floating. For example, 40.7 percent of Sony's shares are held by its top ten shareholders and 13.1 percent are considered floating shares, while 33 percent of Nissan's shares are owned by the top ten but only 8.7 percent are floating.

Because so many shares are locked away, some analysts have concluded that investors have to pay a premium for the scarce amount of equity that is available for trading. The smaller the float of freely marketable stock, the higher the mark-up. Carrying this argument further, they argue that the true market capitalization of any company is the freely floating shares times the share price. This would reduce the PER of Mitsubishi Bank, for example, from 47 to 4, little different from that of U.S. money-center banks. Furthermore, if the entire market were treated as a single company and cross-held shares were disregarded, the PER would fall from 49 in March 1990 to 25.

It is true that cross-held shares constrain supply, but this does not justify their PER. To do so, it would have to be assumed that floating shares are entitled to all of a company's earnings. This is the case in the United States, where a buy-back of shares raises the earnings and dividends accruing to remaining shareholders. In Japan, the cross-held shares are entitled to earnings and dividends in the same way as the floating shares. And as has been shown, cross-shareholding lessens the value of shares owned by outsiders because management is free to ignore them. If anything, investors should give low PERs to companies with high levels of stable shareholders, not high PERs.

Limits on the Supply of Shares

Although stable shareholders have cut the proportion of shares actively traded in the market, the total amount of shares outstanding has grown rapidly. At the end of 1970 the number of shares listed on the TSE was 114 billion; by 1989 it was 313 billion. This was an increase of 174 percent during a period when the number of listed companies increased by only 25 percent, to 1,597. Much of the increase in shares has come in the form of untradable gratis issues while new issues have been tucked away in the vaults of stable shareholders.

Gratis issues totalled 51 billion shares in 1975–89 out of a net increase of 156 billion shares. This number is deceiving, however, because gratis issues do not add to the supply of tradable shares unless they are in large lots. The smallest unit of trading is 1,000 shares for stocks with a par value of ¥50, and 100 shares for those with a par value of ¥500. Shares received through a gratis issue with a lot size below these amounts can only be sold back to the issuing company. Thus, a gratis issue of 5–10 percent of a company's total outstanding shares has a negligible impact on the overall supply of tradable shares. Small investors cannot sell their gratis issues on the

Sources of New Shares

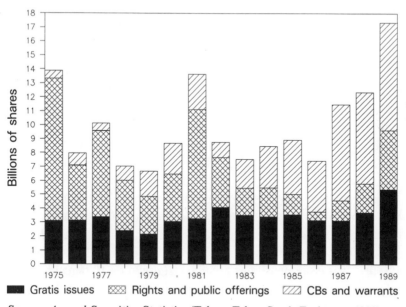

Source: Annual Securities Statistics (Tokyo: Tokyo Stock Exchange, 1989)

open market, while the large long-term shareholders have no interest in doing so.

Stock splits, of course, would increase the outstanding number of shares dramatically, but these occur rarely. A company must amend its articles of incorporation by a special resolution of shareholders in order to split its par-value. Although non-par stock can be split merely by a resolution of the board of directors, non-par shares are uncommon, and only five listed companies have had such splits.

To facilitate stock splits, the commercial code was revised in October 1982 to enable companies to switch between par and non-par shares. Since then there have been about 20 stock splits, but most of these have involved companies with ¥500 par-value stock initiating a ten-for-one split to reduce their par to ¥50. This raises the number of shares tenfold, but the minimum trading unit also jumps by the same multiple, from one hundred to one thousand shares. Stock splits are expensive because of the way dividends are fixed. Having a two-for-one stock split would require a company to double its dividend payment if it were at the ¥5 minimum. By contrast, stock splits are frequent on the NYSE, where there were more than 200 in 1986, because U.S. companies want their shares to be marketable. The NYSE also has no minimum trading unit.

A company can choose not to issue share certificates if the gratis issue to the stockholder is less than the standard trading unit. This acts to prevent investors from trading gratis shares over the counter and thus outside the ambit of the stock market. The company registrar keeps a record of their beneficial ownership on his books. Owners of shares of less than the minimum unit are also denied voting rights.

Japanese investors welcome gratis issues despite their lack of marketability. In theory a gratis issue cannot create wealth since a company can give nothing to its shareholders that they do not already own. In practice they do just that. If a quoted firm has a 10 percent gratis issue, its shares are marked down by 10 percent on the following day, leaving its market capitalization unchanged. Yet share prices are known to bounce back quickly. In fact the effect of gratis issues on share prices is so well known to investors that share prices tend to rise in anticipation of them. This reflects the fact that Japanese investors value shares more in terms of a stock's nominal share price rather than earnings per share. A 10 percent gratis issue simply makes a stock 10 percent cheaper.

Now, consider the new shares that are not offered gratis—in all, 105 billion shares of this kind were issued in 1975–89. The majority of these shares has also been kept off the market. This is because issuers usually ask their underwriters to place public offerings in the hands of stable shareholders. Alternatively, they arrange for stable shareholders to buy in the secondary market following an issue. It is estimated that 30–40 percent of public offerings end up in the hands of stable shareholders. Some 90 percent of all overseas issues of convertible bonds and warrant bonds are eventually owned by Japanese investors.

Japanese companies also try hard to ensure that new issues do not come to the secondary market quickly. One such case is Showa Highpolymer, a chemical company which had a public offering of

five million shares in August 1988. Since stable shareholders held 64
percent of its shares, the company did not need to increase this proportion but wanted to make sure excess supply did not affect its share
price. It was therefore arranged for Showa Highpolymer to buy the
shares of five other companies, four of which also had recent issues,
who in turn bought Showa Highpolymer's shares.

Limits on the Supply of Companies

The structure of the stock market promotes higher prices in
another way—by limiting the number of publicly quoted companies.
At the end of 1989, 2,019 companies were listed in Japan, of which
1,597 were quoted on the TSE. In addition, 286 companies were
traded on the OTC market. This is significantly fewer than the 17,000
publicly traded companies in the United States.

The TSE-quoted companies form an elite group that has grown
much more slowly than the economy. The employees of TSE-listed
companies comprise less than 10 percent of the labor force, but they
generate 29 percent of total corporate sales and a quarter of total corporate earnings. Despite the meteoric growth of the economy and the
number of registered companies in Japan (1.8 million at the last
count), total listings on the TSE have increased by only 59 percent
since 1961, when the Second Section was established. Since 1949
there has been a net increase of only 16 issues a year.

There have been 285 delistings from the TSE since 1961. These
have come about through bankruptcy, merger, or failure to meet
listing requirements. The stable shareholding system is one important
reason for the low failure rate. In contrast, there are many more com-
ings and goings on the NYSE: an average of 93 new listings and 87
delistings each year in 1978–87.

There ought to be a long queue of firms waiting to float because the
TSE offers companies such a cheap source of capital. Shares tend to
soar when they are listed for the same reason that supply is limited.
Kissei Pharmaceutical, for example, was listed on the TSE Second
Section on December 21, 1988, at an offering price of ¥3,820. Buy
orders so outnumbered sell orders that the issue did not trade for
three days; by December 28, the price was ¥6,130. Koito Industries
was listed on the TSE Second Section in February 1988 at an offer

price of ¥810; by March 4, the price reached ¥2,020. In many countries, the underwriter would have been criticized heavily for underpricing the initial offering. Not in Japan. The price of initial public offerings is set in a rather mechanical fashion by comparison with a listed "twin" rather than based on demand. A good share price performance after a listing also ensures that a company's next public offering will be well received. This practice has the added bonus of minimizing an underwriter's risk and allowing it to reward a few special customers.

The lack of quoted firms can be attributed, first, to the fact that there are few good small companies in Japan. The policies of MITI favor large companies. A 1989 survey of 20,000 of the largest unlisted companies by Teikoku Data Bank in Japan found that only 721 companies met the TSE Second Section listing criteria. Moreover, the venture capital market in Japan is poorly developed.

The largest venture capital company in Japan is JAFCO, a company 41 percent owned by Nomura Securities and its affiliates. Listed on the OTC market, it had a market capitalization close to ¥1 trillion in January 1990 and a PER of 280. JAFCO is interesting not so much for its skills in floating companies but rather for the way it is used by Nomura Securities to build relations. Nomura has underwritten a majority of the initial public offerings of companies in which JAFCO has invested. In the long term, JAFCO may be the vehicle by which Nomura builds its own *keiretsu*, in preparation for the day securities companies are allowed into the banking business.

Second, a company wishing to be listed must also conform to the customs of the exchange. This includes competing for stable shareholders among banks and clients to support the share price and to ensure that the shares are in friendly hands. Many small companies have put off going public for fear of being taken over. But big Japanese banks have helped to "shelter" many newly listed companies. Japanese banks held 10 percent of the shares of the 133 initial public offerings between April 1989 and February 1990. At the top of the list was Sanwa Bank, which held shares in 56 of the companies, followed by Long-Term Credit Bank and IBJ.

Third, the requirements for a company to be listed are severe and the test of admission is more rigorous the higher a company rises. On the Second Section, the minimum standard for listing is share-holders' equity of ¥1 billion, pretax profit of ¥400 million, and at least six million shares outstanding. This implies a return on equity of 20 percent for a company that meets the minimum capital require-ment. The official reason for these stringent listing requirements is the protection of the individual investor from risky businesses. But the effect is to benefit handsomely those firms fortunate enough to have passed the test of admission years earlier. It also confers great prestige on the companies that make it onto the First Section of the TSE.

Since the OTC listing requirements were liberalized in November 1983, registration on this market has become similar to Nasdaq's. Only 66 companies newly registered their shares between then and the end of 1987. In 1988, however, 53 companies came to market, and in 1989, 73 companies did. One hundred twenty initial public offerings are expected in 1990. The reasons for the sudden increase are varied. One is that because the current generation of founders is nearing retirement age, the inheritance tax benefits to owning a public, rather than private, company grow in importance. Another is that until 1989, an OTC company was only permitted to have a single public offering of new shares after listing. Thus, a company that thereafter failed to graduate to the stock exchange would be unable to enjoy the financial benefits of being a public company. Also, valua-tions on the OTC have gone up so sharply that registration now looks much more attractive than before. At the same time, it should be noted that many of the new growth companies on the OTC market are little more than the subsidiaries of major corporations. The development of the OTC market has been promoted, some may con-clude, so that these major corporations can sell off minority stakes in undesirable subsidiaries at outrageously high prices.

KEEPING UP APPEARANCES

There are other reasons beside the framework of Japan's stock market to help explain why PERs are so high. One is the accounting principles used by companies. Three principals are important: con-solidation, depreciation, and reserves.

Consolidation

In the United States, the financial report of a listed firm is consolidated to include subsidiaries. Consolidated figures have been required in Japan since 1984, but only if subsidiaries contribute more than 10 percent of group assets, sales, and net income. Until 1989, though, consolidated results did not have to be published together with the results of the parent company. Consolidation has never been important in Japan because it is not allowed for tax purposes; the tax authorities fear that revenues would drop if profitable parent companies' earnings were consolidated with those of loss-making subsidiaries. As an outcome, published PER figures are generally based on parent-only results, not those of the consolidated entity.

The difference between the financial report of the parent company and the group is significant for *keiretsu* leaders like Toyota, Hitachi, and Nippon Steel, but it is negligible for many others. Japanese firms may in fact be more profitable than consolidated results indicate because companies need to consolidate a subsidiary only if it contributes more than 10 percent to profits. But if a firm can leave its profits in unconsolidated subsidiaries, it can do the same for its losses as

Parent and Consolidated Earnings
(FY89)

	Parent		Consolidated	
	Net income (¥ mn)	EPS (¥)	Net income (¥ mn)	EPS (¥)
Hitachi	115,006	37	210,963	62
Sony	58,192	175	102,808	307
Honda	53,224	55	81,684	83
Mazda	26,581	25	23,438	22
Mitsui & Co.	22,049	14	36,414	24
Asahi Beer	6,034	17	3,889	11
Fuji Heavy Industries	5,741	10	(6,005)	−10
Daihatsu	5,665	13	1,471	4
Arabian Oil	2,416	48	(1,470)	−29

Source: Annual reports

well. The troubled shipping industry has been particularly adept at transferring money-losing ships to overseas subsidiaries. It is because consolidation standards are so fluid and disclosure so poor that investors have tended to ignore them.

Results of the 592 nonfinancial companies that issued consolidated results for the year ending March 1990 showed consolidated income 24 percent higher than parent income. While a substantial difference, this does not mean that the PER of the market should be reduced by this amount. These companies only accounted for 33 percent of all listed companies' profits; companies that do not issue consolidated reports accounted for much of the rest. Thus, the market's PER on a consolidated basis should be only 8 percent less than its parent-company level, that is, a reduction from 48 to 44. This is still not large enough to make the valuation of shares understandable.

High Depreciation Charges

Most companies in the United States reduce their tax liabilities through a process called accelerated depreciation. Proportionately more of the investment in plant and equipment is charged against earnings earlier rather than later, and so taxes are deferred. In reports to their shareholders, though, companies use straight-line depreciation, charging against earnings a constant amount over the life of an asset, to give a fairer representation of their trend in earnings.

In Japan, firms use accelerated depreciation in their reports to shareholders as well as to the tax authorities. Deferred taxes are not allowed under Japanese accounting standards; therefore, a Japanese company's reported income to shareholders is understated relative to a U.S. company's. Since capital spending by Japanese companies has grown steadily, it is only on those rare occassions when capital expenditures fall, as in 1986, that earnings of Japanese companies are overstated and their PERs are understated compared to that of U.S. companies.

Probably more important than the method of depreciation is the fact that Japanese companies' invest more than do their counterparts in the United States. Japanese levels of depreciation are consequently higher and their profits lower. When one looks at the cash flow in relation to share prices, defined as net income plus depreciation, the gap

Comparison of PER and Price-to-Cash Flow

	Japan	US	UK	France	West Germany
PER	57.7	13.1	11.8	10.3	12.4
Price/Cash flow	16.4	6.5	7.3	4.5	3.9

Source: Morgan Stanley Capital International Perspectives, May 1988

between U.S. shares and Japanese shares narrows considerably. Yet the PER gap is as large as ever compared to West Germany, which has similar corporate share ownership patterns and similarly conservative accounting practices.

Reserves

Japanese authorities also allow companies to maintain certain reserves for potential losses due to "price fluctuations," "interest rate fluctuations," and "overseas investment." These reserves sometimes reduce a company's tax burden, but often they are taxable with the result that net income is reduced by the full amount of the reserve. U.S. companies can take such contingency reserves only when it is probable that an asset has been impaired or a liability incurred and the amount of loss can be reasonably estimated.

Among the most effective exponents of the art of understatement are the heavily protected casualty insurers which minimize their reported profits so that they will not be pressured to lower the premiums charged to policyholders. Premiums for automobile and fire insurance are fixed by industry cartel, always at a level where the least efficient company can make a profit in underwriting. But since catastrophes are always a possibility in Japan, all companies place a portion of their underwriting profits in a "catastrophe reserve." The catastrophe in this case, however, is not an earthquake or typhoon, but that their earnings could be too high. The largest of these insurers, Tokio Marine & Fire, has accumulated ¥279 billion in its catastrophe reserve. It reported to the government that its pretax profits were ¥152 billion in the year ending in March 1989 while its shareholders were told that pretax profits were ¥122 billion.

Elastic Accounting

If all these accounting differences are taken together, it is apparent that Japanese earnings figures are indeed understated relative to U.S. companies—though probably not by 40 percent as some suggest. Even if the effect of the disparity between U.S. and Japanese PERs is exaggerated, there is a subtler point in that Japanese investors and managers place less store in reported profits than is the case in the United States. Japan's accounting rules allow companies to manipulate their earnings by putting profits into reserves, through sales to subsidiaries, and by treating extraordinary gains as recurring income.

A good example of this is the use of one-time stock market gains (loosely called *zaiteku* profits) to bolster a company's recurring profits from time to time, especially when its main business is going sour. When its margins were being squeezed by the high yen, Sony earned ¥16 billion from its operations (before interest payments and taxes) in the year ending March 1988, but reported net income of ¥30 billion, thanks to nonoperating profits from *zaiteku*. More than 90 percent of Mitsubishi Bank's ¥271 billion in pretax income in the year ending March 1990 came from the sale of its equity holdings.

The sales figures of Japanese companies are also massaged. The nine general trading companies buy and sell huge amounts of commodities at the end of each accounting year in order to bloat their sales and maintain their place in the annually published rankings. In the year ending March 1990, C. Itoh & Co. had sales of ¥21 trillion, Mitsui & Co. had sales of ¥19.5 trillion, and Mitsubishi Corp. had sales of ¥18.5 trillion.

In fact, a company with extremely high profits is accused of not investing for the future or is said to have taken advantage of customers and suppliers. Moreover, the stock market does not reward high profits. The two most profitable firms in Japan, Toyota and Nomura Securities, have among the lowest PERs on the TSE, at 22 and 25 respectively.

Japanese firms would probably take the profit-and-loss account more seriously if earnings were a more important corporate objective. But market share is the primary goal, and capital spending and

Economic Performance of Japan and United States

	1984	1985	1986	1987	1988	1989
Real GNP growth (%)						
United States	6.8	3.4	2.7	3.7	4.4	3.0
Japan	5.1	4.9	2.5	4.5	5.7	4.9
Consumer price inflation (%)						
United States	4.3	3.6	1.9	3.6	4.1	4.8
Japan	2.3	2.0	0.6	0.1	0.7	2.3
Unemployment rate (%)						
United States	7.4	7.1	6.9	6.2	5.5	5.3
Japan	2.8	2.6	2.8	2.8	2.5	2.3
10-year bond yields (%)						
United States	12.4	10.6	7.7	8.4	8.9	8.5
Japan	6.5	5.9	5.2	5.1	4.7	5.7
Private nonresidential investment to GNP (%)						
United States	11.0	11.0	10.3	9.8	10.0	9.8
Japan	15.4	16.3	16.1	16.2	17.5	19.4
Current account ($ bn)						
United States	−104	−112	−133	−143	−126	−106
Japan	35	49	86	87	77	57

Source: International Monetary Fund

price cutting are the means to achieve this. To buy stocks on the basis of the PER or earnings per share is inconsistent with how Japanese companies are managed. This creates a dilemma for investors. For if reported earnings cannot be used as a basis of measuring perform-ance, then they must either assume all companies are much more profitable than stated or else rely on broker-generated market themes for investment decisions.

THE REWARD FOR RAPID GROWTH

Appearances are one thing; reality is another. There is another reason for thinking that Japan's stock market deserves a higher rating than the U.S. market—the Japanese economy is considerably stronger than America's. Indeed, until the early 1980s, this was the reason most cited for Japan's high PERs. As seen here, it is clear that Japan has grown faster with a lower rate of inflation than the United States through most of the 1980s.

The stock market boom in 1986–87 was regarded by many as a speculative bubble caused by the dramatic revaluation of the yen. But the rapid recovery in corporate earnings in the following two years suggests that investors were remarkably prescient. Since then, Japanese industry has emerged considerably stronger in almost every respect. They have cut costs and strengthened their balance sheets. Economic growth slackened to 2.5 percent in 1986, the lowest since 1974, and business leaders bewailed the rise in the yen and the 15 percent fall in profits. But the stock market knew better.

Where's the Growth?

Japan's corporate recovery has been far less spectacular when viewed over the long term. Operating profits for TSE-listed manufacturers have grown by 2.8 percent a year since 1981, and for non-manufacturers (other than financials), the rate has been even less— 0.6 percent. In fact, falling interest rates and reduced debt were the biggest contributors to the 5 percent annual increase in net income for all nonfinancial companies. But the number of shares increased rapidly, so earnings per share grew only 2.8 percent a year. By contrast, listed companies on the NYSE saw their profits grow by 4.1 percent annually in 1981–89 and earnings per share rose even more rapidly due to share buy-backs.

PER Expansion

The main stimulus behind the appreciation of the market in the 1980s therefore was not earnings growth, but higher share prices. These rose on average by 21 percent a year in 1981–89, a process called PER expansion. But it is impossible to tell whether PER expansion causes share prices to go up or vice versa. If PERs had remained at 1981 levels, share prices would have only increased by 11 percent a year.

Falling interest rates caused Japanese investors to value earnings more highly in the mid-1980s than at the beginning of the decade. Declining interest rates imply that future earnings are worth more in

Profits of TSE Manufacturers

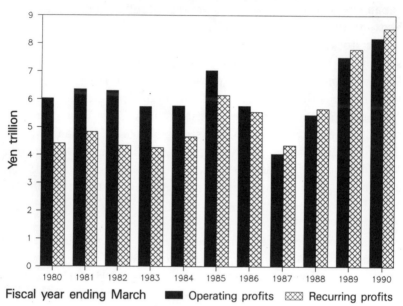

Profits of TSE Nonmanufacturers

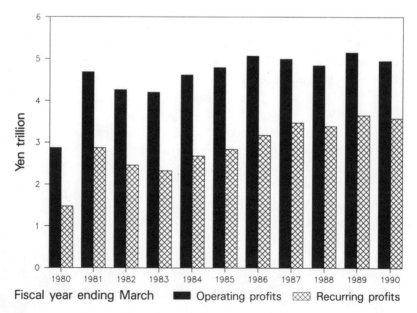

today's money, so investors should be willing to pay a higher price for the shares of companies which produce those profits. Hence, PERs (or share prices) should rise to reflect falling interest rates. The rule of thumb for stock investors was that if interest rates halved, the PER should double, and prices duly rose. Even Japanese brokers become PER advocates when it could be demonstrated that higher PERs were justified.

Graphically, the relationship between PERs and interest rates can be seen by comparing the yield on long-term government bonds to the earnings yield on equities (1/PER).

If the Tokyo market and its PERs had stayed down after 1987, then it might have been true to say that Japanese investors were conscious of PERs. The high PERs of 1987 could then have been explained by Japan's accounting practices, low interest rates, and rapid economic growth. In 1988–89, the combination of PER contraction due to rising interest rates and fast earnings growth would have brought Japan's PERs down to 20 by the end of the decade. But this did not happen. Instead, the stock market rose by 70 percent between January 4, 1988, and January 4, 1990, even though interest rates

Earnings—Bond Yield

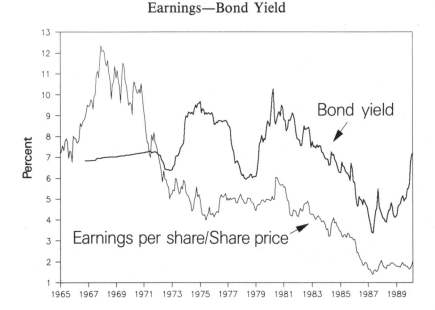

were rising. The market did drop sharply at the beginning of 1990, but this happened two years after interest rates had started climbing. Interest rates are thus not the only determinant of Japan's high share prices.

Awash in Liquidity

Another justification for higher share prices in Japan is excess liquidity, particularly so in 1985–87. This was a time when Japan's rising tide of cash washed over the stock market. Investors chased after steel shares for no other reason than that they were highly liquid. Excess liquidity is an elusive concept, because there is no direct link between stock prices and money supply. Whether a lot or a little cash is circulating, money will head towards those investments whose returns, adjusted for risk, are highest. In Japan, the best gains to be made were in stocks and real estate.

One indication of the rate at which cash flows through the economy is to compare the growth rate of the money supply to the growth rate of nominal gross national product. If the ratio is low, money is circulating through the economy rapidly to keep up with the level of business activity, suggesting tight monetary conditions. If the ratio is high, the opposite is the case: there is excess liquidity in the economy.

The ratio of money supply to GNP growth certainly rose sharply, doubling to 1.8 between 1980 and 1983, dropping a bit in 1984 before resuming its climb to a peak of liquidity at 2.5 in 1987. Share prices, in contrast, increased almost continuously from 1982 until the October 1987 crash. Not a perfect match between liquidity and share performance, but the liquidity ratio in 1987–88 bears a close resemblance to its level during the 1971–72 share boom.

To understand where this excess liquidity came from, it is necessary to understand that the Japanese economy of the early 1980s had simply become too successful. Japan was running a chronic current account surplus, but the country could not reflate its economy to stimulate domestic demand because the government wanted to cut its budget deficit. In 1985, it was decided that the yen should be revalued in order to make foreign goods more competitive against Japanese goods. When the revaluation left the yen stronger

Growth in GNP and Money Supply

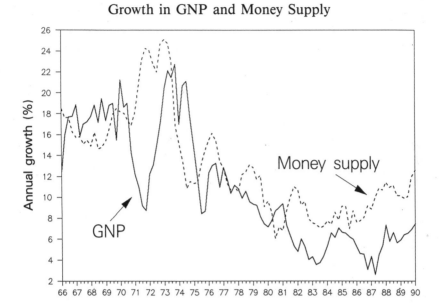

than expected, excess liquidity was created on a scale not seen before. Since the market for imported goods remained as impenetrable as ever, Japan's trade surplus increased, propelled by a worldwide slump in commodity prices. Japan's current account surplus grew from $35 billion in 1984 to $86 billion in 1986. Meanwhile the domestic economy was weakened, and The Bank of Japan kept reducing interest rates lest the economy fall into a recession and the yen strengthen further. Yet because of the strength of the yen, Japanese capital tended to stay at home.

The rise in liquidity could have resulted in higher inflation, but this was checked by lower import costs. Instead the result was inflation in the prices of assets like real estate and stocks. Land prices in the Tokyo metropolitan area skyrocketed 45 percent in 1986 and 61 percent in 1987. Much of the excess liquidity poured into shares.

Cash-swollen companies and rich landowners were not the only investors in Japan's stock market. The sudden increase in wealth caused individuals as well to increase their investment in the market. Sales of equity investment trusts went from ¥5.8 trillion in 1985 to ¥22.3 trillion in 1987. The Japanese could afford to invest more than before because a third of the country's households had financial assets exceeding ¥10 million by the end of 1988. As houses became unaffordable for the average salaryman (a suburban dwelling, at one and a half hours commuting distance, cost ¥60 million, 10 times the average salary), the only way to keep up with asset inflation was to invest in Japanese stocks.

Instead of raising interest rates to choke off asset inflation, the Japanese authorities kept them low to help prevent the U.S. dollar from weakening too much. So money supply continued to grow at a rapid rate in 1988–89.

Land Prices and Stock Prices

Property is expensive in Japan because the supply of land is limited just as with shares. According to the government, the high price of real estate is the result of high population density and high living standards. All this is true, but there are at least two other reasons why property prices have shot up in recent years. The first relates to demand. Just as lower interest rates caused investors to revalue equities, it also caused them to revalue land; panic buying ensued. And Japan's rise as a financial center greatly increased demand for office space and housing relative to what was available.

The second factor is the artificial restraint of supply. A distorted system of land taxation and antediluvian planning regulations keep real estate off the market. Extremely low fixed property taxes, plus a law which makes it virtually impossible for owners of buildings to evict sitting tenants, causes landowners to hoard their land rather then sell or redevelop it.

At the same time, transaction taxes are severe, with the government continually trying to control prices, despite a few much-publicized sales. In central Tokyo, only a handful of properties has changed hands in recent years, even fewer in the Marunouchi business district where many top companies are headquartered. At the end of 1987, the Economic Planning Agency valued the national stock of real estate at ¥1,686 trillion, about four times more than the value of real estate in the United States, which has 25 times the area of Japan.

The land-price spiral has a few additional twists. One is the heavily protected agricultural system which allows part-time farmers to grow rice and vegetables on 10 percent of the land in Tokyo. The other is the extraordinary degree to which economic activity and wealth is concentrated around Tokyo. About half of Japan's gross national product—7 percent of the world's output—is generated within a 100-mile radius of the Imperial Palace in the heart of Tokyo. It has proven a magnet for jobs for the rest of Japan, as well as for workers from overseas. The Tokyo metropolis itself accounts for 20 percent of Japan's gross domestic product.

Landowners began to use their property as collateral for bank loans, and the banks were only to happy to lend. These funds were used to invest in the Tokyo stock market as well as to speculate further in the property market. When Tokyo real estate prices peaked in 1987, land speculators moved into overseas markets on which the yield far exceeded anything Japan had to offer, as well as to other areas within Japan. In 1989, land prices in Osaka, Japan's second largest city, rose 50 percent.

Booms in the stock market have coincided historically with booms in the real estate market. The first postwar real estate boom occurred in 1960–61, led by a surge in industrial land prices; the second, in 1971–73, was led by residential land prices. A brief boom occurred in 1980, followed by the 1986–89 surge led by commercial real estate.

One way to show that land prices rose too far is to compare the nominal value of land prices to that of nominal GNP. In the United States, this ratio has fluctuated between 0.56 and 0.86 since 1970. In Japan, it stayed between 2.2 and 3.2 in 1970–75, and then surged to 5.7 by the end of 1989.

The Bank of Japan estimated that the increase in capital gains in equities and land in 1987 totaled ¥480 trillion, roughly 40 percent more than the gross national product, while in 1986 the increase was 10 percent greater. By the end of the decade, each Japanese had more than three times as many assets by value as each American, even though their gross national product per head was similar.

The Q-Ratio

The spiral in share and property prices made popular a theory of valuing stocks called the Q-ratio. Based upon studies first conducted in the United States, it was used to justify the high value of shares in Japan's stock market. The Q-ratio refers to the relationship between a company's market value and the value of its assets. While earnings may have become expensive on a PER basis, the purchase of shares could still be justified if they cost less than the underlying value of a company's real estate and equity holdings. The further the Q-ratio was below one, the more that could be gained by acquiring the firm and selling off the constituent parts.

Because hostile takeover bids are almost unheard of in Japan, the concept has limited practical application, and so the break-up value of a quoted Japanese company has little relevance. As a result, estimates of the Q-ratio vary widely. An academic at Osaka University found that the Q-ratio for shares quoted on the TSE was 1.73 in 1986, while the Japan Securities Research Institute reckoned it at 0.45.

Nonetheless, the Q-ratio was an appealing concept particularly in

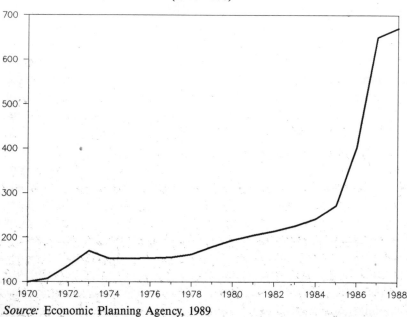

Tokyo Commercial Real Estate Prices
(1970=100)

Source: Economic Planning Agency, 1989

light of the enormous assets that most Japanese companies hold. It was argued that an investor was actually buying two square meters of land in Tokyo worth ¥295,000 with each 1,000 shares of Nippon Steel. Asset valuations for accounting purposes are conservative in most countries. Firms book items like real estate and equity holdings at cost of acquisition. Since many assets were acquired decades ago, the disparity between book value and market value is enormous. Mitsubishi Estate, a part owner of New York's Rockefeller Center, acquired in 1892 a large tract of land next to the Imperial Palace in Tokyo called Marunouchi. Its total landholdings in 1989 were estimated to be worth ¥8.96 trillion and were valued on its books at only ¥193 billion.

The Q-ratio was used by Japanese investors as a way of looking for stocks that sold for less than the value of their assets, particularly land. Many of the stocks selected were of companies whose headquarters or plants were located in Tokyo, where land prices had risen furthest. Some 900 of the TSE's 1,600 issues are based there. Ishikawajima-Harima Industries, with a shipbuilding yard on Tokyo Bay, saw its price quadruple in 1986—a year when it reported a net loss of ¥21 billion.

Perhaps the most convincing reason for ignoring the disparity between the book value of assets and their market value is that it is highly suspect to do otherwise. If a quoted company's share portfolio rises in value, then its own stock price should rise, boosting the value of its shares held by other firms. If their shares rise to reflect their increased worth, then so should the first company's, and so on ad infinitum. That has not stopped investors from using Q-ratios, of course, but it does infer that much of Japan's newfound wealth is merely recorded on paper.

The Q-ratio even implies that a Japanese company is worthless as a source of revenues and profits in comparison to its land holdings. But there is one good reason why share prices had to keep up with real estate values. If they had not, much of Japanese industry could have ended up being owned by the urban farmers of Tokyo.

Golf course memberships are another example of the inflation of assets in Japan. Because of the scarcity of land as well as the popularity of golf, the price of membership in a golf club has soared. Memberships are actively traded over the counter and the *Nihon Keizai Shimbun* has designed an index based on the membership prices of 500 major courses. Indexed to 100 in 1982, the index rose to 487 by 1988 and then soared to 831 by the end of 1989. Of these 500 courses, 20 now cost more than ¥100 million to join, while only 51 cost less than ¥10 million.

One problem with valuing shares based on hidden asset values is that the managers and employees of companies consider hidden assets to be their own property, not that of shareholders. In their opinion, shareholders only own shareholders' equity and earnings—and only receive a token dividend in cash. This is why managers keep hidden assets hidden: to realize the gains would make them someone else's property. Hidden assets are reserves that allow managers to conceal their mistakes.

Excess Liquidity and Financings

One additional source of funds to the market came from the surge in equity-linked financings in 1988 and 1989, when ¥14 trillion and ¥25 trillion were raised respectively. Companies did raise funds for legitimate reasons such as capital spending. However, many issued shares, warrants and convertible bonds simply because they were so cheap. Securities companies used guarantees of an 8 percent return on *tokkin* funds and the bargain cost of financing at 2 percent or less to entice companies to issue. Proceeds went into the stock market. Despite the huge amounts of funds raised by manufacturers in the stock market over the past six years, in no year did capital spending exceed manufacturers' cash flow. In other words, they could have done without issuing any new shares whatsoever.

An Attitude of Mind

There is no clearcut answer to the question why Japanese share prices are so high. Companies have reduced the amount of shares actively traded. Earnings are understated in some respects but overstated in others. Share prices have been inflated by the general updraft of asset prices, but these in turn reflect the economic, as well as narrowly financial, strength of Japan.

The most important factor is that Japanese investors have confidence in the ability of the stock market and Japanese companies
to perform well in the future because they have succeeded in the past.
This notion has enabled investors to buy almost any firm, regardless
of quality, and make a profit. The TSE is a speculator's market and
always has been. Investors speculate about what a company's true
earnings are, what its hidden assets are worth, what stock the Big
Four will promote, and what company the speculative groups are
targeting. It is a rare investor who tries to relate a company's true
worth to that of its market capitalization.

A 29 percent fall in the stock market at the beginning of 1990
would suggest that Japanese investors have realized how overvalued
their stock market is. But this is most unlikely.

Many of the factors that supported high share prices before 1990
will continue to operate. The main difference is that interest rates are
now higher. Prices would have to fall a lot further than 29 percent
from their 1989 peak (which still left share prices twice as high as they
were at the end of 1985) for investors' faith to be shaken. Instead, it
would take a collapse in real estate prices to shake Japan. A fall in
land values would be the clearest sign that Japan's speculative bubble
had burst.

Chapter 6

SERVANT OF INDUSTRY

The structure of share ownership, the behavior of the stock market, and the resulting high share prices have a common aim: they serve Japanese industry. The listed companies in Japan have access to the cheapest capital in the world, and this gives them a big competitive advantage over their foreign counterparts. In 1989, it cost listed Japanese companies an average of 0.4 percent a year to raise money by issuing shares domestically and even less if they sold warrant bonds or convertible bonds overseas and swapped the proceeds into yen. Listed companies raised ¥25 trillion through such issues in 1989, more than twice their total net profits.

Because of these low-cost funds, Japanese manufacturers are more cost competitive than their U.S. counterparts. The net interest expense paid by listed manufacturers in the six months to September 1989 was a negative 0.09 percent of sales; that is, they received more from interest-bearing instruments than they paid out on borrowings. Not only is Japanese debt less expensive because of lower interest rates, Japanese companies also have large cash positions due to their active fund-raising in the stock market. They can spend more on plant and equipment, even to the point of overcapacity, and they need not be concerned about profits, dividends, or a favorable return on their investment immediately.

They can afford to wait, because the payback period on equity at 0.4 percent per annum is 250 years. They can relentlessly compete on price, thus raising their market share which further reduces their unit costs. Eventually, their foreign competitors abandon market after market because it is not profitable enough for them to remain in them. Once their foreign competitors are gone, Japanese companies are then in a position to employ the same price-fixing cartels and agreements to limit industry output that are prevalent in the Japanese domestic market. Subsequent competition is no longer based on price but on quality and service, permitting Japanese companies ultimately to earn good returns on their investment.

The cheap and abundant capital of Japanese companies is not simply the result of Japan's high savings rate but rests in part on deliberate action taken by the government to channel funds into companies. In th 1950s and 1960s, when the pretax cost of equity issues was close to 20 percent per annum, companies relied heavily on debt. The interest rate on loans was fixed at a low level, funds were strategically allocated to large companies, and the financial risk normally associated with high debt levels was borne by the banking industry. But when dividend yields fell below debt costs in the late 1960s, companies began switching to equity financings.

Shareholders do not complain about either earnings-per-share dilution or low dividend yields since, to a large degree, they are themselves listed companies. With no pressure to produce short-term returns, companies can concentrate on long-range competitive advantage. They can plow more money back into their businesses. And they are in a stronger position to cut prices, if necessary, because they can be confident that their share price will not suffer.

If cheap finance were the sole advantage of the Japanese stock market, then it has earned its keep. But there have been other benefits offered by the stock market. First, it gives companies tremendous financial strength by virtue of their shareholdings. Second, the realization of capital gains by occasional sales of stock are a convenient source of cash, which can smooth out profits to compensate for the ups and downs of a company's year-to-year operations. Share sales can even provide a permanent source of revenue to conceal structural weaknesses in a firm's operations.

Third, the stock market helps defend a company from a takeover. High share prices make it prohibitive to launch an unwanted bid for a company. Conversely, an agreed-upon merger between two listed companies is cheap in Japan since it can be accomplished merely by exchanging shares or buying a small stake to win control. All that is necessary is the agreement of the long-term shareholders. Even if hostile takeovers were acceptable in Japan, there are more attractive and cheaper targets overseas where corporate acquisitions are a way of life.

A listing on the stock market gives a significant competitive advantage to a Japanese company over its foreign rival. Yet along with enormous benefits, there are huge costs borne by the Japanese economy, some of them obvious, others less so. The biggest of these is the misallocation of resources. Listed companies are favored at the expense of unquoted firms, which may be better managed and have better growth prospects. This is one reason why there are few rapidly growing, young companies in Japan. The big listed companies control the allocation of funds, the distribution channels, and the growing markets as well.

Cheap capital and a focus on market share rather than profits also lead to chronic overinvestment in plant and equipment. But the ill effects of overcapacity have been borne until now by those firms whose cost of capital is highest—namely, foreign companies. In the domestic market, MITI still attempts to regulate industry's capacity additions and reductions and permits cartels to cope with this situation. Japan's stock market has produced an unparalleled concentration of wealth and power in the hands of a few companies, recreating in a different form the *zaibatsu* that the American Occupation forces sought to dismantle. While this is all to the good of Japan-as-producer, it is another matter whether it helps Japan-as-consumer or the world at large.

U.S. companies face the opposite predicament. For the most part, they are the servants of the investment community, continually trying to satisfy the demand for higher returns. Wall Street's influence has become so strong that managers run their businesses for the benefit of short-term speculators rather than as long-term competitors. Managers are under relentless pressure to ensure that their shareholders receive a high immediate return, achieved either by boosting net income, paying higher dividends, or buying back their own shares. Likewise, a manager's performance is measured by how well the company's share price does. Lest managers forget their goals, they are often compensated in the form of stock options.

Since the investment community is the final judge of U.S. corporate performance, companies must provide a constant flow of information to it. Listed companies are required to release quarterly results and provide a great deal more information about their business and long-term strategy than Japanese ones. Since these quarterly figures are held in great esteem by Wall Street, they can have a substantial influence on a company's share price, particularly if they undershoot analysts' estimates. A U.S. company has 90 days to measure up to the market. A Japanese one has 250 years. Japanese companies have used Wall Street's short-term view to their own advantage by applying financial pressure on U.S. corporations for a few years and forcing them out of key markets.

U.S. companies that fail to live up to expectations are put on the auction block, and after being sold to the highest bidder are often dismembered. To prevent this, managers have to keep a close watch on their profit levels from one quarter to the next. Cash that would be better spent on investing in growth and combating the competition goes to the shareholders instead. For the past eight years, there has in fact been a net cash outflow from the NYSE. In some cases, managers acting solely for the short-term interest of shareholders will tend to load companies with debt, increase dividends and share buybacks, and shift the business risk to creditors. Research and development spending is cut, maintenance of equipment is reduced, and advertising is slashed as managers take cash out of a company. In the extreme case of a leveraged buyout, the shareholders put up very little capital in return for the low probability of a big payoff.

Given the treatment of listed companies in the United States, it should come as no surprise that U.S. managers are becoming more interested in their own financial gain than in the growth of their company. Management-led buyouts and takeovers, where managers receive golden parachutes, have increased dramatically in the 1980s. There is more to be lost than gained by listing on a U.S. stock exchange. In 1988 alone, takeovers cut the value of the NYSE by 5 percent.

The Cash Cow

Cheap Debt

It has taken the Japanese stock market not years but decades to achieve its highly unusual position in the economy. For more than a century after the Meiji Restoration, it was a marginal source of capital. Companies only resorted to equity financings when their banks could not provide the money for growth. In the early 1970s, when equity financings became cheaper than bank loans, the balance was tipped in the other direction.

It is important to understand exactly how U.S. and Japanese companies determine the cost of capital since Japan's lower cost is crucial to its industrial success. In the United States, the cost of capital is defined as a company's weighted-average cost of debt and equity. The cost of debt is the after-tax interest expense, and the cost of equity is the annual expected return on a company's shares, that is, the opportunity cost of issuing equity now rather than next year. Consider a company whose capital structure is 50 percent debt and 50 percent equity at its stated market value. If it can borrow at 10 percent before tax (effectively 6 percent after taxes) and its stock is priced to offer a 15 percent annual return, then its cost of capital is 10.5 percent.

Since debt provides a tax shield, a company can lower its cost of capital by increasing its debt, though eventually the risk of financial distress causes equity investors to demand a higher return. Determining this optimal level for debt and equity is at the heart of corporate finance. The cost of capital in turn determines the minimum acceptable rate that a company must earn on its investments.

For Japanese companies, the cost of capital is also the average weighted cost of debt and equity. The significant difference, though, is that Japanese managers view the cost of equity merely in terms of the dividend that they must pay, not the expected return on the shares. This attitude prevails because the structure of shareholding makes common stock the virtual equivalent of preferred shares. Because businesses are not answerable to the stock market in the same sense as are U.S. companies, their objective is not to maximize profits for shareholders but to minimize the cost of capital.

Before the 1980s, Japanese companies were regarded by foreigners as recklessly indebted, although this was not a matter of choice. Until the 1930s, Japanese companies had conservative capital structures, relying primarily on internal sources of funds and occasional equity offerings, but when Japan started to prepare for war, companies were forced to borrow heavily to expand their production facilities. Firms remained dependent on bank finance to reconstruct the economy after 1945 and then to help fuel its rapid expansion.

The financial markets played a significant role in the government's control over industry until the mid-1970s. This control was achieved through the allocation of credit to companies. Japanese companies were almost totally dependent on bank credit since they could not finance their growth by retained earnings and depreciation following the devastation of World War II. Nor could they turn to the stock market; it was too shallow and prohibitively expensive due to the requirement of issuing new shares at par value. The corporate bond market was not a viable alternative since the government kept the fixed-income market to itself by fixing coupons at yields below those prevailing in the secondary market.

The government's control over the extension of credit by private banks was achieved during the 1950s and 1960s by denying the financial markets their function of allocating the amount and cost of capital. The Bank of Japan, the central bank, determined on a quarterly basis how much new lending banks could extend. As open market operations were virtually unknown, this was the major means of managing the money supply, and guaranteed a sufficient supply of funds to the corporate sector to achieve growth, investments, and exports. To ensure that the banks lent to those industries at the top of MITI's list of priorities, financial institutions were strictly segmented into categories for long-term industrial loans, short-term commercial loans, regional economies, and small businesses. The major banks heeded the guidance of the government since they chronically lent an amount greater than their deposits, and thus had to borrow from the Bank of Japan to make up for their shortfall.

Control over credit was also achieved through strict management of domestic interest rates. In December 1947, the Temporary Money Rates Adjustment Law was passed imposing state controls on interest rates for both lending and deposits. Eventually, a direct link was created between the Official Discount Rate, the rate at which banks borrow from the central bank, and lending and deposit rates. The interest rate on one-year time deposits was fixed at 5.5 percent from April 1961 to April 1970 even though the consumer price index rose 5.9 percent annually throughout this period.

The fact that Japanese interest rates were fixed by monetary policy, not by demand for money, stunted the development of the capital markets and caused companies to rely heavily on indirect financing. Call rates, the rate at which banks borrow from one another, were set above the short-term prime lending rate in order to encourage the flow of funds from regional banks to the city banks, which in turn lent to major companies.

The authorities used their powers to channel capital into the priority areas of the economy: the large corporations in strategic sectors such as steel, petrochemicals, shipbuilding, automobiles, and electronics. With capital abundant at artificially low interest rates, priority industries could undertake costly research and development, capital investment, and quality control that unsubsidized companies could not hope to match. Capital-intensive industries, which would ordinarily have been stifled by high interest rates, were encouraged and nurtured. This system not only accelerated the pace of economic development but determined its direction and structure. Once industrial policy was formulated and industries targeted, capital poured out of Japanese banks to meet their needs.

The primary source of the funds for industry came from individual savings. Savings were encouraged in a number of ways: interest income on savings of up to ¥3 million was tax exempt until 1988; deposits were accepted through the 22,000 post offices in Japan; companies paid a large proportion of wages in the form of semiannual bonuses; pensions were paid in a lump sum; and few safety nets were provided in case of unemployment or old age. Consumer borrowing was discouraged by limiting consumer credit through banks and not allowing individuals to deduct interest payments, even for home mortgages, from their taxable income. In addition, to avoid competing for money with industry, the government kept its fiscal deficit low and introduced a rigorous system of capital controls to prevent money from leaving the country.

Only the largest firms could obtain unsecured credit, while some form of collateral—such as securities, mortgages, or the guarantee of a third party—was required from other borrowers. However, in the 1960s when the demand for funds was particularly strong, the banks demanded substantial compensating balances as partial collateral in order to circumvent interest-rate controls. Companies that were members of a *keiretsu* were at an advantage since they had ready access to credit from one of the major banks. They could also bear more financial risk since the *keiretsu* ties provided a safety net through sales and purchase agreements with the major trading companies.

As a result of this heavy dependence on indirect finance, equity ratios for major companies fell dramatically. In fiscal 1970, net worth comprised only 18.5 percent of total capital for 565 companies on the TSE First Section. Debt was stretched to the limit to achieve Japan's objective of high economic growth. Companies were not vulnerable, however, as most of the financial risks were borne by the banks rather than shareholders. The Bank of Japan, in turn, stood behind the banking industry.

Through most of the high-growth period, the stock market was a minor source of funds. Equity issues were expensive, and the capacity of the equity market to absorb new issues was limited. Almost all new equity was issued at par value to current shareholders, and since companies tried to maintain a dividend of 10 percent of par value, the cost of equity was over twice that of debt when the tax shield of interest payments was taken into account. Because the stock market was poorly developed, the authorities were able to control the allocation of capital through indirect means. This also allowed the banking industry to wield great influence over industrial Japan.

Despite the disadvantages, firms continued to issue shares at par value because it enabled them to borrow more from the bond market (fixed-rate debt could not exceed paid-in capital) and because an issue was seen as a sign of confidence. However, even access to the equity market was restricted from the latter half of 1961 until the first half of 1964. A committee composed of representatives of the central bank, the financial industry, and corporations oversaw new issues in order to cope with the bear market.

Cheap Equity

The switch to issues at market price, which made equity financings much more attractive, could not have come at a better time. Among the traumas of the oil crisis of 1973 was the realization that indebted firms were critically vulnerable to a sudden recession. The financial strategy of heavy borrowing had worked well during the era of double-digit economic growth from 1955 to 1973 because rapidly increasing output provided the cash flow to finance the debt.

When economic growth contracted under the impact of the oil crisis, however, companies faced a cash squeeze. The situation was exacerbated when the Bank of Japan raised the Official Discount Rate to control inflation. Over a period of nine months in 1973, this rate went from 4.25 percent to 9 percent, while inflation shot up to 25 percent. Even though the banking industry stood firmly behind corporate Japan, firms were required to pay more for their debt to reflect the banks' higher funding costs. When companies which had borrowed heavily to speculate in property could not pay the interest, there were bankruptcies. Daiwa Bank wrote off Eidai Sangyo, a big housing company, and Dai-Ichi Kangyo Bank stopped lending to Kohjin, a textile manufacturer.

Japan's rate of real economic growth dropped from 10 percent a year in 1960–73 to an annual expansion of less than 4 percent since then. This was an opportunity for companies to reduce their debt burden. For the 965 manufacturers listed on the TSE, new long-term borrowing peaked at ¥4.8 trillion in fiscal 1975. Although it rose after the second oil crisis in 1979, it declined steadily thereafter to only ¥1.6 trillion by fiscal 1988. Since 1978, long-term debt repayments have exceeded new borrowings; by fiscal 1988 net interest expenses were only ¥394 billion compared with more than ¥2.1 trillion eight years earlier.

The shift in corporate borrowing patterns coincided with an equally important change in the government's own financial position. In the early 1970s and particularly after the 1973 oil crisis, the government's fiscal deficit began to grow sharply as it took a larger role in propelling economic growth. From a level of ¥550 billion in the late 1960s, new government borrowing doubled in the early 1970s, reached ¥5 trillion by 1975 and ¥14 trillion by 1979. The amount of government bonds outstanding rose from ¥10 trillion in 1975 to ¥72 trillion five years later.

Like corporate borrowers, the Japanese government benefited from the controlled financial structure. In the United States, the government must price its debt instruments at a competitive interest rate in order to sell them; but in Japan, commercial banks were obliged to purchase and hold for one year the major share of government bonds. The Finance Ministry decided on the allocation of bonds to each bank.

Nevertheless, in the late 1970s, the Ministry began to deregulate interest rates. This was done to create a market for its debt because the burden of purchasing government bonds by the banks had grown too great. The city banks, for example, saw their holdings of government bonds balloon from ¥388 billion in 1970 to ¥6.8 trillion by 1979. The banks' financial soundness was threatened when high interest rates in 1979 and 1980 caused bond prices to fall far below their face value. In 1980, the Finance Ministry required banks to hold government bonds only until they were listed and also to value their bonds at cost.

The process of interest-rate deregulation began by legitimizing the *gensaki* market, the conditional purchase of government or corporate bonds with resale or repurchase agreements at specific prices. For three years, this was the only free money market. In 1979 commercial banks were permitted to offer negotiable certificates of deposit in order to halt the erosion of their deposit base as increasingly yield-conscious depositors turned to postal savings. In 1980, the Finance Ministry allowed Nomura Securities to sell open-end bond investment trusts that offered higher rates and more liquidity than bank deposits.

To keep companies from being crowded out by government borrowing, the Ministry of Finance eased the regulations concerning the issue of securities. The subsequent reduction in company debt decreased their vulnerability to the now more volatile, deregulated interest rates.

Freer Money

To stimulate capital growth, companies were now free to issue securities other than either straight bonds or equities. Two of the most important were convertible bonds and bonds with equity warrants attached. Convertible bonds have been in existence since 1966, but they did not become de rigueur until the stock market surged in 1980. Warrants only started trading after the Commercial Code was amended in 1981 to allow companies to issue them.

Convertible bonds are bonds that can be converted into shares at a fixed price; they carry a coupon lower than a straight bond to reflect the potential increase in their value should the underlying share price rise. Although the coupon is higher than the company's dividend yield, convertible bonds allow the issuer to raise funds at a rate cheaper than for a straight bond, to have an equity-linked financing without suddenly upsetting the supply of shares in the market, and to tap a broader base of investors, particularly bond investors. For the investor, convertible bonds limit downside risk since their price behaves like that of any normal bond if the share price falls below the conversion price.

Bonds with equity warrants are similar to convertible bonds except that the right to buy shares at a fixed price can be detached from the bond and traded separately. Most convertible bonds are issued in Japan, but warrant bonds are mostly issued in the Euromarkets denominated in a foreign currency.

These two types of issues have become the most popular forms of securities finance. In 1989, listed firms raised ¥6.8 trillion worth through domestic convertible bonds, ¥9.3 trillion through overseas warrant bonds, and ¥5.8 trillion through public offerings of equities. Straight bonds, which totalled only ¥1.4 trillion in 1989, have never been popular for firms other than utilities, primarily because long-term credit banks have discouraged firms from issuing them. Long-term credit banks are the largest issuers of fixed-rate bonds in Japan; in essence these banks take the place of the corporate bond market.

Companies have quickly taken advantage of deregulation of

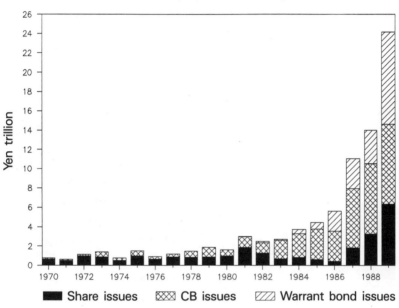

Equity Financing by Listed Companies

Share issues   **CB issues**   **Warrant bond issues**

Source: Annual Securities Statistics (Tokyo: Tokyo Stock Exchange, 1989)

Japan's financial markets and the surge in share prices to issue huge amounts of equities. TSE-listed companies raised a total of ¥4 trillion between 1960 and 1969 through the stock market. This increased to ¥11.6 trillion in the 1970s and then surged to ¥73 trillion in the 1980s. In 1989 alone, listed companies raised an astounding ¥25 trillion.

Bank loans to major corporations, meanwhile, have fallen steeply. According to a 1985 survey of Japanese executives, bank loans were the preferred source of cash in the 1970s but in the following decade they were ranked last—in seventh place—while stock issues went from fourth to third place. Long-term borrowing by listed manufacturers, which stood at ¥12.3 trillion in March 1983, fell to ¥7.1 trillion by March 1989. For TSE-listed nonmanufacturers, excluding financial firms, long-term debt levels have continued to rise. However, here too an improvement in their capital structure can be seen.

Changing Capital Structure
TSE manufacturers

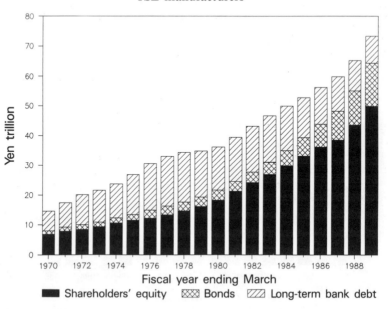

Source: Nikkei Needs

In fiscal year 1988, listed companies raised their long-term capital by ¥25.4 trillion through equity-linked issues, retaining earnings and reserves. New long-term debt only amounted to ¥300 billion. Because plant and equipment investment only totalled ¥13.9 trillion, listed companies raised an excess of funds, much of which found its way into large-denomination deposits and *tokkin* funds. Manufacturers also reduced their long-term and short-term debt by ¥1.9 trillion, which reduced their net interest burden to a negative 0.09 percent of sales in 1989.

The source of the improvement in the balance sheets of Japanese companies has not only come from increased equity financings. Internal sources of cash from retained earnings and depreciation have been sizable contributors. Manufacturers' net income rose from ¥980 billion in the year ending March 1973 to ¥3.6 trillion by March 1989, an 8.6 percent annual increase. Depreciation expenses meanwhile increased by 7 percent a year over the same period.

Why have Japanese companies not raised even more money in the stock market? After all, share prices appear to be unaffected by new issues and in fact tend to rise in anticipation of them. And with stocks selling at high multiples of book value and earnings, new issues can raise book value per share and earnings per share, even if the funds are just deposited in a bank account.

The reason why there are limits to equity financing has to do with a company's stable shareholders, who buy 30–40 percent of most new issues. A company issues new shares to its stable shareholders to keep supply off the stock market, to keep a high percentage of shares in friendly hands, and to maintain the relative position of the top shareholders. In return, an issuer is obliged to buy the issues of other companies in which it is a stable shareholder.

This arrangement sets a ceiling for new equity financings. Stable shareholders will not commit unlimited amounts of money to shares since the return on the investment has fallen to 0.4 percent annually. In addition, a company's investment in equities cannot exceed its own shareholders' equity. Thus, they can only buy new issues if they themselves tap the equity market for funds. As a result, around 40 percent of the money raised in the equity market is eventually plowed back into the stock market to answer reciprocal calls for cash from cross-shareholders. The rest of the proceeds are for use as the issuer sees fit. Japanese corporations have thus been helping each other improve their equity ratios by shifting capital back and forth.

Three categories of stable shareholders have been heavily burdened by this process. The first is the life insurers, which do not issue shares themselves because they are owned by their policyholders. The second is companies that lead *keiretsu*. Many of these have had to regulate financings by their group companies in order to control their own equity purchases. The third is the big banks, which buy the new issues of their corporate clients only to see them use the proceeds to repay bank borrowing. Thus, a bank loan yielding 7 percent is replaced with an equity investment yielding 0.4 percent. The major banks have compensated for this by issuing ¥5.5 trillion worth of capital in 1987–89.

For this process to continue in the 1990s depends on a further rise in share prices. The Big Four had to place a moratorium on all new equity financings because of the stock market's plunge in early 1990. If share prices quickly recover, then equity financings will resume albeit at a slower pace than before. Many Japanese companies have improved their financial position so much that they have no need for new issues in the next few years. Moreover, the higher coupons that convertible bonds and warrant bonds now carry make them less attractive as a source of *zaiteku* profits. At the same time, strong loan demand and high bond yields make equities a less attractive investment for financial institutions.

If share prices continue to drift down for an extended period then financings will be extremely difficult. Issuers will have problems convincing stable shareholders to buy more shares if, as is likely, buyers lost money on the previous issue. Many companies will also be forced to redeem unexercised convertible bonds for cash. This will create an imbalance among stable shareholders because some will have issued convertible bonds and others straight equities. The ability of companies to continue selling equities is likely to be curbed also by further financial deregulation and a large overhang of unexercised convertible bonds and warrants.

Financial deregulation in Japan has lagged behind the development of the country's economic power. The stock market has undoubtedly benefited from this. Currently, Japanese investors still lack a wide array of financial instruments to choose from compared with the United States. The secondary market for straight bonds is virtually nonexistent, and the amount of newly issued government bonds is on the decline as the Japanese government improves its fiscal structure. Almost half of all bank deposits still carry regulated interest rates, and the tax and regulatory structure has pumped up the property market, rendering it unaffordable to most Japanese. If investors had more alternatives from which to choose, money that currently goes into equities might find its way into fixed-income instruments. The lack of financial choice is one reason why Japanese institutional investors have turned to overseas investments. They bought a net $112 billion in securities in 1989 alone.

It is clear that a more competitive market for investment products would make life harder for stocks. Even so, with other alternatives available for several years now, there has been no sign of the stock market suffering from lack of investor interest. This, however, was due to the fact that interest rates were low and falling. Once interest rates began to rise sharply in mid-1989 (and the stock market began to look shaky), there was a shift in individuals' savings out of term deposits and into money market certificates. Corporations began cancelling their *tokkin* funds in order to take advantage of high rates on certificates of deposits.

Unexercised convertible bonds and warrants probably pose a greater threat than deregulation to the stock market's role as Japan's financier. Although the total amount of these issues was only ¥25 trillion in a market worth ¥600 trillion in January 1990, it nonetheless represents a growing concern to issuers. It is not known who holds many of these instruments and for what purposes, particularly warrants which are traded in London. There is no way to predict their effect on the supply of shares available when these instruments are exercised. The amount outstanding may be small compared to the market's capitalization, but it is large compared to the amount of actively traded shares.

In May 1989, the *Nihon Keizai Shimbun* estimated that the total number of outstanding convertible bonds and warrants amounted to 18.2 billion shares if converted. This represented 5.8 percent of all shares outstanding at that time, a sharp increase from 3.2 percent a year earlier. It also comprised 7.1 percent of the outstanding shares of the 977 issuers. Unexercised warrants and convertible bonds equalled more than 40 percent of the shares outstanding for five companies and more than 10 percent for 392 companies.

UNYIELDING DIVIDENDS

Equity finance is cheap for issuers because dividend yields are low and declining. Dividends have been on the decline since 1951 when the average yield peaked at 11.9 percent. In 1989, the average yield reached an all-time low of 0.43 percent. A primary reason for the drop is the fact that share prices have risen at a much faster rate than dividends. Equally important, though, is the way in which dividends are set by companies. Rather than having dividends reflect the level

Average Dividend Yield on the TSE First Section

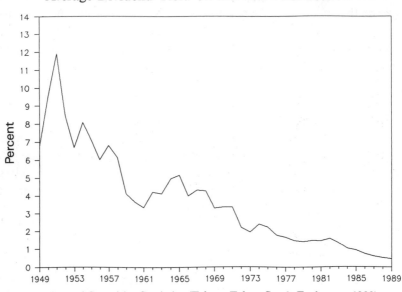

Source: Annual Securities Statistics (Tokyo: Tokyo Stock Exchange, 1989)

of earnings, companies normally set their dividends at a fixed percentage of their share's par value, which is ¥50 for most companies. Currently, the par value of a share has little meaning since this was merely the face value of a share at the time a company was established, although it often represents the acquisition cost of shares for stable shareholders.

Japanese companies usually set their dividend at ¥5, which represents a 10 percent return on the par value of a share. Managers regard this as a reasonable level in relation to the cost of a bank loan. Stable shareholders accept this level, as they too have to pay dividends. Although dividends are raised on occasion in increments of ¥0.5 or ¥1, it is usually because earnings per share have grown very rapidly or because a competitor in the same industry has raised its dividend. By the same token, when a company has a gratis issue it maintains its dividend per share; thus, a 10 percent gratis issue results in a 10 percent increase in dividends.

Even for shares acquired by stable shareholders at higher prices, there is no urgent call for higher dividends. If one side of the cross-shareholding arrangement were to raise its dividend, then the other side of the arrangement would have to follow suit. Since half of the shares in the stock market are held by listed companies, raising the general level of dividends of all companies would not benefit listed companies but would merely create a net outflow of cash to insurance policyholders, owners of investment trusts, individuals, and foreigners—investors that are least important to Japanese companies. Managers can thus retain more of their earnings to invest in their business or to deposit in a bank.

The proportion of net profits paid out as dividends by all listed firms has plunged from 44 percent in 1977 to only 29 percent in 1988. The top 400 quoted firms in the United States paid out 53 percent of post-tax income. The Japanese payout is even lower if, as some argue, firms understate their earnings. Even highly profitable companies in mature industries—the proverbial cash cows—continue to retain most of their earnings.

Payout Ratio
TSE listed companies

Source: Annual Securities Statistics (Tokyo: Tokyo Stock Exchange, 1989)

Companies with Low Payout Ratios
(FY88)

	EPS (¥)	Dividend (¥)	Payout (%)
Toyo Seikan	139	8	5
Fujitsu Business System	162	9	6
Aoyama Shoji	318	20	6
Fuji Photo	219	14	6
Sumitomo Bank	82	8	10
Toyota Motor	117	19	16
Ito-Yokado	127	22	17
Sony	242	45	18
Kyocera	183	44	24

Companies with High Payout Ratios
(FY88)

	EPS (¥)	Dividend (¥)	Payout (%)
Kobe Steel	10.0	5	50
Kanebo	9.1	5	55
Tobu Railway	8.0	5	63
Tokyu Car	6.3	4	63
Toho Rayon	7.6	5	66
Sumitomo Coal Mining	7.2	5	69
Meiji Seika	8.1	6	74
Prima Meat Packers	5.7	5	88
Nippon Yusen	2.6	4	154

Source: Company reports; based on consolidated earnings if available

For companies with low earnings per share, even a ¥5 dividend can be a strain. This is particularly true for industries such as steel and textile spinning which have a large number of shares outstanding;

their payout ratios tend to be high. Once a dividend level is established, there is considerable loss of face if the dividend is lowered.

A SHOW OF STRENGTH

Another major benefit that Japanese companies derive from high share prices is financial strength. Listed Japanese companies own 50 percent of all shares outstanding, worth ¥219 trillion at the end of April 1990. The acquisition cost of these shares is around one-quarter of this amount. Theoretically, they could sell their holdings and use the proceeds to purchase half the companies on the NYSE. Toyota, for example, has unrealized capital gains of ¥2.2 trillion and ¥1.5 trillion in cash on its balance sheet, more than enough to buy Ford Motor Co. or Chrysler. The unrealized capital gains held by Mitsubishi Bank are greater than the equity capital of J.P. Morgan, Citicorp, Bank America, and Chase Manhattan combined. Altogether, there were 159 listed industrial companies in Japan with unrealized capital gains in excess of ¥100 billion as of March 1989.

It is difficult, though, to imagine these companies ever realizing their wealth suddenly, since it is their act of holding shares that helps the stock market maintain high share prices. However, it is not uncommon for a single company to sell part of its holdings or to borrow against the value of its holdings. When Ataka Trading Co. went bankrupt in 1977, Sumitomo Bank covered its ¥106 billion in losses through the sale of equities. And when Sanko Steamship collapsed in 1985, Daiwa Bank sold 30 million of the 42 million shares it owned in Nomura Securities to raise ¥40 billion.

Because investors tend to place a higher value on shares of companies that have large hidden assets, companies indirectly benefit by virtue of higher share prices. The greatest hidden assets are held, first, by the big banks and, second, by the main companies in each of the industrial groups. These holdings provide them with a big advantage over other Japanese companies and allow them to control those companies in which they own a large stake. Nippon Steel has a ratio of equity to total capital of 47 percent based on its stated accounts. After adding in the value of its hidden assets and removing deferred

Corporate Financial Strength
(March 1989)

	Shareholders equity (¥)	Equity Hidden Assets (¥)
Hitachi	1,131	2,188
Toyota Motor	2,955	2,146
Matsushita Electric	1,764	2,132
Nippon Steel	626	1,854
Mitsubishi Corp.	468	1,496
Mitsubishi Heavy	667	1,325
Nissan Motor	1,502	1,243
Mitsui & Co.	320	1,016
Fujitsu	753	911
NEC	677	896
Toshiba	803	849
Ito-Yokado	296	574
Nisshinbo Industries	127	449
Nippon Suisan	71	330
Taiyo Fisheries	31	103

Source: *Japan Company Handbook* (Tokyo: Toyo Keizai, 1989)

capital gains taxes, its equity ratio rises to 68 percent. For smaller companies the difference is even more dramatic. Japan Wool Textile, a manufacturer of woolen textiles and yarns, has shareholders' equity of ¥33.7 billion but has unrealized capital gains of ¥118 billion.

Although a company's hidden assets have become more popular as a means of valuing shares, the price of many issues is less than the value per share of the firm's stockholdings. This implies that the company's main business could be purchased for nothing. The cheapest shares on the market are those of the casualty insurance companies which sell at discounts of up to 50 percent of their hidden asset value. Other examples include Nippon Flour Mills, which had hidden assets of ¥1,020 a share and a stock price of ¥800 at the end of April 1990. Tokyo Printing Ink had hidden assets of ¥844 a share and a share price of ¥1,000. These equity holdings would be critical in determining the value of a company if there were an active merger-and-acquisition market in Japan, since they could be sold to finance a takeover. The fact that these shares are not for sale makes M&A less likely.

The high price of real estate in Japan fulfills a similar function as hidden assets in shares. Although rarely sold, real estate provides collateral for most loans made in Japan and helps to support share prices. To be sure, the financial benefits of land holdings are even greater than shares since the total value of land held by corporations is much greater than that of shares. Land prices have moved so far out of line with a company's earning power that when a private business is sold in Japan its price is normally set at the value of its landholdings. The intrinsic business is essentially worthless.

If equity and real estate prices had risen less rapidly, Japanese companies would not have been able to grow as fast as they did, either through the use of debt or equity financing. This is a virtuous circle: the success of Japanese companies has led to higher stock and land prices which in turn permitted Japanese companies to grow faster. This raises the question of whether high share prices and real estate prices are the result of their high growth or are, in fact, a major contributor to it.

INVESTMENT INCOME FOR CORPORATIONS

Despite the need to maintain stable business relationships, Japanese companies have become major investors and traders in equities. They boost their earnings by buying and selling shares through *tokkin* and fund trusts. Alternatively, they sell off portions of their long-term holdings to realize capital gains but this is rarely resorted to. A less direct method is to issue new shares with a low dividend yield and then deposit the proceeds in the bank.

The active management of surplus cash is referred to as *zaiteku*, literally financial engineering. But the nonoperating income of most companies comes from far less spectacular forms of investment. Poor standards of disclosure do not permit an outsider to ascertain the true exposure of companies to equity investment.

Investment in *tokkin* and fund trusts is normally treated on the balance sheet as a bank deposit and on the income statement as interest income. Companies have also been known to transfer portions of their long-term holdings into their *tokkin* and fund trust accounts in order to bolster their returns. Gains from sales of securities, which would be treated as an extraordinary gain in the US, are treated as recurring profits under Japanese accounting standards.

The spectacular growth of investment in *tokkin* and fund trusts—from ¥12 trillion in 1986 to ¥43 trillion in early 1990, shows that companies are using the strength of the stock market to improve their performance. This was particularly true in 1986–87 when operating profits were squeezed by the sudden revaluation of the yen. Approximately half of the investment in *tokkin* and fund trusts comes from nonfinancial companies, although this percentage has dropped with the recovery of the economy in mid-1987.

Among listed companies, Toyota had the largest net nonoperating income of ¥169 billion in the year ending June 1989. Of this sum, ¥114 billion was derived from interest on bank deposits and notes receivable, ¥25 billion from equity dividends and ¥30 billion from sales of stocks and bonds. The firms with the biggest *zaiteku* profits tend to be large and international.

Top Twenty Companies by Net Financial Income
(¥ bn, FY89)

Toyota Motor	139.0	Hanwa Kogyo	21.4
Matsushita Electric	115.0	Nippon Oil	19.2
Hitachi	61.9	Nippon Denso	19.1
Kirin Breweries	28.4	Mitsubishi Corp.	18.4
Sharp	26.6	Sanyo Electric	17.9
Fuji Photo	25.8	Asahi Glass	16.4
Sumitomo Corp.	25.0	Sekisui Chemical	15.6
Sony	23.7	Mitsubishi Electric	15.3
Mitsubishi Heavy	23.6	Komatsu	15.0
Nissan Motor	22.7	Kyocera	14.6

Source: Nihon Keizai Shimbun

While some companies are able to show a steady surplus in nonoperating income, others only generate a surplus when absolutely necessary. Steel companies' *zaiteku* profits shot up in 1986 when earnings from their steel business fell sharply due to the rise in the yen. Isuzu went from a non-operating loss of ¥4.4 billion in 1986 to a surplus of ¥16.4 billion in 1987, even though its operating profits fell from ¥2.7 billion to a loss of ¥15.6 billion.

Gains on sales of assets, primarily securities, for listed manufacturers went from ¥240 billion in the year ending March 1985 to ¥952 billion two years later. Over the same period, operating profits fell 42 percent. By March 1989 manufacturers' operating profits had recovered to the levels of four years earlier, while gains from asset sales declined to ¥480 billion.

The existence of these large nonoperating profit gains, whether from aggressive equity trading or merely bank deposits, raises some important issues. First, it demonstrates how the lack of shareholder rights in Japan has enabled Japanese companies to hoard their cash even when they have nothing better to do with it than put it in a bank. This is demonstrated by the deteriorating return on equity for Japanese companies, which went from 12 percent in the year to March 1980 to 7 percent nine years later—an indication of too-high a ratio of equity to debt within their capital structure and the low return on fund management relative to the company's business.

Second, the large amount of nonoperating income calls into question the valuation of shares in the market. If nonoperating income is a large contributor to net income, then for a share on a PER of, say, 50, an investor is paying 50 times the interest income earned from a bank deposit. A company can thus deposit ¥1,000 in a bank, earn ¥30 per year after tax, and then have the market capitalize these earnings at ¥1,500. If the market were efficient and capitalized these earnings at only ¥1,000, this means that the PER of a company's operating business is valued even higher than 50 times earnings.

Third, the growth in earnings of Japanese companies can be shown to be the result of an improvement in financial position rather than better operating profits. Between March 1980 and March 1989, listed manufacturers' operating profits grew only 2.5 percent a year. Their recurring profits grew 6.5 percent annually, leading to the conclusion that an improved financial position provided 4 percent of annual earnings growth. Between March 1970 and 1980, operating profits and recurring profits grew at approximately the same rate of 8.8 percent a year.

TOUGH ON PREDATORS

The structure of Japan's stock market helps to defend companies from predators by making them too expensive. At the end of 1988, there were 209 Japanese companies among the world's top 500 in terms of market capitalization. It would cost $14 billion to buy Mitsubishi Estate, Japan's major commercial real estate owner, yet it only cost Mitsubishi Estate $846 million to buy half of the Rockefeller Group. It is difficult to justify the purchase of a Japanese firm based on the expected cash flow alone, the usual method for valuing a takeover target, because share prices are so high.

A company's stable shareholders can also block a takeover. Of all listed companies, the top ten shareholders control an average of 37.6 percent of shares outstanding in a given company, and the top twenty control 40.6 percent. Unless an outsider can gain the consent of these shareholders, the target for acquisition is impregnable. Hostile takeovers in Japan, by domestic or foreign firms, are therefore very rare. In 1989, the Finance Ministry revised the takeover rules in Japan, abolishing the requirement that a buyer apply for a takeover bid 10 days in advance and extending the offer beyond the 30-day limit. The requirement to appoint a soliciting agent was also done away with and the threshold for reporting the accumulation of a company's stock lowered from 10 percent to 5 percent. These changes, though useful, do not attack the root of the difficulty in buying and selling companies.

By contrast, it is cheap for a Japanese company to acquire another Japanese company by exchanging shares. The implied cost of Mitsui Bank's acquisition of Taiyo Bank was ¥3.5 trillion. But it was merely effected by exchanging shares, eight of Mitsui Bank for ten of Taiyo Kobe Bank. No company would have paid this amount of money in cash for Taiyo Kobe Bank.

A foreign company is cheap compared with a Japanese company.

The acquisitions of Columbia Pictures by Sony, the Rockefeller Group by Mitsubishi Estate, and Firestone by Bridgestone are therefore perfectly logical. Japanese buyers can raise money cheaply and thus lower the minimum return needed to justify the investment.

The ease with which U.S. companies can be bought has changed the attitudes of Japanese managers toward M&A dramatically. In the early 1980s, the American practice of buying and selling companies was considered shortsighted, but no longer. The new thinking is based on the need to move more of Japan's production overseas and upon the fact that no foreign competitor could afford to buy a Japanese company.

A survey of 623 major listed companies conducted by *Nikkei* in January 1990 found that one-third of those questioned had already engaged in some type of M&A activity and that 60 percent felt it would be necessary in the future. Manufacturing companies, which tend to depend more on overseas markets, have been much more active in acquiring other companies, particularly as a means of diversifying and acquiring technology. Some 43 percent of nonmanufacturers reported that they were looking to buy domestic companies. By contrast, only 14 percent of manufacturers had the same view. It should come as no surprise that there were only two cases of a U.S. company buying a Japanese company in the first half of 1989 and 84 cases of a Japanese company buying a U.S. one.

One symbol of the change in attitudes is that the market jargon is softening. The Japanese words for takeover, *nottori* (which means hi-

Japanese Acquisitions at Home and Abroad
(No. of cases)

	1985	1986	1987	1988	1989
Purely domestic	161	226	219	223	240
Japan buys foreign company	100	204	228	315	405
Foreigner buys Japanese company	26	21	22	17	15
Total acquisitions	287	451	469	555	660
Disclosed amount ($ bn)	NA	3.9	5.5	8.1	9.2

Source: Yamaichi Securities

jack), and divestiture, *miuri* (selling one's body), have given way to then less pejorative acronym "M&A"—although this is applied to both greenmail and conventional merger activity. Executives remain ambivalent; they see the practice as both an opportunity and a threat.

Money is pivotal in the U.S. takeovers: a rich suitor prepared to pay the highest price for a company will usually win his quarry. U.S. courts have ruled that a company must give its shareholders the opportunity to accept or reject a well-financed bid. A company must also hold a fair auction among all bidders instead of simply seeking a friendly deal with a white knight. Japanese companies can therefore exploit the legal framework in the United States to their advantage.

As long as U.S. companies are cheap and Japanese financing costs low, the flow of M&A activity will continue in one direction. Even if a foreign company were able to buy a major Japanese company, the Japanese government would probably step in to thwart such a move.

CHECKS AND BALANCES

In a competitive market, price is the signal of scarcity or abundance. If a stock market is flooded with new equity, share prices should fall, thus raising the cost of finance. This does not happen in Japan because stable shareholders take a large proportion of newly issued shares and keep them off the secondary market. Nor do they clamor for higher dividends, because they themselves are managers of companies which also pay low dividends.

The position for listed Japanese companies could not be better: cheap finance with no strings attached. The implications are worrisome for the United States. There companies do not have the access to cheap finance, so they tend to grow more slowly than in Japan. In 1989, non-residential fixed investment in Japan overtook that of the United States even though the Japanese economy is one-third smaller. Over 20 percent of Japan's GNP went into investment in that year, a level unheard of in a large developed economy. The price of capital would be low in Japan even if the stock market did not exist because of an excess of domestic savings over domestic investment, but Japan's stock market has reduced the cost to almost zero.

The structure of the Japanese stock market also promotes overcapacity in important industries, notably automobiles, semiconductors, and electronics. As financial discipline common to other capitalist countries does not exist in Japan, Japanese companies are prepared to overinvest and to sell their products at marginal cost. MITI often imposes restrictions on domestic capacity expansion and permits price cartels to prevent a bloodbath in the domestic market.

The excess capacity of Japan is therefore exported. In 1985, it was estimated that 58 percent of Japan's automobile industry was dependent on overseas sales, as was 49 percent of its consumer electronics industry, 48 percent of its machinery industry, and 42 percent of its steel industry. The largest proportion of this went to the United States, whose markets are among the most accessible and whose companies are the least protected. When Japan had a small economy, its drive to raise its standard of living through industrial policy could be commended. Now, however, Japan's continued heavy dependence on exports and unwillingness to increase imports has endangered free markets throughout the world.

For the most part, the United States has willingly accepted this inflow of low cost goods into its market based on the view that it is good for consumers and forces U.S. companies to be competitive. No matter how hard U.S. companies try to compete with Japan, however, their higher capital costs continually put them at a disadvantage. Should this situation continue, in the near future it is likely that MITI will be fixing capacity and prices in the U.S. market as well as in Japan. The benefits that U.S. consumers have received for so long may eventually be replaced by the the high prices Japanese consumers have had to endure for the past 40 years.

This is not the only result of a stock market where outside shareholders are ignored. Japanese companies in mature markets are hoarding cash, rather than paying it back to investors in the form of higher dividends, and raising money that they have no use for. In such industries, Japanese companies are using their financing advantage to take over companies in the United States, that by many measures are more efficient and better managed. U.S. companies, meanwhile, are kept out of the Japanese domestic market by the high cost of acquiring a Japanese company as well as the impossibility of overcoming the network of cross-shareholdings. If the United States cannot break into the Japanese market, the trade deficit between the two countries is likely to show little improvement until the day arrives that Japanese companies have moved most of their assembly operations to the United States.

Foreign countries and companies are not alone in their concern. Japan is also affected. The stock market has helped concentrate economic power in the hands of the managers of capital, not the owners of it. Unlisted firms have lost out at the expense of publicly quoted businesses because they cannot tap the same source of cash. It has reinforced Japan as a nation of producers rather than consumers at a time when Japan should be trying to achieve a greater balance between the two. The interests of producers hold sway because of the belief that stronger companies mean higher wages. The result, however, is that the managers of capital are only answerable to themselves and other managers.

The question arises whether this balance of power is appropriate for Japan's size and level of development. If the answer is no, then it suggests that the stock market will have to be changed along with other aspects of Japan. For in order to strengthen consumers' power, the influence of outside shareholders has to be boosted as well—at the expense of the insiders.

Japan's financial strategy also raises the question of whether it is playing by the rules of free-market economies. Much of the success of Japan in world competition has been the result of heavy financial subsidies orchestrated by the government. In the 1950s and 1960s, this was achieved through artificially low interest rates and protection against the financial risks of high leverage. In the 1980s, however, it was the stock market which provided the boost with cheap funds and hidden assets.

Chapter 7

A SHARPER EDGE

The stock market has given Japanese companies an almost unbeatable financial advantage—the ability to raise huge amounts of money at virtually no cost, to retain most of their profits, to increase profits during hard times, and to bolster net worth by means of hidden assets. This has helped Japanese companies to cut their export prices relentlessly just as they did when they relied on cheap loans before the mid-1970s.

Japanese companies were quick to exploit the benefits of their stock market, possibly recognizing that share prices could not go up forever. By the end of the 1980s' bull market, Japanese companies had largely achieved their goal of financial self-sufficiency. Even if the stock market performs miserably in the 1990s, they are in a strong position to continue their rapid expansion overseas and their domestic consolidation. Once their position in key markets is solidified and competitors are driven out, the ability of Japanese equities to perform well in the future will matter less to issuers.

BANKS AND THE BIS

The massive amounts of equity capital the banks raised in 1987–89 shows the degree to which Japan's stock market is underestimated in the West. The story of Japanese banks' rise to power should begin not in Tokyo but in Basel, Switzerland, the location of the Bank for International Settlements (BIS), the organization which acts as banker to the world's main central banks.

The BIS is responsible not only for the smooth flow of payments between central banks, but for regulating how commercial banks borrow and lend across borders, beyond the jurisdiction of individual monetary authorities. In the decade that followed the first oil shock of 1973, the BIS had grown increasingly concerned about the risky loans made by commercial banks to developing countries. To safeguard the soundness of the international banking system, it sought commitment among its member countries to raise the ratio of capital to assets for all commercial banks conducting cross-border lending. Countries tightened their banks' regulations, but they did so with no uniformity. Japanese banks were required by the Ministry of Finance to have capital to back only 4 percent of assets by 1990, whereas the standard set by the Federal Reserve Board in the United States was 6 percent.

A lower capital-asset ratio meant more leverage: Japanese banks could hold assets to a level 25 times their capital base, compared with 16 times in the United States. This leverage meant that lower lending spreads—the gap between the cost of funds and the rate charged to the borrower—could give the same return on equity. Japanese banks could also lend a greater amount of moray than their overseas competitors.

Ever since the end of World War II, Japanese banks have expanded their assets at the expense of profits. Six of the largest banking institutions were at the center of rapidly growing industrial groups. Banks were eager to consolidate their position within each *keiretsu*, and loans were the cheapest form of finance. For much of the time, the big bankers acted as quasi-venture capitalists, lending money at low interest rates to new businesses and taking an equity stake in return. In this sense, banks were little different from the companies they served, relying on a high leverage in their balance sheet to maximize market share. This was encouraged by the Ministry of Finance.

Old habits die hard. When Japanese banks began to expand abroad in the late 1970s, they took their loose capital regulations with them. At a time when developing nations found themselves incapable of paying back loans, U.S. banks were particularly

Banks' International Assets
($ bn)

	1984	Share (%)	1988	Share (%)
Japan	518	23	1,756	38
United States	595	26	675	15
France	201	9	384	8
West Germany	143	6	354	8
United Kingdom	169	8	239	5
Switzerland	83	4	182	4
Italy	91	4	201	4
Others	451	20	807	18
TOTAL	2,249	100	4,598	100

Source: "International Banking and Financial Market Development," BIS

The World's Largest Banks

1981	Assets ($ bn)	1988	Assets ($ bn)
Citicorp (US)	110	Dai-Ichi Kangyo Bank (J)	353
Bank of America (US)	107	Sumitomo Bank (J)	335
Credit Agricole (FR)	107	Fuji Bank (J)	328
Banque Nationale de Paris (FR)	106	Mitsubishi Bank (J)	318
		Sanwa Bank (J)	307
Credit Lyonnais (FR)	99	IBJ (J)	262
Societe Generale (FR)	91	Norin Chukin (J)	232
Barclays (UK)	89	Credit Agricole (FR)	214
Deutsche Bank (FRG)	88	Tokai Bank (J)	214
National Westminster (UK)	82	Mitsubishi Trust (J)	206
Dai-Ichi Kangyo Bank (J)	80	Citicorp (US)	204
Chase Manhattan (US)	76	Banque Nationale de Paris (FR)	197
Fuji Bank (J)	70		
Sumitomo Bank (J)	69	Mitsui Bank (J)	196
Sanwa Bank (J)	64	Barclays (UK)	189
Dresdner Bank (FRG)	63	Sumitomo Trust (J)	181

Source: *The Banker*

vulnerable. Their capital base heavily damaged, U.S. banks were forced to keep spreads high. This allowed Japanese banks to undercut the competition. By 1988, Japanese banks had captured 38 percent of all international lending, 12 percent of the U.S. banking market, and 23 percent of the U.K. banking market.

Trade friction ensued. Unhappy with the apparent inequities, the central banks of several countries, particularly the United States and Britain, sought to level the playing field. After two years of negotiation, agreement was reached in July 1988 on an international equity ratio standard. All international banks would be required to maintain enough equity to cover at least 8 percent of risk-weighted assets from 1993. This was double the level Japanese banks had to comply with before. The severity of this new requirement was mitigated,

Capital Base of Japanese Banks
(March 1990)

	Shareholders equity (¥)	Hidden assets (¥)	BIS equity ratio (%)	BIS ratio without HA (%)
Dai-Ichi Kangyo Bank	1,750	3,346	8.3	4.5
Sumitomo Bank	1,937	2,903	8.4	5.0
Fuji Bank	1,753	3,107	8.3	4.6
Mitsubishi Bank	1,601	3,382	8.4	4.3
Sanwa Bank	1,668	3,099	8.5	4.6
Tokai Bank	964	2,485	7.8	3.9
Taiyo Kobe Mitsui Bank	1,489	4,194	7.0	3.5
Bank of Tokyo	775	1,145	8.0	4.8
Kyowa Bank	473	1,514	8.8	4.4
Daiwa Bank	523	1,642	8.4	4.2
Saitama Bank	451	848	8.3	4.5
Hokkaido Takushoku Bank	320	711	8.3	4.2
Industrial Bank of Japan	1,205	4,120	7.8	3.9
Long-Term Credit Bank	969	2,990	8.2	4.1
Nippon Credit Bank	457	1,520	7.3	3.7

however, by the allowance that 45 percent of unrealized capital gains in stock portfolios could be counted toward banks' equity, on the condition that unrealized gains do not contribute more to the BIS equity ratio than do normal shareholders' equity. That is to say, for a bank with an 8 percent equity ratio, 4 percent or less could come from unrealized capital gains.

This stipulation cleared the way for Japan's stock market to help Japanese banks. Unlike U.S. commercial banks, which are not allowed to hold shares in other companies, Japanese banks have for decades accumulated shares in the firms they have made loans to. And their unrealized profits on these stocks have risen with each uptick of the stock market. Negotiators in the BIS agreement were aware of this, but the Japanese side prevailed.

The Japanese had actually pressed for inclusion of 70 percent of paper profits in the new equity ratio on the ground that the stock market had never fallen much more than 30 percent at any one time. The Bank of England was said to have argued strongly against any hidden share profits. The value of hidden assets can fluctuate sharply and share prices can drop in anticipation of a bank having to sell its holdings to cover a big loan default. Why allow even 45 percent to be counted toward banks' equity ratio? The reasoning was impeccable, but in this case, with the 45 percent agreed upon, financial might proved to be right.

Bank Shares for Sale

Japan's banks sat on well-padded reserves, but in order to meet the BIS ratio without retarding growth in their assets, there was the immediate need for funds. This is where the stock market came in useful again—by absorbing an unprecedented amount of new issues.

Before international pressure forced them to raise capital in a hurry, Japanese banks were not big equity issuers. When money was needed in the past, they relied on the safer method of rights issues, which left them indifferent to the market value of their shares. In fact until 1983, the market considered bank shares the equivalent of bonds, with a fixed price and yield. Although they comprised 15 percent of the stock market's entire capitalization, their shares were extremely illiquid. This illiquidity, coupled with a lackluster business performance, caused outside investors to shun bank shares. Securities companies discouraged orders in bank shares because banks insisted on knowing the identities of the buyer and seller, and their purpose. Banks, in effect, controlled their share price. In 1978, the Industrial Bank of Japan's share price hit a high of ¥253 and a low of ¥248. In 1982–83, Sumitomo Bank's share price traded within a range of ¥495 to ¥511, while Fuji Bank traded between ¥490 and ¥510.

By the early 1980s, when the need to raise money in the stock market became obvious, banks moved to lift their market price so as to issue equity at the cheapest rate. On one day in January 1984, the share price of Sumitomo Bank—the most admired of the city banks—jumped by ¥100, a rise of 20 percent. The following day, the prices of the other major banks' stocks also jumped ¥100. This was extraordinary. For the previous two years, bank shares had barely budged. By the end of 1984, Sumitomo Bank shares were priced at ¥1,830, and shares of other banks had risen at a similar rate. In early 1987, bank share prices peaked at a level 10 times higher than they were in January 1984.

Bank stocks would not have risen so quickly if investors did not have reason to think them undervalued. Sure enough, bank profits began to rise sharply after 1986. Interest rates were falling, improving the banks' bottom line considerably as funding costs declined faster than revenues. Net profits for the 12 city banks rose by 83 percent to ¥920 billion between fiscal 1984 and fiscal 1987. The rise in their share prices, however, far exceeded this increase in profits. At the end of 1989, city bank shares carried an average PER of 61, and if one excludes the contribution to earnings from the sale of equities or gains from *tokkin* funds, their PER was 514. The elite Industrial Bank of Japan sold for 166 times its earnings.

With their share prices inflated, the banks proceeded with a full-scale program of equity financings. The city banks alone raised ¥5.6 trillion in 1986–89, more than any other industry. The bank's pattern of raising money followed the well-defined hierarchical order of the industry. The city banks issued shares first, usually starting with Sumitomo Bank; then came the regional banks. The same amount of funds tended to be raised by each bank each year, so as not to fall

Fuji Bank, Sumitomo Bank

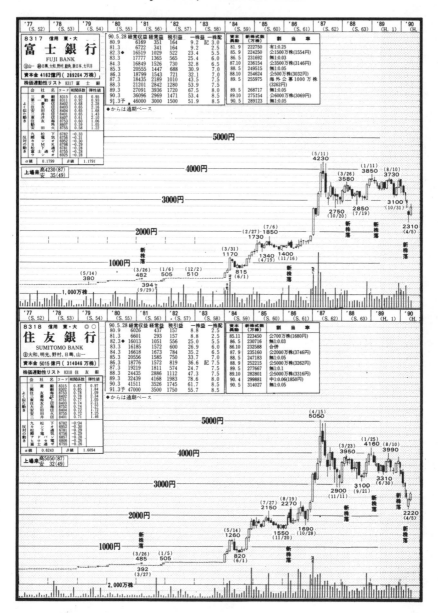

Source: Tsukiashi shu, vol. 894 (Tokyo: Golden Chart Company, June 1990); reprinted by permission of the publisher

behind one's competitors. Only IBJ broke the pattern. Rather than have an underwriter sell its shares to the public, it chose to have two massive rights offerings instead, raising ¥496 billion.

This ability to raise capital derives from the banks' central position in the Japanese economy, particularly within the system of corporate cross-shareholdings. Although companies have grown less dependent on banks for finance, banks remain a vital link between companies in their respective groups and are consequently an invaluable source of business information. Banks were counted on to help out in the past when the going got tough; then it was the turn of the banks' major borrowers to help the banks. After the banks increased their capital base, they returned the favor to their clients and bought their new equity issues. The city banks increased their investment in equities from ¥6.1 trillion in March 1985 to ¥17.2 trillion by March 1990. Mutual support has paid dividends for all concerned.

Banks have also sold some of their shareholdings so that they could count the profit in their BIS equity ratio. In the year ending

Equity Financing by Major Banks
(¥ bn)

	1985	86	87	88	89	TOTAL
Dai-Ichi Kangyo Bank	53	0	126	314	357	851
Sanwa Bank	58	0	178	195	343	774
Fuji Bank	60	0	178	252	249	738
Mitsubishi Bank	51	0	173	268	233	724
Sumitomo Bank	51	0	75	288	282	696
Taiyo Kobe Mitsui Bank	34	28	70	256	222	611
IBJ	0	0	218	279	0	496
Bank of Tokyo	47	0	40	163	151	401
Tokai Bank	0	36	0	181	153	369
Daiwa Bank	0	66	10	90	99	265
Kyowa Bank	0	0	78	78	55	211
Hokkaido Takushoku Bank	8	0	45	55	62	170
Saitama Bank	16	0	44	60	49	168
TOTAL	377	130	1,234	2,478	2,256	6,475

Note: Total of public offerings, rights offerings, CBs

March 1990, net gains from sales of equity holdings amounted to ¥1.8 trillion for the city banks or 85 percent of their recurring profits. This in turn allowed them to count more hidden assets toward their overall capital base.

In order to avoid disturbing their stable shareholdings, the banks repurchased most of the shares they had sold. From a financial standpoint, this represented a loss in the form of higher corporate taxes. The banks were asked by the Finance Ministry in September 1989 to slow down the pace of their sales and to disclose in their financial statements the extent of profits from sales of equities and *tokkin* accounts. This showed that in March 1990, the city banks had ¥2.8 trillion in *tokkin* funds, and the three long-term credit banks ¥1.1 trillion.

Hidden assets also helped the banks to offset the impact of the less developed country (LDC) debt crisis. Japan had the second-largest exposure, after the United States, to heavily indebted countries, but it was insignificant in relation to the value of their hidden assets. Bank of Tokyo, the bank most exposed to the LDC debt crisis, had ¥573 billion in loans outstanding versus hidden assets of ¥1.2 trillion.

The fortunes of U.S. banks have waned as Japan's have flourished. While Japanese banks raised fresh capital in the market, U.S. banks have been forced to cut back and sell assets—to the Japanese. Manufacturers Hanover Trust sold 60 percent of its most valuable asset, CIT, to Dai-Ichi Kangyo Bank for $1.3 billion to raise its equity base. Citicorp sold a half share of its New York headquarters building to a Japanese life insurer. And Bank of America received a capital injection from Japanese financial institutions in 1987 to help it restructure.

The stock market crash in early 1990 has reversed the fortunes of the Japanese banks. They were the largest beneficiaries of the 1980s' bull market, and they were the big losers from the market's fall. The banks are heavily dependent on the market to maintain their growth plans, unlike industrial companies which can continue business as usual despite turbulence in the stock market. Equity financings and hidden assets have been needed to support the growth of the banks' assets, while *tokkin* profits and equity sales hid their low profitability.

New equity offerings by the banks were put on hold in early 1990 and were expected to be held up until their share prices recovered to the level of their previous issues. The value of their hidden assets had shrunk as well. The stock market would have had to fall by more than one-third from its peak at the end of 1989 to cause banks' equity ratios to drop below the 8 percent level required by the BIS. An even bigger decline in the stock market would force the banks to reduce their assets in order to conform with BIS rules. This would affect overseas loans first because they yield least. Around 25–35 percent of the assets of major Japanese banks are non-yen denominated, mostly in U.S. dollars. Half of this is in the form of interbank deposits—borrowing from one bank to lend to another—and one-third in U.S. Treasury bonds and convertible bonds. Sales of these assets would probably drive up U.S. interest rates.

MICROCHIPS AND THE MARKET

The semiconductor industry has become a symbol of the growth of Japan's economic power and of the business decline of the United States. Semiconductors are at the heart of the electronics industry, and leadership in semiconductor production is viewed on both sides of the Pacific as a measure of virility. The stock market played an important part in helping Japanese companies drive all but two U.S. semiconductor makers out of the market for memory chips.

Until the 1980s, U.S. companies were the undisputed leaders of the semiconductor industry. In 1975, MITI organized Japan's major computer makers—such as Hitachi, Toshiba, and NEC—into a consortium, with the aim of developing the next generation of microchips and of leap-frogging U.S. competitors. At that time, 4-kilobit random access memory (RAM) chips were under mass production. These chips were capable of storing 4,000 bits of information of a single piece of silicon. The next generation of chips, 16K RAM, was expected shortly. MITI set 1980 as the date by which Japan would beat the United States to production of the 64K RAM.

To ensure success, the Japanese domestic market was almost completely closed to U.S. semiconductor makers, and Japanese producers were granted special subsidies. Japanese chip makers introduced their first 16K RAMs in 1978–79, three years later than in the United States, yet by cutting their prices they were quickly able to take a 40 percent share of the world market.

In 1980, Japanese companies shipped their first commercial samples of 64K RAMs, beating production in the United States by six months. Due to massive Japanese investment and ruthless price cutting, all but two U.S. chip producers were driven out of the market. In late 1984, the next generation of 256K RAM chips flooded the U.S. market. Japan's excess production capacity and an attendant slump in the U.S. computer industry caused prices to plummet even faster than for 64K RAMs. Although every Japanese chip maker was losing money, they continued doggedly to invest. Before long, Japan controlled 90 percent of the global RAM market as their U.S. competitors scaled back.

By 1987, with the market securely in Japanese hands, a recovery in demand helped push up prices for microchips. Agreements with the United States and the European Community ensured that prices

Investment in Semiconductor Plant and Equipment

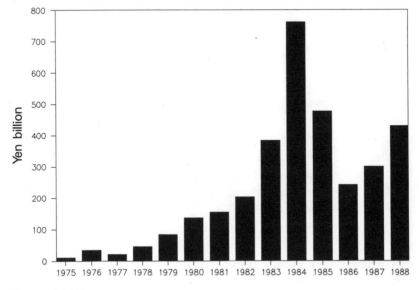

Source: MITI

would not fall through the floor. Japanese semiconductor makers have been reporting profits since the second half of 1987. Performance in 1988 improved further, owing to a rise in capacity-utilization rates and the introduction of high-priced 1-megabit dynamic random-access memories (DRAMs).

Japan's success was largely the result of the financial advantages its companies enjoyed over their U.S. competitors. The semiconductor industry is capital-intensive. Because raw material costs are negligible, production costs fall rapidly as total output increases. Growth in market share is therefore critical for long-term success. Since memory chips are a commodity, the main way to compete is on price. This has meant that the companies that win are likely to be those that are best financed. Thanks to Japan's stock market, those companies are Japanese.

Unlike their U.S. competitors, which were independent producers specializing in semiconductors, all of the Japanese companies designated to lead the drive into the semiconductor industry were large electronics companies as well as core members of their *keiretsu*. NEC was from the Sumitomo *keiretsu*, Toshiba from the Mitsui *keiretsu*, Mitsubishi Electric from the Mitsubishi *keiretsu*, Hitachi from the Sanwa *keiretsu*, and Fujitsu from the Dai-Ichi Kangyo *keiretsu*. Each of these companies also leads its own industrial group.

As the champions of their respective *keiretsu*, these companies could depend on related companies to purchase their products and to supply the necessary support equipment and materials. The main bank of each company stood by to help, providing cheap loans for research and development. Hidden assets in equity holdings and real estate were a cushion for the companies and also reduced the risk exposure of the banks. And fellow companies in a *keiretsu* could be counted on to purchase their numerous equity financings in the 1980s. Stable shareholders wanted only to see a long-term improvement in the performance of the company whose shares they held, so a rapid return on investment was unnecessary. Heavy investment and severe price cutting could therefore be sustained for as long as required to increase market share.

Contrast this to the circumstances facing their U.S. competitors: independent companies without a tight network of helpful companies and no bank to offer the equivalent of venture capital. Nor would they have hidden assets to soften the blow. And unlike in Japan, the American market was wide open.

Once it was clear, from about 1980, that Japanese firms could succeed in the semiconductor industry, they began to tap the equity market for ever larger amounts of money. In 1981–88, the five largest semiconductor producers raised a total of ¥2.36 trillion through the equity market. The combined consolidated operating profits of the five largest Japanese semiconductor makers only grew from ¥656 billion in fiscal year 1980 to ¥1.2 trillion in fiscal year 1988, but their market capitalization increased from ¥2.7 trillion to ¥16.8 trillion over the same period. The share price of Hitachi went up 523 percent, and NEC's rose 350 percent. Even if these companies had not been able to tap the equity market, it is possible they might still have been successful. But it is also true that without equity financings their debt burden would have increased—to a combined total of ¥142 billion in annual interest payments.

The United States must depend on Japan for memory chips, now that the market is dominated by Japanese companies. This was evident in the battering that U.S. computer makers took in 1988 and early 1989 when Japanese suppliers failed to meet their requirements for 1-megabit RAMs, of which Japan supplies 80 percent of the market. The shortage of chips led to a quadrupling of prices and forced American computer companies to raise their own prices and cut back production. Consequently, profits of Japanese chip makers surged, as the long-term vision of Japan's stock market began to materialize.

For a brief period in 1989, it appeared that U.S. companies were finally responding to the Japanese challenge. IBM and AT&T, the two biggest computer companies in the United States, together with three of America's largest chip makers proposed the creation of U.S. Memories. The new enterprise would vertically integrate suppliers and users and produce DRAMs in huge quantities, aiming to capture 7–10 percent of the world market by the mid-1990s. U.S. Memories would be free from the American preoccupation with profits and would focus on long-term growth. The original business plan for the company called for an investment of $500 million to build four fabrication lines over four years that would produce 4-megabit and

Equity Financings by Semiconductor Producers

	Amount	Type of issue
Hitachi		
1981	$150 million	Convertible bond
1982	¥29 billion	Public offering
1984	¥80 billion	Convertible bond
1985	¥100 billion	Convertible bond
1987	¥120 billion	Convertible bond
1988	¥120 billion	Convertible bond
1989	¥250 billion	Convertible bond
Toshiba		
1981	¥81.6 billion	Public offering
1983	¥30 billion	Convertible bond
	SF200 million	Convertible bond
1984	¥50 billion	Convertible bond
	SF200 million	Convertible bond
1985	¥80 billion	Convertible bond
1987	¥100 billion	Convertible bond
1989	¥250 billion	Convertible bond
	$1.2 billion	Warrant bond
NEC		
1981	£30 million	Convertible bond
1982	¥49.3 billion	Public offering
	$80 million	Convertible bond
1983	SF250 million	Convertible bond
	¥80 billion	Convertible bond
1984	¥50 billion	Convertible bond
	¥62.7 billion	Public offering
	$150 million	Convertible bond
1986	¥60 billion	Convertible bond
1987	¥100 billion	Convertible bond
1988	¥120 billion	Convertible bond
1989	$700 million	Warrant bond
Mitsubishi Electric		
1981	$80 million	Convertible bond
1982	¥30 billion	Convertible bond

1983	$100 million	Convertible bond
	SF15 million	Convertible bond
1984	SF200 million	Convertible bond
	¥50 billion	Convertible bond
1985	¥39 billion	Public offering
	$100 million	Convertible bond
1988	$300 million	Warrant bond
	¥80 billion	Convertible bond
1989	$800 million	Warrant bond

Fujitsu

1981	$80 million	Convertible bond
1982	SF30 million	European Depository Receipt
	¥36.3 billion	Public offering
1983	¥40 billion	Convertible bond
	SF250 million	Convertible bond
1984	¥60.7 billion	Convertible bond
	SF150 million	Convertible bond
	$180 million	Convertible bond
1985	DM300 million	Convertible bond
	SF400 million	Convertible bond
	¥60 billion	Convertible bond
1986	$200 million	Warrant bond
1987	$300 million	Warrant bond
1988	$500 million	Warrant bond
1989	¥80 billion	Convertible bond

Source: *Shikiho* (Tokyo: Toyo Keizai, summer 1990)

16-megabit chips, based on technology licensed from IBM. The computer makers would be required to buy a minimum of 20 percent of their DRAMs from the venture.

However, the idea was abandoned in early January 1990. Most of the computer makers were unwilling to make the financial and purchasing commitments. By mid-1989, fears of a chip shortage were allayed by a glut and the consortium members wanted a quick return on their investment.

While U.S. Memories was folding, the major Japanese chip

makers were reducing chip production because of low prices and a plan to switch to more advanced chips. Now that the market is controlled by Japan, the gluts and rampant price cutting of the early 1980s are unlikely to reappear. From now on competition will be based on technology, quality, and service—not price—just as it is in virtually every Japanese domestic industry.

In the absence of foreign competition, Japanese semiconductor makers can improve their profitability. Toshiba generates about 45 percent of its profits from integrated circuits and Hitachi 35 percent. There is little to be gained by Japanese companies competing among themselves on price, as none of them would be forced by a lack of resources to drop out of the market.

THE NEW BIG THREE

If the banks and chip makers appear formidable, then the Japanese automobile manufacturers look unstoppable—particularly when viewed from the other side of the Pacific. Japan's motor vehicle exports totalled ¥56.6 trillion in 1988, representing 23 percent of Japan's total exports. Nearly half of these vehicles went to the United States. As the Japanese car firms gear up to produce cars abroad, American car manufacturers have seen that their call to curb automobile imports into the United States has merely postponed the day of reckoning. Their deadliest rivals are now in their backyard.

Japanese automakers have succeeded so well against their U.S. rivals that Toyota, Nissan, and Honda are being proclaimed by the Tokyo press as the "new Big Three." Japan's share of the U.S. automobile market has grown from 21 percent in 1983 to 26 percent in 1989. Over the same period, General Motors' share of its own domestic market has fallen from 44 percent to 36 percent, a slide that is continuing. There are a number of reasons for the success of the Japanese automakers, such as rapid new model introductions, superior engineering, attention to quality, and low prices. There are also a number of reasons for the failure of the U.S. automobile industry, such as poor workmanship, slow model changes, and too great an emphasis on short-term profitability.

Japanese car makers are less dependent on the stock market than

League Table of Automakers in 1988

	No. of vehicles (000)	Sales ($ bn)	Net income ($ mn)	Employees (000)
General Motors	5,147	121	4,856	766
Toyota	3,969	51	2,315	86
Ford	3,329	92	5,300	358
Nissan	2,164	29	463	108
Fiat	2,035	34	2,325	277
Peugeot	2,018	23	1,486	158
Volkswagen	1,880	34	420	252
Chrysler	1,718	36	1,050	130
Renault	1,681	27	1,497	182
Honda	1,293	22	820	58

Source: *Analysis of Japanese Industries for Investors* (Tokyo: Nikko Research Center, 1990)

Comparison of Performance

	Japanese Big Three	American Big Three
New model development speed	24 months	36–48 months
Development costs	$1–1.5 billion	$3.2–4 billion
Capital costs	0–2%	9–11%
Plant operating rates	85–105%	70–75%
Vehicles per employee	80–105	50–85
Years between model changes	4 years	5–6 years
Outside sourcing of parts	70%	40%

Source: *Nikkei Business*

the banks and the semiconductor companies, but the market has still been important. It has provided cheap funds and *zaiteku* profits. It has also enabled automakers to control their parts suppliers. And it has helped finance a glut of capacity, both in Japan and in the United States.

How Nissan Survived the Strong Yen

Heavily dependent on exports, Japanese car companies bore the brunt of the rise in the yen, which doubled in value against the dollar in 1985–88. In 1986, 59 percent of the 7.8 million motor vehicles produced in Japan were shipped abroad, but instead of raising export prices to reflect the yen's strength, automakers kept prices steady to hold on to their overseas market share. Operating profits took a beating at all three firms: Toyota's consolidated operating profits fell 48 percent in 1985–87, Nissan's profits went from ¥237 billion to a loss of ¥31 billion, and Honda's profits fell 43 percent. But their share prices hardly suffered at all.

One reason the market was so forgiving and generous was that automakers' recurring profits were considerably better than their operating income. This sleight of hand was achieved by dipping into the companies' war chest of securities to realize some of the capital gains made over the years. Nissan's operations were affected particularly harshly by the yen's strength: the parent company's operating profits fell from ¥71 billion to a loss of ¥8 billion. But recurring profits, which include earnings from *zaiteku*, only fell from ¥148 billion to ¥118 billion. Once Nissan's operating profits began to recover in the middle of 1987, the stock market rewarded it by more than doubling its share price in just over a year. Between January 1987 and June 1989, in fact, the share price tripled.

For these automakers, it was crucial to avoid a fall in their share price because they were tapping the capital market at home and abroad for funds. Keeping their prices up helped to ensure that the issues received a good reception from investors. Honda went to the market five times in 1985–89, Toyota four times, and Nissan three.

Timing was important too, as Nissan and Toyota were just beginning to invest overseas. Honda was in a different position, having embarked on overseas expansion as early as 1978. By the time its larger Japanese competitors had set up their first factory in the United States, Honda was pursuing its strategy of overtaking Chrysler on the latter's home turf.

The Stock Market As Vertical Integrator

As well as providing car companies with a source of finance—both from *zaiteku* and securities issues—Japan's stock market has brought the assembler and its component suppliers together through stable shareholdings. Component manufacturers are obliged to supply their output on time and at the right price to companies that hold their shares. Conversely, assemblers are committed to steady purchases over the years, to collaborate on research and design of car parts, and to provide assistance in upgrading the facilities of component producers.

These ties do not just extend to and from parts makers and final assemblers, but also exist among the assemblers themselves. Toyota and Nissan have traditionally relied on their affiliates, Daihatsu and Fuji Heavy Industries (Subaru) respectively, for the production of the smallest cars in their model ranges. When demand outstrips their capacity, Toyota and Nissan farmed out production of larger cars to their affiliates in order to meet demand.

Of the 46 manufacturers of automobile parts listed on the TSE, 37 have at least one carmaker among their main shareholders. In many cases, these companies behave like subsidiaries, even though the nominal shareholding by the "parent" may be a lot less than 50 percent. Toyota Auto Body, Nissan Shatai, and Kanto Auto Works are merely former factories established as separate companies after the war. Beyond the car industry itself, the "new Big Three" have extended their reach, through share stakes, into every relevant business, from machine tool companies to trading firms. Each represents an industrial group of its own.

Cross-shareholdings denote mutual obligations, but this does not imply that the members of the groups are equals. The conglomerates are hierarchical, often ruthlessly so, with the car assemblers themselves at the top of the pyramid. During a recession, it is the components makers and subcontractors which must take up the slack, laying off workers until demand picks up again. Only the biggest companies can afford to employ their staff "for life." The system of "just-in-time" inventory control, made famous by Toyota, is another example of how the cross-holdings work. The system aims to ensure that components arrive when the assembler needs them, but this is often achieved by shifting the burden of large inventories onto the shoulders of the subcontractors.

Keiretsu of the Automakers

		% owned by *keiretsu* leader
TOYOTA MOTOR		
Kanto Auto Works	Assembler of Toyota's small cars	49.0
Toyota Auto Body	Car assembler	40.7
Toyota Gosei	Rubber and plastic products	40.4
Jeco	Car clocks	34.2
Kyowa Leather	Synthetic leather for upholstery	33.5
Trinity Industrial	Painting plants and equipment	30.2
Aisan Industry	Carburetors	30.1
Tokai Rika	Switches and seat belts	29.5
Tokyo Sintered Metal	Sintered machinery parts	25.0
Chuo Spring	Chassis springs	24.0
Toyota Automatic Loom	Industrial machinery, car assembly	23.4
Nippondenso	Car electronics	22.9
Aisin Seiki	Transmissions, clutches, brakes	21.7
Toyota Tsusho	Trading arm of Toyota Group	21.3
Aichi Steel Works	Rolled steel products	21.3
Toyoda Machine Works	Machine tools, automobile parts	21.2
Koyo Seiko	Bearings and steerings	20.5
Koito Mfg.	Automobile lighting	19.0
Daihatsu Motor	Minicars, small passenger cars	14.0
Futaba Industrial	Automobile mufflers	13.4
Akebono Brake Ind.	Disc brakes	13.1
Shiroki Corp.	Door sashes, moldings	11.5
Hino Motors	Truck manufacturer	10.1
Toyoda Boshoku	Filters, interior materials	8.9
Kayaba Industry	Hydraulic shock absorbers	8.8
Ichiko Industry	Lamps, mirrors	6.2

Owari Precise Products	Forged automobile parts	5.2
Chuo Malleable Iron	Malleable iron parts for cars	5.1
Toyo Radiator	Automobile ratiators	4.7
NOK	Car oil seals	4.0

NISSAN MOTOR

Kiriu Machine Mfg.	Automobile parts	59.3
Tokyo Sokuhan	Automobile parts	49.0
Ikeda Bussan	Automobile seats and interiors	43.0
Nissan Shatai	Assembles Nissan cars	42.5
Nissan Diesel	Truck and bus manufacturer	40.2
Shin Nippon Forging	Precision forged parts	34.8
Fuji Tekko	Transmissions	34.1
Daikin Mfg.	Automobile clutches	33.5
Calsonic	Radiators, heaters, air conditioners	33.2
Kanto Seiki	Car meters and electronic parts	31.5
Atsugi Unisia	Engine and transmission parts	29.6
Kinugawa Rubber Ind.	Antivibration rubber for engine mounts	25.3
Hashimoto Forming Ind.	Automobile trim	24.8
Kasai Kogyo	Door interior products	24.4
Fuji Kiko	Automobile parts	23.8
Aichi Machine Ind.	Auto assembler, engines	23.8
Jidosha Denki Kogyo	Motors and control equipment	23.8
Nippon Carbureter	Automobile carburetors	23.7
Tachi-S	Car seats	20.9
Ichikoh Industries	Lamps, mirrors	20.7
Tochigi Fuji Industrial	Differential gear locks	20.2
Akebono Brake Ind.	Disc brakes	13.3
Clarion	Car audio equipment	12.7
Diesel Kiki	Fuel injection pumps, air conditioners	10.5

Sanoh Industrial	Automobile parts	9.6
Kayaba Industry	Hydraulic shock absorbers	8.4
Koito	Automobile lighting	5.9
Shin-Kobe Electric	Car batteries	3.9
HONDA MOTOR		
Keihin Seiki Mfg.	Carburetors and injectors	39.7
Showa Manufacturing	Shock absorbers	29.8
Nippon Seiki	Automotive instruments	7.3
Mitsuba Electric Mfg.	Fuel pumps, wiper motors, starters	5.4

Source: *Shikiho* (Tokyo: Toyo Keizai, summer 1990)

Because of their control over their parts suppliers, the "new Big Three" are able to squeeze profits ruthlessly from them. As a group, Japan's autoparts makers are among the least profitable of listed companies. Toyota had a 6 percent operating profit margin in 1989, while Toyota Auto Body and Kanto Auto Works had a 1.8 percent margin. The smaller companies suffer most because they have no alternative but to supply a single automaker.

Protecting Their Own

The system may be highly disciplined, even paternalistic, but it has proven to be very effective in repelling unwanted outsiders, whether Japanese or not. In April 1989, an affiliate of Toyota which manufactured car headlamps found that it had a stranger in its midst—none other than the U.S. oil raider, T. Boone Pickens. His merchant bank, Boone Co., acquired 20.2 percent of Koito, making him the largest shareholder, slightly ahead of Toyota with 19.9 percent. Nissan was another sizable shareholder with a 5.9 percent stake.

Many jumped to the conclusion that this was an attempt by Pickens to "greenmail" Koito, by cornering a large proportion of the company's stock and forcing friendly shareholders to buy out the greenmailer at a higher price than the shares cost. It was a charge Pickens strongly denied; he was there for the long term, he said. Suspicions were aroused when it was learned that Pickens had bought his shares in a block from Azabu Motors, which is run by a well-known greenmailer, Kitaro Watanabe, a former motorcycle mechanic who built up a profitable car business and then bought several hotels in Hawaii.

If the motivation had been to make a quick profit, Koito seemed a tempting target because Toyota had bought out a greenmailer once before, in April 1987, when a speculative group acquired 17 million shares in Toyota Automatic Loom, the original parent company of the car giant. The greenmailing group made a profit of ¥20 billion from the deal. Koito does not have the same historical ties with Toyota as does the textile machinery maker, but it is a longstanding supplier of components.

Koito's share price began rising in July 1987, from ¥510 to a peak of ¥5,470, just before the Pickens purchase became known. Toyota refused to buy him out, saying that "to buy the shares at a price that is higher than their true worth would be a betrayal to our shareholders." This was an extraordinary statement for a company not noted for its concern toward outside stockholders. Koito was far from undervalued at the time, with a PER of 250.

Despite increasing his stake later to 26 percent at a total cost of ¥170 billion, Pickens failed to exert any control over Koito's management. He asked for directorships for himself and three others. This was rejected at the annual general meeting in June 1989. He asked the court to force Koito to disclose more financial information, but this too was turned down. In November 1989, Koito's board rejected a request to raise its interim dividend from ¥4 to ¥7.

Although Pickens was the largest individual shareholder, Toyota and five other stable shareholders controlled 63 percent of the company. The car firm has supplied Koito's president, a vice-president, and one director. But the relationship goes much deeper than that. According to the Pickens camp, Toyota effectively controls the price, the delivery time, and, thus, the profits of Koito. If Koito makes too much profit in one year, it will be asked to reduce it in the next period by discounting its sales—hence, the low dividend.

Even if Pickens were to succeed in gaining board representation, Toyota could always respond by switching its orders to rival headlamp makers, which are also caught in the web of cross-shareholdings woven by the automakers. The experience of T. Boone

Pickens illustrates the fact that investors other than the big, stable shareholders have no influence in Japan. After Koito's annual meeting, Pickens said, "When you buy a stock in a company, you're one of the owners. You don't have to work your way in with the management; the management has to work its way in with you. You're the owner, they're the employee."

Feeding Automobile Overcapacity

The most dangerous aspect of the stock market is that it imposes very little financial discipline on the automakers and permits them to invest as much as they can in new automobile production capacity. Despite their high profitability, Japanese automakers are not required to pay out much of their earnings in the form of dividends to shareholders, allowing them to retain more for investment. The worst offender is Toyota, which paid out a mere 16 percent of its income as dividends in 1989, even when it had no better use for the funds than to deposit them in a bank. Nissan's payout ratio was higher at 30 percent, though this was primarily because its earnings had dropped, while Honda's was 15 percent. General Motors, in contrast, paid out 47 percent of its earnings, Chrysler paid out 77 percent, and Ford 36 percent. The fact that profits are not important to share prices suggests that high depreciation charges are of little concern, even though they might reduce current profits. All the main car companies can tap the stock market regularly for low-cost funds. Toyota raised ¥913 billion from the equity market between 1981 and 1989, while returning only ¥318 billion in the form of dividends. The net result is chronic overinvestment by the industry, particularly since the mid-1970s when growth in demand for vehicles in the domestic market slowed.

Japanese automakers have less flexibility in controlling the output of their factories than their U.S. counterparts, since their longstanding labor practices prevent them from laying off or firing full-time workers. Labor therefore represents a fixed cost. Moreover, none of the automakers have diversified sufficiently into unrelated sectors to keep redundant employees gainfully working during periods of weak demand. Thus, these companies are compelled to maintain high-capacity utilization rates. During periods of weak automobile demand in the domestic market, the classic response of these companies has been ruthless price competition and a high volume of exports to overseas markets in order to maintain capacity utilization rates. Domestic sales of automobiles generate little in the way of profits except during periods of strong demand.

Because of the appreciation of the yen since 1985 and growing protectionism in overseas markets, the export option for Japanese companies has been curtailed. Instead of facing the fact that their markets are maturing, the Japanese automakers are merely shifting their investment to overseas markets, particularly the United States and Europe.

These factories are convenient because they are mainly assembling operations. They therefore help to maintain domestic capacity utilization rates until they are forced to raise local content. Moreover, profits from overseas operations can offset low domestic earnings, because margins on automobile sales in the United States are much higher than in Japan owing to the pricing umbrella of General Motors, Ford, and Chrysler. The managers of Japanese car companies continue to want to expand their market share.

Despite signs of a slowdown in sales in the Japanese domestic market after three years of strong growth, followed by a sharp downturn in the United States market, major Japanese automakers and autoparts companies are expected to invest over ¥1.4 trillion in new plant and equipment in fiscal 1990. Much of their new production capacity is being built in the United States at a time when American automakers are seeing their inventories balloon and their profits squeezed. As American automakers close plants and lay off workers, Japanese automakers continue to expand. The eight assembly plants built solely by the Japanese in the 1980s have put the same number of U.S. Big Three plants out of business in the past three years.

Because their cost of capital is lower, their labor force younger and nonunionized, and their production facilities more modern, Japanese automakers know that they can underprice their U.S. competitors when the inevitable industry shakeout occurs. By 1994, total automobile production capacity in North America is expected to climb to 16 million cars annually, from 14 million today, while sales

North American Production Bases of Japanese Automakers

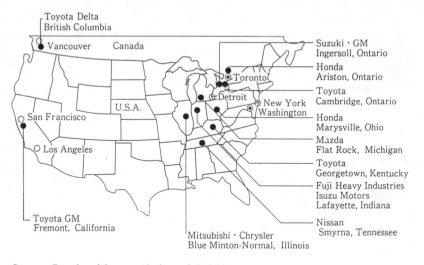

Source: Reprinted by permission of JAMA

are expected to reach only 13 million. U.S. automakers, driven by the need to maintain profits and dividends, will gradually scale back their operations. By 1995 Japanese automakers are forecast to have capacity for more than 3.5 million automobiles and light trucks in North America. Already they account for 15 percent of U.S. automobile production.

Not only are U.S. automakers threatened; their parts suppliers are as well. Japanese automakers depend on imports of Japanese-made parts from their related autoparts companies, unless these companies produce them locally. As the output of U.S. carmakers falls, U.S. autoparts makers will attempt to sell to the Japanese carmakers. But given their lack of shareholding ties and probable unwillingness to have their profits controlled, a happy, lasting business relationship seems unlikely.

DEFENSE OF THE GROUP

When a Japanese company comes under attack from a corporate raider, as happens occasionally, it turns first for help to its stable shareholders. And because their combined strength is almost always greater than 50 percent of the outstanding equity, a successful takeover bid is well-nigh impossible. Yet sometimes a company will take its stable shareholders for granted or fail to take steps to ensure a majority vote in its favor. One such case was the Tokyu Group, a conglomerate of 300 companies with combined annual revenues of ¥2 trillion in 1989. At the heart of the group is a railway company that operates and owns lines running west of Tokyo.

Railway lines are not the most exciting way to make money. In Japan, their fares are fixed by the government and passenger usage rises only slowly. Even in Tokyo, there is a limit to the number of people a commuter train can carry. But what makes the railway business attractive is the many other activities it spawns. Each railway runs through a given territory in which it has the sole license to operate. Tokyu accordingly developed areas along its railway line, building houses and apartment blocks to fill with commuters and to be sold through a real-estate subsidiary. It built department stores near railway stations; it built hotels, resorts, even a television station whose cable runs along the railway line.

Such was the empire founded by the strong-willed Noboru Gotoh, who, because of the power of his personality, was able to wield control without the need for large share stakes in his affiliates (14 of which are quoted). The group companies owned only a total of 12 percent of Tokyu Department Store.

When the founder died in March 1989, corporate predators began to nibble at the edges of the group. Its most tempting asset was the land held by member firms. These landholdings became the first target of Dai-Ichi Real Estate, a large property firm which disclosed that it had acquired 2.7 million shares—almost 3 percent—in Tokyu Hotel, the second largest chain in Japan. To prevent further encroachment, Tokyu bought off Dai-Ichi off by allowing it to operate the new Tokyu hotel near Tokyo Disneyland and by promising it more collaboration in the future.

Fearing that the entire group was in danger of being dismembered by other outsiders, the members of Gotoh's family and other stable shareholders agreed to raise their cross-shareholdings. The railway company was to hold more than 15 percent of the shares in four big

Listed Tokyu Group Companies

	Percent owned by Tokyu Corp.	Percent owned by Tokyu Group
Fujita Tourist	9.9	9.9
Japan Air System	25.6	25.6
Izukyu	37.5	49.7
Shiroki	19.9	29.5
Sotetsu Transportation	25.0	31.8
Tokyu Car	18.0	23.3
Tokyu Construction	9.6	22.7
Tokyu Corp.	—	3.2
Tokyu Department Store	10.1	12.8
Tokyu Hotel Chain	22.6	27.3
Tokyu Land	13.9	16.2
Tokyu Recreation	23.6	33.7
Tokyu Store Chain	19.9	41.0
Tokyu Tourist	30.8	35.4

Source: *Shikiho* (Tokyo: Toyo Keizai)

group firms—construction, real estate, retailing, and rolling-stock manufacture. The group as a whole would own 25 percent of their shares. For the remaining eight listed group companies, Tokyu Corp. intended to hold 20 percent of the equity and the overall group 35 percent.

News of this plan to increase cross-shareholding levels appeared on the front page of the *Nikkei*, and the share price of Tokyu Corp. rose by 50 percent in a matter of days. The reason is unclear. Either investors hoped to take advantage of the buying of Tokyu's shares by the group or they expected more takeover activity within the group. Nor is it known why the story was leaked to the newspapers. Perhaps the group planned to use the story to make its shares so expensive that it would not have to buy any after all.

Tokyu Corp.

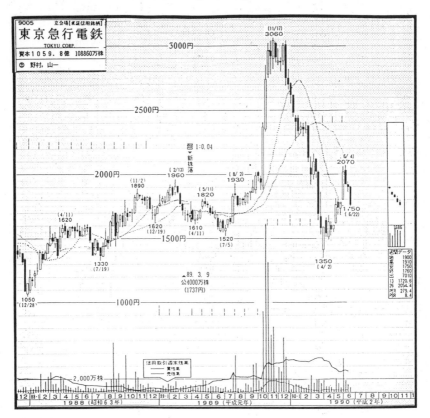

Source: First Section Chart Book, no. 745 (Tokyo: Toshi Radar, July 2, 1990);
reprinted by permission of the publisher

RESTRUCTURING INDUSTRY

Every economy in the world is in the process of restructuring. The
most successful are those which see the need early on and take steps
to make the change smoothly. The stock market can play a central
role in helping companies adapt. In the United States, firms weakened by their failure to move with the times are taken over by
stronger ones and dismantled in order to realize their full value.

Japan's stock market is much more patient, giving industries time
to restructure themselves. Rather than punishing weak companies

through falling share prices, share prices remain stable until prospects improve. Hostile takeovers are almost impossible. If a company is in trouble, its main bank will lend it money. The bank will supply expertise and a watchful eye, and if all else fails, it will find a suitable corporate partner to take over the business. During the 1980s, when much of the developed world was writing off its heavy industry, Japan's was clinging on tenaciously; by the end of the decade, it had staged a comeback by taking advantage of the country's economic boom.

The Japanese steel industry, the biggest in the capitalist world, has made the most remarkable recovery of all, helped by a boom in the stock market. Like the automobile manufacturers, the big five steel producers—Nippon Steel, NKK, Sumitomo Metal, Kawasaki Steel, and Kobe Steel—were struck hard by the yen's rise from 1985. Almost a quarter of Japan's annual output of more than 100 million tonnes is exported. In the year ending March 1987, the net loss of the big five producers totalled ¥64 billion, yet none of them saw a fall in their share price. Investors' patience was rewarded with combined net profits of ¥302 billion two years later, by which time their share prices had risen six to eight times their 1985 levels.

This dramatic improvement came about through harsh cost-cutting and rationalization by the steel companies in order to claw back export markets lost to South Korean, British, and U.S. producers. They were also helped by the surge in demand from such domestic customers as car and construction firms. But the real savior was the stock market. At the end of 1985, Japan's five leading steel firms had bank borrowings of ¥5.3 trillion, equal to 65 percent of annual sales. Most of these liabilities were in the form of long-term loans, costing them more than ¥500 billion a year to service. From mid-1988 through early 1990, however, they raised a total of ¥2.3 trillion from issues of warrant bonds, convertible bonds, and public offerings. Debt was retired, interest charges fell 40 percent by the end of 1989, and profits surged. The cost of these financings averaged around 0.5 percent owing to the dramatic rise of share prices on the numerous stockmarket waves and the turnaround of their business. These five steel companies were all scheduled to have more financings in 1990 and 1991 until the crash of the stock market curtailed those plans.

In 1986, steelmakers were in the limelight as "excess liquidity stocks" because of their large number of shares outstanding and because investors were flush with cash. The sales pitch was extremely simple: how could such a fine company as Nippon Steel have a share price of only ¥150? Next, when "hidden assets" and Tokyo Bay redevelopment were the rage, steel shares climbed higher, buoyed by the rising value of their landholdings. Eventually, industry earnings recovered on the strength of domestic demand, and steel makers were transformed into "earnings stocks." Following equity financings in early 1989, however, share prices began to fall as earnings appeared to have peaked. And so in September 1989, the steel shares became "rescue stocks" since their share prices had to be rescued, both for the sake of the companies and of domestic investors who held large positions. When Nippon Steel issued ¥300 billion in convertible bonds in June 1989, its prospective PER was 59. At the time, the ratio for USX (formerly U.S. Steel) was 6.

The Japanese industry with the weakest finances—shipping—stands next in line for financings after the steelmakers. In March 1989, the 13 shipping companies listed on the TSE's First Section carried total debt of ¥1.8 trillion but had shareholders' equity of only ¥460 billion. Profits in the year ending March 1989 amounted to only ¥18 billion.

Japan's shipping companies are no strangers to financial trouble. They were forced to restructure under government decree in 1964, forming six groups as a result. The only company to refuse to toe the line was Sanko Steamship, whose ¥520 billion bankruptcy in 1985 was the largest in Japan's postwar history. Shipping has never been a profitable business in Japan because the government decided that it should not be so. To keep Japan's exports price-competitive, shipping companies were not allowed to charge high shipping rates. Moreover, they were required to buy their ships from Japanese shipyards in order to maintain the shipbuilding industry's operating rate, and to use expensive Japanese crews.

Like shipping companies elsewhere, Japan's were glutted with ships after the 1979 oil crisis, their problems compounded by the soaring yen after 1985. Revenues were denominated in U.S. dollars, but costs for wages, depreciation, and borrowings were all in yen.

Net losses for the 13 companies totalled ¥117 billion in the three years to March 1987. To staunch the wound, ships and land were sold, foreign crews hired, and flags of convenience flown—all with the support from their creditors, the Japanese banks. And two of the largest and financially weakest firms, Japan Line and Yamashita Shinnihon Steamship, were merged.

Despite their history of losses, shipping firms' share prices moved up sharply from the end of 1984. NYK, with the soundest finances of the shipping companies, saw its price rise from ¥208 in 1984 to a peak of ¥1,250 at the end of 1989, when its PER was 220. Kawasaki Steamship's price rose from ¥106 to ¥1,200, Inui Steamship went from ¥75 to ¥1,940, and Meiji Shipping rose from ¥83 to ¥4,900. At its peak price, Meiji Shipping had a market capitalization of ¥176 billion, 29 times its annual sales revenue and 90 times its net worth.

Only two companies were able to take advantage of the robust stock market, because they were the only ones which had paid the minimum ¥4 dividend required for a company to issue new shares. Despite the recovery in profits, only two more companies were able to restore their dividend in the year ending March 1990. If their earnings continue to improve and they are able to have equity financings, Lazarus will have been outdone.

IT'S A SONY CB!

Despite his harsh criticism of American companies' business practices and their adoration of Wall Street, Sony's Chairman Akio Morita has nonetheless made good use of Japan's stock market to fund his firm's takeovers of two big U.S. companies, CBS Records and Columbia Pictures Entertainment. In fact, since the start of 1987, Sony has raised the second largest amount of funds from the stock market of any company in Japan—a staggering ¥908 billion.

The cost of these funds was extremely cheap. Sony's three convertible bond issues carried a coupon of less than 1.5 percent annually and the dividend yield on the shares sold through its two public offerings was under 1 percent. Sony's counterpart raiders in the United States must pay 15 percent or more when they raise their takeover war chest through junk bonds.

Leading Issuers in Japan
(¥ bn, Jan 1987–Mar 1990)

Sumitomo Bank	959
Sony	908
Nippon Steel	810
Dai-Ichi Kangyo Bank	798
Fuji Bank	710
Mitsubishi Bank	656
Toyota	632
Matsushita Electric	568
Sanwa Bank	526
Toshiba	524
Sumitomo Corp.	503

Note: Total of CBs, warrant bonds, public offerings, rights offerings

In fact, Sony's purchases of CBS Records for $2.3 billion and Columbia Pictures for $3.4 billion were predicated on the strength of the Japanese stock market. Since CBS Records was only marginally profitable and Columbia Pictures was losing money, Sony could not have easily bought these companies with debt financing. To do so would have caused its own earnings to drop by at least one-third. Morita may have a long-term vision, but it is easier to think ahead if there is access to unlimited funds at virtually no cost.

TRADING PLACES

How would U.S. companies compete and their shares be valued if they operated in an economic environment similar to Japanese companies'? If IBM were a listed company on a new NYSE and a core component of America Inc., it is likely that its reported net income would be about $2 billion a year rather than the current level of $5 billion. This would still allow it to rank first in profits among all listed companies, while reducing its tax bill to $2 billion. This would give it an additional $3 billion to spend on new equipment and on research. It would need to pay only $400 million a year in dividends, rather than $2.8 billion as it did in 1989.

It would have equity-linked financings of at least $2 billion a year, the opposite of the $5 billion worth of its own shares it planned to buy back from 1990. The money would be placed in a term deposht at Chemical Bank, one of its major stable shareholders, to increase its earnings. Its cost of debt would be halved as well, if interest rates were controlled in the United States in the same way as they are in Japan.

Beneath IBM would be a group of companies supporting its operations bound together by cross-shareholdings. It would never have to fear a shortage of semiconductor chips since it would hold a large proportion of the shares of chip suppliers such as Texas Instruments. It could also farm out labor intensive operations to small sub-contractors totally dependent on IBM for their sales.

Foreign competition would never be a problem because the domestic market would be closed to protect the "fledgling" computer industry. Even if the market were opened, foreigners would lack the distribution channels as well as the business ties necessary for a sale.

If the computer industry were to slump, IBM would not have to curtail its equipment-spending plans or close factories since profits from the stock market would make up for any losses on its business. It could ruthlessly engage in dumping its computers in Japan to keep its factories running at peak efficiency in the United States. If the slump became too severe, the American version of MITI would step in to fix prices in the domestic U.S. market and ensure adequate profits for all companies.

IBM would also be able to pay its employees less since wage rates would be fixed throughout the industry, rising a standard 5 percent a year during the spring wage offensive. It would not have to worry about its best researchers leaving since the venture capital industry would be nonexistent and other major companies such as DEC and Hewlett-Packard would refuse to hire such disloyal employees. Of course, IBM's employees would have to make sacrifices to ensure IBM's success. Promotions within IBM would be based on seniority rather than ability, and employees would have to live in tiny IBM-supplied houses, ride a company bus to work, and go out drinking together nightly in order to work out problems harmoniously. Still, the quality of the employee would rise since the top graduates of Harvard University would line up outside its headquarters on the first day of the annual recruiting season.

There would of course be guidelines to abide by. IBM employees would have to keep in constant contact with the U.S. version of MITI to ensure compliance with the government's vision for the computer industry in the year 2000. Capacity expansions as well as new product introductions would have to be coordinated. IBM's technology would be available to all its competitors since most products would be jointly developed and patent protection nonexistent. IBM's top executives would be constantly making trips to Japan to explain American business practices, in particular why the U.S. domestic market is not really a closed market. And if the Japanese expressed doubts, the U.S. visitors could criticize Japanese managers for their short-sighted practices of maximizing shareholder wealth.

IBM would also require a budget for acquiring the shares of other American companies to promote good group relations and drive away unwanted outside investors. If Dupont issued new shares on the NYSE, IBM would be obliged to take its required 5 percent of the issue. Even so, the increase in unrealized capital gains on its holdings in Bethlehem Steel, Chemical Bank, and Dupont would be very large and would help to support IBM's own share price.

For a company with such a bright outlook, the market would have to value IBM at a PER of 100, giving it a market capitalization of $200 billion. While this may be high, analysts would argue that in fact IBM's real PER is much lower as it hides its profits in reserves set aside for "computer price fluctuations." Moreover, its shares would be caught up on a number of market themes such as "Manhattan Redevelopment" and "Dream Computers."

On the other hand, if Toyota were to operate in the same environment as General Motors, imagine the following prospect. Toyota's shareholders would demand that it pay out more of its earnings as dividends, rather than retaining its profits. They would demand that Toyota make a special dividend or at least buy back its shares in order to reduce its cash account from the current ¥2 trillion. Its annual fund raising on the TSE would be replaced with annual share buybacks.

Toyota could no longer count on its parts suppliers to deliver those parts just-in-time and at a low price since market forces would dictate price and delivery schedules. The quality would also deteriorate as its parts suppliers tried to maximize profits. As a result, Toyota would be forced to produce more of its parts in-house.

Its employees would be less efficient as the Japanese Auto Workers would determine strict job classifications. Strikes would be frequent as workers balked at the pace of the production line and refused to sing the company song. Only half of Toyota's workers in fact would be able to read the words.

Toyota would face stiff competition in the Japanese domestic market from imported American cars built by Ford and Chrysler. They would cost less, since the American companies have lower capital costs, and they would be roomier as well, quickly capturing the high end of the Japanese auto market and then trickling down. This in turn would put profit pressure on Toyota, forcing it to abandon the high-end market and reduce its capital outlays.

The situation would become so difficult for Toyota that the U.S. MITI would have to restrain exports voluntarily to Japan. But Chrysler, driven by market share, not profits, would soon begin assembling Omni's in Japan, with parts supplied by its *keiretsu* companies and financing from Citicorp. To reduce costs, Chrysler would only hire young Japanese workers, and locate its factories in northern Japan rather in Nagoya, whose high unemployment levels have made it a concrete jungle.

Toyota would not find a ready market in the United States since its steering wheel would be on the wrong side and the bureaucrats at the U.S. MITI would use every ploy imaginable to block imports. It would be difficult to establish a sales network as well, since the price of U.S. real estate would be exorbitant. Even if Toyota could afford it, none would be for sale in any case.

Toyota's managers would have to spend most of their time apologizing to investors as to why they lost the Japanese auto market to the Americans. They would regularly have to endure Lee Iacocca on Japanese television discussing poor management practices in Japan. Toyota would also have to keep up its earnings and offer a hefty dividend in order to keep the company from being put into play by raiders.

Although Toyota's profits might be initially higher than it now reports, investors would be wary of its ability to maintain them in the light of the gains being made by American automakers in the Japanese market. They would be concerned about a looming slump in the U.S. auto market which would lead to the dumping of cars in Japan. At best, Toyota could expect a PER of 5.

This comparison, amusing as it is, may not be as farfetched as imagined, for the success of a company and the vision of its management are greatly influenced by the environment in which they operate. Friction occurs when one company with certain advantages competes with another that lacks the same benefits. Until these are made more similar, it is impossible to determine how much better one company is than another or how much more its shares are worth. Japanese companies look expensive from the other side of the Pacific. But if Chrysler were suddenly transplanted to Japan, its performance would almost certainly improve and its shares rise.

Chapter 8

POWER AND RISK

Japan's stock market, once a prime asset, has become a liability since the start of 1990. Because the price of shares and the value of land are so closely related, any sharp equity sell-off could feed through to the property market, and the whole of corporate Japan would be endangered. This is not a localized difficulty. When the world's richest country feels the pinch, the rest of the world shudders.

Even if Japan's stock market quickly recovers from the slump of early 1990, the threat to the country's finances would only have been postponed. A return to the old days of ever-rising share prices would only fuel more property and stock speculation and lead to more equity issues by corporations. The threat to foreign companies posed by Japan's excessively low capital costs would aggravate trade friction; retaliation against Japan would be almost unavoidable.

The growth of Japan's stock market cannot continue indefinitely. A simple piece of arithmetic can demonstrate this. If the stock market were to go on expanding at an annual rate of 20 percent as it did between 1949 and 1989, its capitalization would reach ¥1,500 trillion by 1995, two-and-a-half times its size at the end of 1989. By then, the stock market would be more than three times the size of Japan's gross national product, assuming GNP grew at 5 percent a year. Even an economy as strong as Japan's could not support so bloated a capital market.

The ice age cometh. The stock market has worked itself out of a

TSE Market Capitalization to GNP

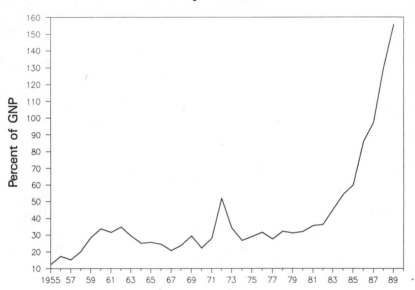

job. Japanese industry no longer needs the help of the stock exchange to catch up with the West because many companies already
outclass their foreign competitors. But more importantly, the crash
of 1990 exposed a design flaw in the system, namely that share prices
must rise continuously in order for the stock market to sustain itself.
If the price of stock stops going up, outside investors have no incentive to hold onto shares that yield next to nothing. They sell; corporate investors do not buy; prices come tumbling down.

Under these circumstances, the best that can be hoped for is a soft
landing for the equity market, a gradual decline in the price of shares
for a couple of years to take some of the inflationary pressure out of
the system. This would give issuers and investors time to adjust to a
new world, one in which share values bear a closer relationship to the
underlying performance of corporate Japan. One of the toughest
challenges for the country's famed bureaucracy will be to achieve as
painless a deflation of asset values as possible.

Most investors may escape less rich but financially intact from the
debacle of 1990. Even if share prices were to halve from their level at

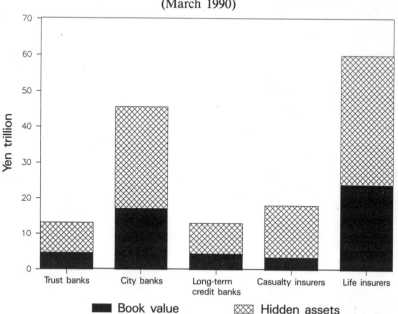

Book and Market Value of Equity Holdings
(March 1990)

the end of 1989, an investor who bought a representative portfolio 20 years earlier would experience a relatively small drop in the annual rate of return on his shares from 16.6 percent to 12.2 percent. This is still a great deal better than the return provided by bonds or bank deposits.

Because many institutional investors have not earmarked their unrealized capital gains for any specific purpose, the distress from the crash ought not to be too debilitating. The conservative accounting practices of the life insurers and the heavy cash weightings of the investment trusts actually benefit policyholders and investors in a bear market. Many financial institutions will still earn a respectable dividend on their holdings, having acquired them so long ago. Individual investors in Japan have a much smaller proportion of their financial assets in equities than is the case in the United States, and so the losses should not be that great, relatively speaking.

The biggest losers will be the companies that have gained the most from the market's rise, namely Japanese banks. The unrealized capital gains on their equity portfolios that will have evaporated are needed to meet international capital-ratio requirements. Lower equity ratios would force them to concentrate on their core business, to stop lending to real-estate speculators, to improve their profitability, and to scale back their overseas operations.

A severe slump in the stock market would affect the financing plans and issuing costs of corporate Japan, but it would not be disastrous. If Japanese corporations are as good as they claim to be, then they can continue to operate their businesses when the cost of capital is 7 percent (the long-term prime lending rate) instead of its rate of less than 1 percent in the late 1980s. U.S. companies have been operating under a 10–15 percent cost of capital for years. Besides, the Japanese manufacturing sector is flush with cash and should easily be able to pay for future growth without recourse to the market.

Although the ¥15 trillion in convertible bonds outstanding at the end of 1989 will not see the light of equity if share prices continue to slide, this represents only 20 percent of the total amount raised in the 1980s. Moreover, the value of convertible bonds due for redemption in 1990–93 is negligible. The balance sheet of corporate Japan would weaken, but not to the extent seen at the start of the 1980s. Even if PERs were to drop to 30 and yields rise to 1 percent, Japanese companies would still enjoy benefits rarely seen in other stock markets.

No Turning Back

Since the late 1960s, Japan has been in a constant state of friction with its trading partners. Its massive trade surplus ($81 billion in 1989) and its targeting of foreign industries has won Japan few friends. Tariffs and quotas are among the lowest in the developed world, but this cuts no ice with countries like the United States. Japan has defended its practices by claiming necessity (Japan does not want to become dependent on imported food) or cultural differences (Japanese consumers demand quality and service). Japan has recently gone on the offensive, countering that the problem lies with the short sightedness of U.S. businesses and with the U.S. fiscal deficit.

But patience abroad is wearing thin. Japan's critics have pointed to the fact that domestic consumer prices failed to drop when the yen rose after 1985. If the home market were as fiercely competitive as the Japanese government claims, shops would have been forced to pass on the lower costs of imported inputs and finished goods to the consumer. The Tokyo government conceded that Japanese consumers received only one-seventh of the ¥35 trillion gain that accrued when the yen doubled in value against the U.S. dollar in 1985–88. Producers and distributors pocketed most of the rest. Even foreign consumers benefited more than Japanese consumers, when companies like Toyota and Toshiba avoided passing on the full impact of the yen's rise in the form of higher foreign-currency denominated export prices. They could afford to do this because they were making such big profits at home.

The primary reason for the insolubility of the trade issue can be traced to the structure of share ownership. Because companies are owned by other companies and are under the control of their managers, they are not driven by profits, as are their foreign competitors, but by market share. Because the financial industry is designed to support companies rather than benefit savers or policyholders, money is always available to bolster industrial expansion. The stock market, in fact, has become a substitute for operating profits, a hidden subsidy to listed companies.

The way in which most of Japanese industry is organized into *keiretsu* makes it very difficult for an outside company (particularly a foreign one) to penetrate the Japanese market. It also makes it impossible for a foreign company to buy a healthy Japanese one without the consent of the main shareholders, which so far has never been given. Supposing a corporate suitor gained permission to buy a Japanese company, the asking price would be prohibitive. This has prevented foreign companies from building up their local market share.

If Japan is serious about working in partnership with the rest of the world, then the Tokyo stock crash provides it with an opportunity to take certain critical steps. There is nothing wrong with employees owning their company or with managers being in control—as long as the company is private. If a company is publicly owned, however, managers should be answerable to shareholders. A new balance of corporate power is required in which the stock market serves shareholders as effectively as it has, in the past, met the needs of corporate management.

UNDER RENOVATION

Three elements have been essential to the evolution of Japan's stock market. Two of them—corporate share ownership and the brokerage oligopoly—are integral to the exchange itself. With seven in ten shares in the hands of corporations, the employers and owners of capital are, in effect, one and the same. The tight concentration of ownership has given the Big Four brokers much more power to steer the market than would have otherwise been the case. External, but no less essential, to the stock exchange is the support given by the Japanese government. Bureaucrats have rarely hesitated to step in to help out when the going got tough. All three elements must be altered to reform the Japanese economy, but of these, one is most important.

The Key: Stable Shareholding

General MacArthur's Occupation forces tried in 1945 to democratize the economy by scattering share ownership as widely as possible. It is time for another try at reforming Japanese business, starting with cross-shareholdings. On present trends, the proportion of equity held by individuals will fall to 13 percent by the end of the 1990s, while that of financial institutions will climb to 53 percent. Japanese companies as a whole would then own nearly 80 percent of all outstanding shares. Such a situation may be awkward, but stable shareholdings make life considerably more predictable and safe for Japanese businesses. An October 1989 survey conducted by the *Nihon Keizai Shimbun* of 300 listed companies found that 41 percent of the companies thought it desirable to have at least 60 percent of their shares in stable hands; one-fifth of respondents wanted long-term shareholders to control more than 70 percent of their stock.

In a similar way, the share of outstanding equity held by the top ten shareholders and by company directors continues to rise, despite the fact that the number of shares outstanding has increased rapidly in recent years. Conversely, there has been a decline in the percentage of shares held by investors in units of less than 50,000 (the "float", so-called because they are deemed to be held by outside investors rather than stable shareholders). Within the Mitsubishi *keiretsu* the amount of shares cross-held has increased from 25.2 percent in 1986 to 26.8 percent in 1989. If the trend continues, the Mitsubishi and other *keiretsu* will have succeeded as did their *zaibatsu* forebears: finance will be generated within the group, with cash flowing to those members of the *keiretsu* in need.

Threatened by Bears

The appetite of a stable shareholder for more shares is not insatiable, despite appearances to the contrary. One of the keys to the maintenance of the stable shareholder system has been a rising stock market. As long as share prices continued to appreciate at their average 20 percent annual rate, there were few incentives for a stable shareholder to sell even if the indirect benefits from this relationship were minimal. In a falling market, though, where the returns on investment are negative, the situation changes dramatically.

This is particularly true for the life insurance companies. The insurers were able to justify their stable shareholdings in the 1960s on the basis of dividend yields, as their accounting practices dictated. Since the mid-1970s, the only justification for continuing to buy equities has been capital gains—a rather flimsy argument in that policyholders do not receive such benefits. Now, with prices falling, there is no justification at all.

The *Nihon Keizai Shimbun* reported on April 2, 1990, that life insurers had decided to sell large portions of their stable shareholdings. This piece of news triggered a 7 per cent drop in the market the same day. Although Dai-Ichi Life, Japan's second largest assurer, held a press conference later to say that it expected to be a net buyer of shares on an annual basis, corporate Japan was put on notice that the life insurers were reassessing their relationship with issuers of shares.

Even before the market crash, stable shareholders appeared to be losing their appetite for more shares. Life insurance companies have refrained from stable shareholding unless an issuer offers the insurer some pension funds to manage or other forms of business in return. Banks and other listed companies only purchase new shares if the issuer will buy a certain share of their own financings.

In the face of a continuing bear market and if capital spending remains strong, companies may choose to sell their shares to raise cash. *Tokkin* accounts and investment trusts would be the first affected. Firms might even start to sell off their long-term holdings as well.

REMEDIAL ACTION

Lower the Ceiling on Corporate Holdings

Japanese financial companies are currently forbidden from holding more than a certain proportion of another firm's equity. Banks cannot own more than 5 percent, and life insurers no more than 10 percent, of the shares in a given firm. Insurers must not invest more than 30 percent of their assets in equities, a ceiling which some casualty insurers have nearly reached. These ceilings should be lowered.

While the banking industry would plead that these shareholdings are a basis for their financial strength, the collapse of the market in early 1990 showed them to be a precarious liability. A cut in banks' share ownership would force banks to improve their asset management practices and to limit their real-estate lending. The risks that Japanese banks faced in the 1990 stock market crisis should cause the Bank for International Settlements, which laid down the international rules for banks' capital adequacy, to reconsider the provision allowing banks to include hidden assets in capital calculations. The stipulation that 45 percent of unrealized gains on their investment portfolio could count toward a bank's required capital proved in 1990 to have been ill-advised. It should be scrapped.

The stock market would benefit from a gradual lowering of the limit on shareholdings by banks. Since banks are at the center of the *keiretsu*, this measure would decisively break the ties that currently bind these companies together. A gradual reduction in the ceiling to zero should be carried out over the next ten years.

The Antimonopoly Law forbids nonfinancial companies from investing more in equities than their own net worth. This in effect limits the amount of shares that they can buy unless they can have issues of their own to raise their own capital. The provision has provided a powerful reason why companies conduct financings, but it defeats the purpose of raising capital if the money is merely plowed back into the stock market.

More to the point would be if the rules were based on the market value of holdings, rather than on their acquisition cost. Most companies would, by the former measure, have exceeded their limits and would, as a consequence, be forced to sell. While bad for share prices in the short run, it would greatly loosen stable shareholdings. In the fiscal year ending March 1991, listed companies will be required to disclose the market value of their equity holdings. This is a step in the right direction.

Outlaw *Tokkin* Funds

Tokkin funds have become among the biggest traders of equities in the market. They should be banned. Although no precise breakdown of their activities is available, a rough idea of their impact can be seen in the banks' overall share trading, which includes *tokkin* and fund trusts. Between 1984 and 1989 the proportion of turnover on the TSE First Section accounted for by banks rose fivefold to 19 percent.

Tokkin funds and fund trusts are used primarily to segregate actively traded shares from stable shareholdings. They permit companies to enjoy the benefits of investing in the stock market without disturbing long-term business ties. Outlawing *tokkin* funds would force corporate managers—of banks and insurance companies in particular—to choose between maximizing investment returns on the one hand and strategic investment on the other. This would result in a decline in liquidity in the short term but stable shareholdings would be pried loose in the long term, thereby increasing the proportion of floating shares. In any case, *tokkin* funds have long been abused as a means by which stable shareholders can conveniently circumvent restrictions on their level of ownership.

Force Fund Managers to Compete

Heightened competition among fund managers would compel institutions to invest in equities for the same reason as their U.S. and British counterparts, that is, to earn a high return. At present, the Finance Ministry wants to improve the poor returns received by investors by opening pension-fund management and investment trusts to newcomers one step at a time. But it does not intend to allow a completely free market.

One reason why fund-management performance is so poor is that the managers have no motivation to try harder. In the past 16 years, financial companies have been the biggest buyers of shares in the market. These investments made sense in the 1960s when dividend yields were high and PERs were low, but these circumstances no longer exist. The pressure building on financial institutions to improve their investment performance may force banks and insurers to stop tying up excessive amounts of their assets in stable shareholdings.

The authorities can promote this. Accounting standards for insurance companies need to be revised and updated. The restrictions on their payout of capital gains, either to policyholders or (in the case of casualty insurers) to shareholders, were imposed originally so that loans could be made to corporate Japan. Now that corporate Japan has all the resources it needs, the regulations are both unnecessary and damaging. As life and casualty insurers have increasingly become long-term investment managers of individuals' assets, they need the freedom to invest for long-term capital gains rather than for current income. A revision of the law would not necessarily result in large-scale sales of their holdings, since equities are still the best long-term investment, but it would make them more active traders of shares.

Banks, like insurers, need to improve their profits, particularly since banks' access to new equity capital has been curtailed by the collapse of the stock market. If the market fall is not arrested and banks' BIS equity ratios fall, they will begin selectively to sell shares of companies which are of less strategic importance. This could be encouraged by offering companies a reduced capital gains tax over a defined period. The investment trust management industry should be reformed by allowing many more companies into the industry and by disclosing performance in a reasonable and timely fashion. If individuals knew how badly these funds performed, the management companies would be forced to compete harder and more honestly to maintain their funds under management.

Permit Share Buy-backs

Allowing companies to purchase their own shares would be instrumental in breaking down stable shareholding. If one of the motivations of stable shareholding is to reduce the supply of floating shares and protect a company from M&A, then a share buy-back could accomplish this. It could be done by stable shareholders exchanging the shares held in each other.

In conjunction with this, the rules on mergers and acquisitions should be modernized to make it easier for companies to change hands. But this ought to be done in such a way as to ensure that the legal weapons to defend a firm against a takeover bid are as powerful and as numerous as the means of attack.

Institute Stricter Delisting Requirements

A company currently faces delisting if more than 70 percent of its shares are held by its ten largest shareholders. In addition, a TSE-listed company must have at least 1,000 shareholders if it has more than 20 million shares outstanding, and at least 2,000 shareholders if it has more than 120 million shares outstanding.

The maximum number of shares that can be held by the ten largest shareholders in any listed company should gradually be reduced from its present level of 70 percent to 49 percent. This would not prevent stable shareholders from finding clever ways to circumvent the rules—such as finding more business allies to lock away shares for them. But it would make control much more difficult than it is now. A minimum level of floating shares should also be introduced to ensure that there is ample liquidity in the market.

If Japanese companies are public companies, then they should be owned by the public. If they are not, then they should not be listed.

Break the Big Four Brokers

Japan's brokerage oligopoly of Nomura, Daiwa, Nikko, and Yamaichi is losing its cartelizing power, and forthcoming regulatory changes could clip their wings permanently. They served the market well when its primary function was to help companies raise cash. But if the stock market is to serve the investor, their controlling role is obsolete.

Japanese banks, which have been prevented from competing directly with the securities houses since 1947, are expected to be allowed into the brokerage industry by around 1992 through the establishment of brokerage subsidiaries. This change is being promoted since no amendment to Article 65 of the Securities and Exchange law would be required. The law only forbids banks, not their subsidiaries, from entering the securities industry. The impact on the brokers is likely to be dramatic, particularly in the area of corporate underwriting, due to the banks' long-term relationships built up through stable shareholding.

The obvious implication is that Japan would resemble the continental European model much more closely. The one similarity already present—the abundance of corporate cross-shareholdings, with banks at the center—would be joined by another, namely universal banking. This would probably make the Tokyo stock market a much duller place than it is today. As the British experience after Big Bang in October 1986 has shown, bankers rarely make good stockbrokers. The former stresses conservatism and the analysis of credit risk, the latter thrives on volatility.

In order to prevent the reappearance of a new Big Four with different names, the Finance Ministry should go further than merely allowing banks in. One way would be to require any bank wishing to enter the securities industry to reduce its equity holdings gradually to zero. The conflicts of interest are too great to allow banks to have the best of both worlds.

There are additional steps that could be taken to promote the interests of shareholders. The first of these—the introduction of floating brokerage commissions for institutional customers—would stimulate trading by big investors and would probably shrink the profits of the Big Four securities houses. Commissions on orders from individual investors should remain fixed and low.

To increase the number of tradable shares, the Finance Ministry should encourage companies to split their stock, possibly by setting a maximum share price for listed shares. This would make shares more accessible to individual investors. Likewise, the minimum trading unit could be reduced from 1,000 shares to 100.

WHO BENEFITS

The attitude of bureaucrats toward the stock market may be changing. Officials appear to have realized that corporate Japan can have too much of a good thing.

The collapse of share prices has demonstrated to the bureaucrats the risks of keeping the current financial structure. Because the market has grown so large, it can no longer be controlled so easily. If the Finance Ministry were to step in to freeze share prices, it would immediately be criticized by the rest of the world. Its task therefore is to engineer change as painlessly as possible.

In addition to the defusing of trade friction, there are a number of benefits to be had from reform of the stock market. The most important is that the stock market of the 1990s could play an important role in helping Japan as a whole, rather than just listed companies.

Japan Reconstructs

A reformed stock market would mean the restructuring of Japan's highly inefficient and cosseted domestic market. Fear is the reason why invisible trade barriers have not been removed. Many Japanese companies are not unaware of their poor management, and they are afraid that allowing foreign competitors into Japan will mean their demise. The distribution system has thus been designed to make penetration by outsiders as difficult as possible.

Japan's trade surplus failed to drop as far as expected, therefore, with the revaluation of the yen against the U.S. dollar in 1985–88. Instead of passing on the benefits of the strong yen to consumers in the form of lower domestic prices, distributors carried on with business as usual. They reaped huge windfall profits that were then invested in the equity and real estate markets.

Subsequent measures taken after the revaluation to stimulate consumer spending and the domestic economy have been inflationary. Imports cannot reach the consumer and so Japanese companies are straining at full capacity to supply the domestic market themselves. As a consequence, Japan has suffered from inflationary pressure when it should be enjoying the benefits of a strong currency and its status as the world's largest foreign creditor.

Uncorrected, the distortion between consumers' wants and the ability of Japanese companies to supply them will worsen. Japan must open up its domestic markets or face the closure of overseas markets in retaliation. The graying of the Japanese population will make it increasingly difficult for Japan to supply its own needs, and yet the entry of young, foreign workers is considered socially unacceptable. If the liberalization of the domestic market is inevitable, the sooner Japanese firms restructure themselves the better.

Changes in the level of stable shareholdings would facilitate mergers and acquisitions and would eliminate the distortion in the value of shares caused by lack of liquidity. Weak management would no longer be able to hide behind a bloated share price. A more active M&A market, brought about by reduced stable shareholdings, would force domestic industries to become more efficient. Aware of the possibility of a takeover, companies would struggle to reduce costs, sell unprofitable businesses, and merge to achieve economies of scale. Japan's exporters are much stronger and more efficient than companies supplying the domestic market because the latter have never faced the cold blast of international competition.

The prospect of more domestic competition is already encouraging more M&A within Japan. In the financial services industry, the Taiyo Kobe Mitsui Bank merger will herald more consolidation for Japan's banks. In the past four years, 20 mergers have taken place among financial institutions, mostly among unlisted firms, but the prospect of bigger banking tie-ups is a continual source of speculation in the stock market. Liberalization of interest rates has made banking a riskier business than it was before.

Japan's labyrinthine distribution system is also seeing a gradual restructuring, partly pressed by the goverment's decision in 1989 to relax controls on the speed with which large department stores can be opened. This has frightened the smaller listed retailers.

While M&A would appear to go against the grain in Japan, attitudes are changing rapidly. Recent surveys of Japanese executives show that the majority are interested, or involved, in M&A themselves. The momentum that is building behind corporate buying and selling could shake loose interlocking shareholdings, as old loyalties are sacrificed in favor of raw market power.

Less Savings to Go 'Round

Until now, the management of financial assets lagged far behind the goal of allocating savings to industry. Financial assets have been inefficiently allocated in Japan because it has enjoyed one of the highest savings rates in the world. But this will not last forever. Some economists have contended that demographic factors underpin Japan's high savings rate. Individuals save during their working years and then spend their savings in retirement. Thus, Japan's high savings rate is based on its lower ratio of old people (spenders) to the working-age population (savers) as well as a lower ratio of young (small spenders) to working people (savers).

Japan's population will grow old at a faster rate than anywhere else in the developed world. The proportion of people aged 65 or over will rise from 11.5 percent in 1989 to 25 percent by 2020. Japan's Economic Planning Agency has forecast that the personal savings rate will halve from the 1985 level of 16 percent of disposable income by the turn of the century.

A lower savings rate and older population will require the better management of financial assets. Financial institutions will no longer be able to get away with deploying huge sums in stable shareholding merely because a company established ties with a bank or insurer a hundred years ago. Money will no longer be available to companies with no immediate need for the cash, particularly given the poor levels of dividend payouts. Fund management will become more of a profession in its own right rather than a stepping-stone in a salaryman's career.

Recycling Capital

In a free economy, resources flow to those areas where demand is strongest. In Japan, the process is short-circuited by excessively high share prices and too-cheap equity finance. Money has flowed into the wrong hands.

Until now, Japanese corporations have been driven by the goal of market share at all costs. This has been achieved because of the benign way the stock market has treated companies. Companies have been free to invest heavily in plant and equipment and to cut prices to the bone. But in a sense, Japan is not a capitalist economy where people invest money with the expectation of earning a reasonable payback. After 40 years, huge amounts of cash continue to flow into the hands of corporations, not outside shareholders.

In future years, however, Japanese companies will have more cash than they know what to do with. The stock market cannot expand indefinitely, nor can Japanese companies. The semiconductor industry has already captured most of the world market and Japanese automakers control 30 percent of the U.S. automarket. Their market share will have to grow more slowly, regardless of how much is invested in new plant and equipment.

This may cause Japanese companies to turn to profitability as their primary goal. But unless changes are made to the stock market, those profits will not be recycled. More and more Japanese firms will come to resemble Toyota, which has been a cash cow for 15 years but still retains 90 percent of its earnings. The benefits to the stock market would be twofold. Higher profits and dividends would make Japanese stocks less speculative and encourage portfolio investors to hold shares for longer periods of time.

Unless stable shareholding is checked, therefore, the financial benefits of the stock market to Japanese companies will be lost. In an illiquid market, *zaiteku* profits would be difficult to come by, as any significant selling would cause tremors in the market. Banks and insurers would see their hidden assets deteriorate in value, even if prices remained fixed, by virtue of the fact that they could not sell them when necessary.

LONG ODDS AGAINST DRAMATIC CHANGE

The main obstacle to reform of the stock market is that it would threaten the foundations of Japan Inc. For it is the stock market's design that has helped foster and prolong these business practices. Employees are loyal to a company because they see themselves as the owners. Lifetime employment is the norm in big companies because the stock market protects them so well. Long-term vision and planning are possible because the stock market and shareholders do not demand quick profits. Bureaucratic guidance is possible because there is no competing interest group of shareholders.

Transferring power to the owners—as in the United States and United Kingdom—would make Japanese companies very similar to their foreign counterparts. But a quick glance at the current economic condition of these two countries might cause the Japanese to question such a change. It would take power away from corporations and bureaucrats and give it to those that have until now mattered least in Japan, the consumer and the individual shareholder.

Even though MacArthur's Occupation forces wielded absolute control over the economy, in crucial respects the system that existed prior to World War II has reemerged intact. *Zaibatsu* disappeared, but *keiretsu* took their place. Expecting corporations and the bureaucrats now to cut their own throats forty years later is asking a little too much, especially now that Japan appears to be winning its economic battle with the United States.

Japan can weather the storm in the stock market in early 1990 just as it did following the crash of the market in 1961 and 1973. Although there are some very good reasons to make radical changes, the Japanese are more likely to patch and mend.

If damage from the 1990 share slump is contained and if Japan's stock market returns to business as usual, then two extreme possibilities present themselves:

Japan Wins

In this case, the stock market suffers a year or two of turbulence, but eventually hits bottom. During the market chaos, individual investors will have reduced their holdings. These have ended up in the hands of stable shareholders. The market as a consequence is more illiquid than before, but once again, speculative funds start to flow into it. The new source of excess liquidity comes from a boom in exports of high-definition television, a decline in interest rates, and from repatriated profits into Japan.

Share prices begin to respond. Corporations work closely with brokers. Underwriters recommend the shares of select corporations so that the convertible bonds issued in the 1980s are exercised. Another era of new equity issues is on its way. Since share prices start from a higher base, the cost of this round of financings is even cheaper than the last.

Whereas funds raised during the previous bull market were primarily directed at setting up operations in the United States and taking over U.S. companies, the money raised in the current bull market is used for Japan's entry into the unified European market.

The level of the stock market shoots up 500 percent as it usually does in a bull market, but this time fundamentals may have something to do with it. Japanese companies are now so much stronger than their foreign competitors they no longer need to invest to expand their market share. Control is complete. Prices are raised without concern over losing market share, and price cartels are established overseas, just as in Japan. Earnings surge in consequence, bringing PERs down to reasonable levels. The expansion of Japan's stock market over the years has been justified.

Trade friction is no longer a problem for Japan, which will have positioned much of its production overseas, close to both the sources of raw materials and consumer demand. Exports decline, though income from overseas investment more than compensates. Japan will have successfully evaded any protectionist barriers that are subsequently erected. At last, Japan opens up its domestic market to imported goods, but all imports are exported by Japanese companies abroad. The largest of these exports are Japanese cars manufactured in the United States and Japanese beef raised in the United States and Australia.

Its goal of national security through economic might secured, Japan sets about reforming the stock market. But the stock market is no longer needed to help companies. Japanese companies have no cause to worry.

The stock market may simply be turned off. Stable shareholdings will have grown to the point where trading on the TSE is choked off. As the individual is driven from the stock market and more shares end up in stable hands, the stock market ceases to function as a place where shares are traded. Companies will be unable to raise more cash from outside investors, but this is a small inconvenience. Corporations will have the cash to finance themselves internally or will turn to their *keiretsu*. The prewar *zaibatsu* will have been rebuilt, the unwanted outside investor will have been eliminated, Japan Inc. will have won.

Japan Loses

In this case, the stock market begins to recover after a bear market lasting a couple of years. Growth is remarkably quick. Increasing sophistication in the use of index funds results in money pouring into the stock market at a rapid rate. Interest rate deregulation has made savers more sensitive to changes in deposit rates, and a sudden shift in assets out of money market certificates and into the stock market occurs. Vast wealth is created overnight. Real estate prices jump sharply as those who missed the last property boom are determined not to miss the next.

Before the bureaucrats are able to act, asset prices surge. Inflation erupts as the prices of goods and services move to catch up. The yen depreciates rapidly against other foreign currencies, reflecting its worthlessness in Japan. One external shock—perhaps a third oil crisis, foreign retaliation against Japanese trade practices, chaos in China—does the trick. Japan Inc. breaks up in a financial implosion. Reverberations from the earthquake are felt around the world.

Selected Bibliography

Abegglen, James C., and George Stalk, Jr. *Kaisha: The Japanese Corporation*. New York: Basic Books, 1985.

Adams, T. F. M. *Japanese Securities Markets: A Historical Survey*. Tokyo: Seihei Okuyama, 1953.

Adams, T. F. M., and Iwao Hoshii. *A Financial History of Modern Japan*. Tokyo: Research Publications, 1964.

Adams, T. F. M., and Iwao Hoshii. *A Financial History of the New Japan*. Tokyo: Kodansha International, 1972.

Annual Securities Statistics. Tokyo: Tokyo Stock Exchange, 1953 through 1989.

Ballon, Robert J., and Iwao Tomita. *The Financial Behavior of Japanese Corporations*. Tokyo: Kodansha International, 1988.

Bronte, Stephen. *Japanese Finance: Markets and Institutions*. London: Euromoney Publications, 1982.

Daiwa International Capital Management. *Tsukiashi nijunen* (Twenty-Year Charts), no. 29. Tokyo: Jitsu Nichi Research Center, 1990.

First Section Chart Book, no. 744. Tokyo: Toshi Radar Co., 1990.

Hadley, Eleanor M. *Antitrust in Japan*. Princeton, NJ: Princeton University Press, 1970.

Hayden, Eric W. *Internationalizing Japan's Financial System*. Stanford, CA: Stanford University, Northeast Asia–United States Forum on International Policy, 1980.

Hollerman, Leon. *Japan Disincorporated: The Economic Liberalization Process*. Stanford, CA: Hoover Insitution Press, Stanford University, 1988.

Japan Company Handbook. Tokyo: Toyo Keizai Shinposha, 1974 through 1990.

Japan Securities Research Institute. *Securities Market in Japan*. Tokyo: Japan Securities Research Institute, 1990.

Kaisha Joho. Tokyo: Nihon Keizai Shimbunsha, 1990.

Kaisha Shikiho. Tokyo: Toyo Keizai Shinposha, 1968 through 1990.

Kigyo Keiretsu Soran 1990. Tokyo: Toyo Keizai Shinposha, 1990.

Machida, Tsuneo. *Kabu no subete* (All About Stocks). Tokyo: Kosaido Shuppan, 1976.

Matsumoto, Kazuo. *Keiki to kabuka* (Economic Cycles and Share Prices). Tokyo: Nihon Keizai Shimbunsha, 1970.

Matsumoto, Kazuo. *Toppu chachisuto ni yoru kabuka yosoku '89* (1989 Stock Price Forecasts by Top Chartists). Tokyo: Nihon Keizai Shimbunsha, 1988.

McCraw, Thomas K., ed. *America Versus Japan*. Boston: Harvard Business School Press, 1986.

Nikko Research Center. *Analysis of Japanese Industries for Investors*. Tokyo: Nikko Research Center, 1990.

Nikko Research Center. *The New Tide of the Japanese Securities Market*. Tokyo: Nikko Research Center, 1988.

Nomura Research Institute, Ltd. *Manual of Securities Statistics*. Tokyo: The Nomura Securities Co., Ltd., 1989.

Okumura, Hiroshi. *Nihon no kabushiki shijo: Toki jidai no kabuka wa ko kimaru* (Japan's Stock Market: How Prices Are Determined in a Speculative Age). Tokyo: Daimondsha 1988.

Prestowitz, Clyde V., Jr. *Trading Places: How We Allowed Japan to Take the Lead*. New York: Basic Books, 1988.

Tsukiashi shu (Monthly Charts), vol. 93. Tokyo: Golden Chart Co., 1990.

Viner, Aron. *Inside Japan's Financial Markets*. Tokyo: The Japan Times, 1987.

Yamashita, Takeji. *Japan's Securities Markets: A Practitioner's Guide*. Singapore: Butterworth, 1989.

Yamashita, Takeji. *Nihon wa naze kabuka ga takai* (Why Are Japanese Share Prices High). Tokyo: Toyo Keizai Shinposha, 1985.

Zaibatsu saihen to shuryoku kabu (Reorganization of the Zaibatsu and Leading Stocks). Tokyo: Toyo Keizai Shinposha, 1954.

Acknowledgments

We are deeply indebted to Craig Nelson, John Donald, and Stephen Marvin for their useful comments on the manuscript; to Su-Chzeng Ong, for guiding us through the publishing world; and to our editor Elmer Luke. We would like to thank Philip Bowring, the editor of the *Far Eastern Economic Review*, for allowing his Tokyo correspondent some time to work on the book. Thanks are also due to colleagues in the *Review*'s Tokyo bureau, Charles Smith, Bob Johntone, and Kazumi Miyazawa, for their professional help and friendship during Nigel Holloway's stint in Tokyo; and to Professor Hiroaki Wakabayashi and the Ministry of Education, which provided Robert Zielinski with the opportunity to come to Japan almost a decade ago. Special thanks must be given to the Industrial Bank of Japan and its Industrial Research Department, which have enriched our understanding of Japan's economy, industry, and stock market, and to *Toyo Keizai* and *Nihon Keizai Shimbun*. And then there are our wives, Harumi and Stella, whose support and encouragement lightened the burden of writing this book.

Index